PROMOTING POSITIVE PARENTING
An Attachment-Based Intervention

MONOGRAPHS IN PARENTING SERIES
Marc H. Bornstein, Series Editor

Borkowski, Ramey, and Bristol-Powers Parenting and the Child's World: Influences on Academic, Intellectual, and Social-Emotional Development

Bornstein and Bradley Socioeconomic Status, Parenting, and Child Development

Kalil and DeLeire Family Investments in Children's Potential Resources and Behaviors That Promote Children's Success

Cowan, Cowan, Ablow, Johnson, and Measelle The Family Context of Parenting in Children's Adaptation to Elementary School

Luster and Okagaki Parenting: An Ecological Perspective (2nd ed.)

Bornstein and Cote Acculturation and Parent-Child Relationships: Measurement and Development

Juffer, Bakermans-Kranenburg, and Van IJzendoorn Promoting Positive Parenting: An Attachment-Based Intervention

Goldberg Father Time: The Timing of Fatherhood in Men's Lives (In Preparation)

Bornstein The Parent: Essential Readings (In Preparation)

For more information on LEA title, please contact
Lawrence Erlbaum Associates, Publishers, at www.erlbaum.com

PROMOTING POSITIVE PARENTING
An Attachment-Based Intervention

EDITED BY
Femmie Juffer
Marian J. Bakermans-Kranenburg
Marinus H. van IJzendoorn

LEA Lawrence Erlbaum Associates
Taylor & Francis Group

New York   London

Cover illustration: Sculpture by Gustav Vigeland, The Vigeland Park, Oslo, Norway. © The Vigeland Museum / Beeldrecht Amsterdam 2007

Lawrence Erlbaum Associates
Taylor & Francis Group
270 Madison Avenue
New York, NY 10016

Lawrence Erlbaum Associates
Taylor & Francis Group
2 Park Square
Milton Park, Abingdon
Oxon OX14 4RN

© 2008 by Taylor & Francis Group, LLC
Lawrence Erlbaum Associates is an imprint of Taylor & Francis Group, an Informa business

Printed in the United States of America on acid-free paper
10 9 8 7 6 5 4 3 2 1

International Standard Book Number-13: 978-0-8058-6352-9 (Softcover) 978-0-8058-6351-2 (Hardcover)

Library of Congress Cataloging-in-Publication Data

Juffer, F. (Femmie), 1950-
    Promoting positive parenting : an attachment-based intervention / Femmie Juffer, Marian J. Bakermans-Kranenburg, and Marinus H. van IJzendoorn.
        p. cm. -- (Monographs in parenting series)
    Includes bibliographical references and index.
    ISBN-13: 978-0-8058-6352-9 (alk. paper)
    ISBN-10: 0-8058-6352-4 (alk. paper)
    ISBN-13: 978-0-8058-6351-2 (alk. paper)
    ISBN-10: 0-8058-6351-6 (alk. paper)
    1. Parenting. 2. Child rearing. I. Bakermans-Kranenburg, Marian J. II. IJzendoorn, Marinus H. van, 1952- III. Title.

HQ755.8.J84 2008
306.874087'4--dc22   2007013604

Visit the Taylor & Francis Web site at
http://www.taylorandfrancis.com

Contents

Series foreword

Parenting is fundamental to the survival and success of the human race. Everyone who has ever lived has had parents, and most adults in the world become parents. Opinions about parenting abound, but surprisingly little solid scientific information or considered reflection exists about parenting. *Monographs in Parenting* intends to redress this imbalance: The chief aim of this series of volumes is to provide a forum for extended and integrated treatments of fundamental and challenging contemporary topics in parenting. Each volume treats a different perspective on parenting and is self-contained, yet the series as a whole endeavors to enhance and interrelate studies in parenting by bringing shared perspectives to bear on a variety of concerns prominent in parenting theory, research, and application. As a consequence of its structure and scope, *Monographs in Parenting* will appeal, individually or as a group, to scientists, professionals, and parents alike. Reflecting the nature and intent of this series, contributing authors are drawn from a broad spectrum of the humanities and sciences — anthropology to zoology — with representational emphasis placed on active contributing authorities to the contemporary literature in parenting.

Parenting is a job whose primary object of attention and action is the child — children do not and cannot grow up as solitary individuals — but parenting is also a status in the life course with consequences for parents themselves. In this forum, parenting is defined by all of children's principal caregivers and their many modes of caregiving. *Monographs in Parenting* encompasses central themes in parenting ...

Who parents?

Biological and adoptive mothers, fathers, single parents, divorced, and remarried parents can be children's principal caregivers, but when siblings, grandparents, and nonfamilial caregivers mind children their "parenting" is pertinent as well.

Whom do parents parent?

Parents parent infants, toddlers, children in middle childhood, and adolescents, but special populations of children include multiple births, preterm, ill, developmentally delayed or talented, and aggressive or withdrawn children.

The scope of parenting

Parenting includes genetic endowment and direct effects of experience that manifest themselves through parents' beliefs and behaviors; parenting's indirect influences take place through parents' relationships with each other and their connections to community networks; the positive and negative effects of parenting are both topics of concern.

Factors that affect parenting

Evolution and history; biology and ethology; family configuration; formal and informal support systems, community ties, and work; social, educational, legal, medical, and governmental institutions; economic class, designed and natural ecology, and culture — as well as children themselves — each helps to define parenting.

The nature, structure, and meaning of parenting

Parenting is pleasures, privileges, and profits as well as frustrations, fears, and failures.

Contemporary parenting studies are diversified, pluralistic, and specialized. This fragmented state needs counterforce in an arena that allows the extended in-depth exploration of cardinal topics in parenting. *Monographs in Parenting* vigorously pursues that goal.

Marc H. Bornstein
Series Editor

Preface

More than 20 years ago we started to experiment with videotaped parental behavior in order to enhance parents' sensitivity to their children's signals. This volume presents the outcome of this effort, Video-feedback Intervention to promote Positive Parenting (VIPP) and its various modalities. The protocol of the VIPP programs is presented in Chapter 2. Our brief and focused parenting intervention program has been successfully implemented in a variety of clinical and nonclinical groups and cultures. This book describes the VIPP approach as one of the few evidence-based parenting intervention protocols to date.

Central to early attachment-based intervention is the assumption that a secure attachment relationship is an important basis for children's future development, especially in domains closely related to attachment, such as social development. Empirical studies have shown significant relations between early childhood attachment security and children's later favorable social development and competence. Secure children tend to trust others, show adequate self-esteem in social interaction, make friends, and experience social support. Therefore, the concept of secure attachment relationships and the related concept of parental sensitivity are highly relevant to the clinical field, as is the development and evaluation of attachment-based interventions for at-risk and clinical families.

In this volume we focus on attachment-based interventions for parents and caregivers, using three perspectives. First, we introduce the VIPP programs and identify their essential components: the video feedback, the intervention themes, the optional written information, and the attachment discussions in one of the VIPP modalities. Second, we paint a picture of the broader field by reviewing existing attachment-based interventions with narrative and meta-analytic approaches. Third, we provide detailed descriptions and case reports of intervention studies based on the VIPP programs designed at Leiden University in the Netherlands and adapted for different cultures, settings, and (clinical) families. The VIPP programs were implemented and tested in families and in childcare settings in several countries, including the Netherlands, Italy, the United Kingdom, and the United States. The various chapters present how the VIPP approach was implemented successfully in samples of insecure mothers, mothers with eating disorders, and childcare providers, and in samples with preterm infants and children suffering from dermatitis, adopted children, and children with early externalizing behavior problems. In the pertinent studies important intervention effects of the VIPP approach were found on maternal sensitive behavior and attitudes, on positive parent-child interaction, and on child behavior (e.g., increases in attachment security, reduction of overactive behavior). However, the evidence base for the VIPP approach is not restricted to the empirical studies reported in this book. Support for the VIPP approach also resides in the findings of several meta-analyses documenting that behaviorally focused and rather brief interventions appear to be most effective in enhancing parental sensitivity as well as in promoting children's attachment security ("less is more").

The work presented in this volume is important for researchers, students, and practitioners in developmental and clinical psychology, human development and family studies, psychiatry, social work, public health and nursing, early childhood education, and related fields. The book may be used in undergraduate and graduate courses on attachment and early childhood development, early childhood education, as well as in courses on (preventive) early childhood interventions.

We hope that bringing together the work on VIPP in a single volume will inspire researchers and clinicians alike to take VIPP into consideration when they work with troubled parents of young children.

About the authors

Lenneke R. A. Alink is assistant professor at the Centre for Child and Family Studies, Leiden University, the Netherlands. She participates in the Leiden Attachment Research Program, focusing on the (biological) precursors, correlates, and consequences of externalizing behavior in early childhood. Her dissertation focused on early childhood physical aggression. She investigated the prevalence and development of physical aggression in one- to three-year-old children and also examined the biological and parenting predictors of this behavior. Besides her work at the Centre for Child and Family Studies she conducts postdoctoral research at the Institute of Child Development at the University of Minnesota.

Erin Bartsch is a doctoral student in child development and family studies at Purdue University, West Lafayette, Indiana. Her primary research interest is in investigating how language plays a part in sensitive responsive caregiving.

Philomeen Breddels-van Baardewijk completed her MA at the Centre for Child and Family Studies, Leiden University, the Netherlands. She participated as a PhD student in the Leiden Attachment Research Program and was involved in several phases of the study examining the effectiveness of the Video-feedback Intervention to promote Positive Parenting (VIPP) and VIPP with representational attachment discussions (VIPP-R) programs in the Netherlands.

Simone Bruno conducted his PhD study at the University of Bari, Italy, examining attachment of mothers and children with recurrent asthmatic bronchitis. As a PhD student he participated in the pilot study that investigated the effectiveness of the Video-feedback Intervention to promote Positive Parenting with representational attachment discussions (VIPP-R) in families with sick children.

Rosalinda Cassibba is professor of developmental psychology at the University of Bari, Italy. In her PhD study at the University of Padua, Italy, her research focused on attachment and play in childcare centers. In her research program she has been studying diverse aspects of early human social, affective, and cognitive development, including language, play, attachment, and at-risk infant development. She supervises various research projects concerning attachment and infant development in families with preterm and dermatitis children, and a study on the effectiveness of the Video-feedback Intervention to promote

Positive Parenting with representational attachment discussions (VIPP-R) aimed at enhancing maternal sensitivity and children's security in low-SES families.

Gabrielle Coppola is a researcher at the Department of Developmental Psychology, University of Chieti, Italy. She conducted her PhD study at the University of Bari, Italy, examining the effectiveness of VIPP-R (Video-feedback Intervention to promote Positive Parenting with representational attachment discussions) in enhancing maternal sensitivity and promoting children's attachment security in families with preterm children. Her research interests include attachment processes throughout the life span and social development in the first years of life.

Alessandro Costantini, psychologist, is a PhD student at the University of Bari, Italy. His thesis focuses on attachment security and language development in preterm infants. He is involved in a research project on the definition of evaluation criteria for foster care.

Lucia Elia, psychologist, is a PhD student at the University of Bari, Italy. Her PhD study focuses on attachment processes, social competence, and theory of mind in the preschool age. She is also involved in a research project on the social development of handicapped children.

James Elicker is associate professor in child development and family studies and director of children's programs at Purdue University, West Lafayette, Indiana. He has been an early childhood teacher, administrator, and researcher for more than 30 years. He completed his graduate education in child development and early education at Harvard University and the University of Minnesota, receiving his PhD in 1991. He teaches courses in child development, early childhood education, and research methods. His research focuses on young children's development in the context of early childhood programs.

Sergio Gatto, clinical psychologist, University of Bari, Italy, is attending the Cognitive-Behavioral School of Psychotherapy (G. Liotti, director). His research interests include attachment processes through the life span and psychopathology. He is involved in a research project on attachment and the social development of handicapped children.

Oana Georgescu has a BA in psychology from St. Mary's University and an MS in child development and family studies from Purdue University, West Lafayette, Indiana. She is working in Bucharest, Romania, with nonprofit organizations focused on child and family development and continuing her work with video feedback in childcare.

Leezah Hertzmann is a psychoanalytic psychotherapist working both in private practice and in schools. She is an honorary research psychotherapist at the Tavistock Clinic and Portman NHS Trust, London, where she has worked on a number of studies investigating interventions for parents and infants. Until recently, she worked as child mental health adviser to the Department for Education and Skills, where she advised on child and family mental health, influencing and shaping policy and practice in this area. She has an interest in the development of psychological interventions for parents and children and, in particular, making such interventions accessible to families in school settings. In addition to supervising and lecturing on psychotherapy training courses, she also consults to various organizations in the area of child and family mental health.

Mariska Klein Velderman studied child and family studies at Leiden University in the Netherlands. At the Centre for Child and Family Studies (Leiden Attachment Research Program) she conducted her PhD study examining the effectiveness of the Video-feedback Intervention to promote Positive Parenting (VIPP) and VIPP with representational attachment discussions (VIPP-R) programs. At the same center she was involved in the Dutch national incidence studies on child abuse and neglect (NIS-R) as a research assistant. She then started to work as a researcher at the Netherlands Organization for Applied Scientific Research (TNO), focusing on several topics including child abuse, public health, bullying, and early childhood intervention programs.

Hans M. Koot is professor of developmental psychology and developmental psychopathology at the Vrije Universiteit, Amsterdam. After his PhD work on problem behavior in pre-school-aged children at Erasmus University, Rotterdam, he was involved in — mostly longitudinal — research projects on emotional development, behavioral and emotional problems, psychopathology, adjustment, and quality of life in both the general population and special clinical samples, including children and adolescents with psychiatric disorders, intellectual disability, and somatic disorders. He supervises the emotional development program concerning the normative and deviant development of children, adolescents, and young adults, with special attention to the development of social skills, emotional competence, and antisocial and prosocial behavior. Studies include longitudinal observations and surveys, experimental work, and (preventive) interventions.

Judi Mesman is associate professor at the Centre for Child and Family Studies, Leiden University, the Netherlands. She participates in the Leiden Attachment Research Program. Her research interests include the role of early parent-child interactions in the development of externalizing problems, early indicators of harsh discipline, and parent-child relationships in a cross-cultural context. She investigates the relative contribution of the main parenting processes described in attachment theory (sensitivity) and coercion theory (social learning) to the development of early childhood externalizing problems. She is also involved in a project examining parental behavioral and physiological hyperreactivity to infant signals as precursors of harsh discipline in high- and low-SES families from different ethnic groups. Her research also focuses on families from different cultural groups in the Netherlands, comparing parent-child interaction, child externalizing problems, and the development of ethnic identification.

Alan Stein is professor of child and adolescent psychiatry at the University of Oxford (Warneford Hospital) and an honorary consultant in child and adolescent psychiatry at both the Oxfordshire Mental Healthcare NHS Trust and the Tavistock and Portman NHS Trust. He received his medical education at the University of Witwatersrand in Johannesburg, South Africa, and did most of his postgraduate training in Oxford. He also held a post at the Winnicott Research Unit at the University of Cambridge for five years. Before taking up his current position he was professor of child and family mental health at the Royal Free and University College Medical School and the Tavistock Centre. The main focus of his research has concerned the development of young children in the face of adversity. The ultimate aim of this work has been to find ways to enhance children's development and helping to support their families. He is also very committed to the training of medical students and other healthcare professionals in these areas of work.

Mirjam N. Stolk completed her PhD study in the Leiden Attachment Research Program at the Centre for Child and Family Studies, Leiden University, the Netherlands. Her thesis focused on the role of the family context in the development and prevention of early externalizing problems. She conducted a process evaluation of the Video-feedback Intervention to promote Positive Parenting and Sensitive Discipline (VIPP-SD) program. She was one of the interveners who implemented the VIPP-SD program in families with children screened for high levels of externalizing behavior problems, and she helped train other interveners.

Alessia Tota, psychologist, is a PhD student at the University of Bari, Italy. Her research focuses on attachment in sick children and interventions with handicapped children.

Jantien van Zeijl is a researcher at Statistics Netherlands (Centraal Bureau voor de Statistiek [CBS]), analyzing national statistics about children's school performance in the Netherlands. She completed her PhD study at the Centre for Child and Family Studies, Leiden University, the Netherlands, within the Leiden Attachment Research Program. Her research focused on evaluating the effectiveness of the Video-feedback Intervention to promote Positive Parenting and Sensitive Discipline (VIPP-SD) program. She was one of the interveners who implemented the VIPP-SD program in families with children screened for high levels of externalizing behavior problems, and she helped train other interveners. She also examined differential susceptibility in the association between negative parenting and child externalizing problems, as well as the nature of externalizing problems in one-year-old children. In addition, she was involved in a study on childcare.

Helen Woolley has combined a career of clinical work within the fields of child and family mental health with research encompassing two particular areas of interest: first, that of evaluating children's hospice care, including hospice staff stress and support, within the context of the wider service provision for children suffering life-limiting illness. The second and main research focus spanning the last 18 years has consisted of an exploration of the impact of maternal eating disorders upon children, particularly through the very early years. In this context she has developed a specific interest in the microanalysis of videoed mother-infant interaction and the use of video feedback as a tool for intervention. She has worked and published in each area of research with Alan Stein both at the Warneford Hospital, University of Oxford, Section of Child and Adolescent Psychiatry in Oxford and in London.

About the editors

Femmie Juffer holds the chair for adoption studies at the Centre for Child and Family Studies, Leiden University, the Netherlands. She completed her PhD study at Utrecht University, the Netherlands, examining the effectiveness of an attachment-based video-feedback intervention program for adoptive families. Since 1993 she has been affiliated with the Leiden Attachment Research Program, specializing in research on adoption and intervention. She is involved in a longitudinal adoption study and several other studies on the development of adopted children and children reared in institutions. Together with Marinus van IJzendoorn she supervises the Adoption Meta-Analysis Project (MAP), examining adopted children's development through meta-analytic syntheses. Her research also focuses on the development and evaluation of attachment-based interventions in adoptive and biological families.

Marian J. Bakermans-Kranenburg, associate professor at the Centre for Child and Family Studies, Leiden University, the Netherlands, participates in the Leiden Attachment Research Program. Since her PhD study on the reliability and discriminant validity of the Adult Attachment Interview she has been involved in studies on disorganized attachment, attachment in children with autism, attachment-based interventions, stress regulation, and the development of compliance and empathic concern. She also contributed to several meta-analyses, including attachment-based interventions, the Attachment Q-Sort, secondary traumatization, attention bias, and physical growth in adopted children. A focus on behavioral and molecular genetics has led to several twin studies on attachment. She is interested in effects of gene-environment interaction (including the dopamine D4 receptor gene polymorphism) and children's differential susceptibility to child-rearing influences.

Marinus H. van IJzendoorn is professor at Leiden University, the Netherlands, Centre for Child and Family Studies, and director of the Leiden Attachment Research Program. After his PhD study on adolescent cognitive, moral and political development at the Free University of Berlin and the Max Planck Institute for Education and Human Development, he specialized in research on attachment across the life span and in meta-analytic syntheses of research on child and family studies. He is involved in attachment studies on nonparental childcare, development of orphaned and adopted children, development of (children of) Holocaust survivors, child maltreatment, autism, and the develop-

ment of compliance and empathic concern. Cultural and neurobiological contributions to variations in children's emotion regulation are emphasized, as well
as evidence-based intervention to optimize child development.

Acknowledgments

The editors gratefully acknowledge the support of Reineke Mom, Joke Scholtens, and Marian Verlaan, all affiliated with the Centre for Child and Family Studies, Leiden University, the Netherlands, in editing and revising this volume. The editors also thank Marc Bornstein, editor of the *Monographs in Parenting* series, for his numerous helpful suggestions to improve previous drafts of the book, and Lori Handelman (Lawrence Erlbaum) for her practical support.

The interventions introduced in this book, VIPP and VIPP with representation attachment discussions (VIPP-R), were developed at the Centre for Child and Family Studies at Leiden University, supported by a Pioneer Award from the Netherlands Organization for Scientific Research NW0 (grant PGS 59-256) to Marinus H. van IJzendoorn. Marian J. Bakermans-Kranenburg and Marinus H. van IJzendoorn are supported by the Netherlands Organization for Scientific Research NWO (VIDI grant and SPINOZA prize, respectively). VIPP-Sensitive Discipline (VIPP-SD) was developed with support from the Netherlands Organization for Health Research and Developments ZON-MW to Marinus H. van IJzendoorn and Femmie Juffer.

Femmie Juffer
Marian J. Bakermans-Kranenburg
Marinus H. van IJzendoorn

1

Promoting positive parenting

An introduction

Femmie Juffer, Marian J.
Bakermans-Kranenburg, and
Marinus H. van IJzendoorn
*Centre for Child and Family Studies,
Leiden University, the Netherlands*

Since Mary Ainsworth (1967) and John Bowlby (1969) discovered that children use their parents as a secure base to fulfill their attachment and exploration needs, an impressive body of empirical research has been devoted to the search for the origins and consequences of (in)secure child-parent attachment relationships. Today attachment security can be characterized as a construct that has proven to be valid across various cultures (Van IJzendoorn & Sagi, 1999); in different contexts, such as family, childcare, and institutional settings (e.g., Goossens & Van IJzendoorn, 1990; Howes, 1999; Vorria et al., 2003; Zeanah, Smyke, Koga, & Carlson, 2005); and in families with different types of genetic kinship (e.g., parents with twins, siblings, or adopted children; Bokhorst et al., 2003; Juffer & Rosenboom, 1997; Van IJzendoorn et al., 2000). Secure attachment relationships have been associated with better social competence (e.g., Stams, Juffer, & Van IJzendoorn, 2002; Weinfield, Sroufe, Egeland, & Carlson, 1999) and with more optimal parent and peer relationships than insecure attachments (e.g., Sroufe, Egeland, Carlson, & Collins, 2005). The concept of secure attachment relationships and the related concept of parental sensitivity appear to be highly significant for the clinical field, including the development and evaluation of attachment-based interventions for at-risk and clinical families. In particular, parental sensitivity as the empirically documented determinant of children's attachment security (De Wolff & Van IJzendoorn, 1997) has been the focus of intervention efforts. Parental sensitivity can be defined as the ability to accurately perceive the child's signals and to respond to these signals in a prompt and adequate way (Ainsworth, Blehar, Waters, & Wall, 1978).

In this volume we focus on attachment-based interventions, reviewing and analyzing attachment-based intervention research and introducing a newly developed and empirically tested attachment-based intervention: VIPP. Also, we describe how the VIPP intervention was adapted for and evaluated in several (clinical) groups and cultures. In this chapter, we discuss the theoretical background of attachment-based interventions in general, followed by an overview of this volume's contents.

Attachment-based intervention: theoretical basis

Departing from an evolutionary perspective and drawing on research that examined the effects of separations of (primate) infants from their parents (e.g., Harlow, 1958; Robertson & Robertson, 1989), Bowlby formulated the main principles of attachment theory in his famous trilogy *Attachment, Separation,* and *Loss* (Bowlby, 1969, 1973, 1980). According to attachment theory, infants are biologically predisposed to use their parents as a haven of safety to provide comfort and protection when they are distressed, and as a secure base from which they can explore the world (Bowlby, 1969, 1988). Securely attached children feel free to play and express their feelings because they trust their parents to comfort and support them whenever they need help. However, not all children experience their parents as a haven of safety and a secure base. It was Mary Ainsworth (1967; Ainsworth et al., 1978) who in her pioneering studies in Uganda and Baltimore discovered that children vary in their quality of attachment security. Consequently, she designed a now-famous paradigm to assess these individual differences: the Strange Situation Procedure (Ainsworth et al., 1978).

Attachment security

In the Strange Situation Procedure children are confronted with several mildly stressful conditions: an unfamiliar room with toys, an unfamiliar person, and two short separations from their mother (or father). Two episodes in this procedure are particularly relevant for the assessment of individual differences in attachment security: the reunions after the two separations. These episodes show whether and how children strike a balance between their attachment needs and exploration behavior. *Secure* (B) children may be distressed by the separation, but they actively seek their mother's proximity and contact at the reunion. After being comforted, these children are able to continue their exploration of the toys and the environment. *Insecure-avoidant* (A) children are not visibly distressed by the separation, although their heart rates during separation are as elevated as those of secure children (Spangler & Grossmann, 1993). On reunion they turn their attention to the toys and the environment or actively avoid their mother's proximity. In other words, avoidant children do not show their attachment needs and they seem to be intensively involved in exploratory behavior. In contrast, *insecure-ambivalent* (C) children show their attachment needs by being visibly upset and distressed by the procedure, but after the mother's return they cannot be settled to play and exploration again. In normative groups, about 65% of the children are securely attached, 21% are insecure-avoidant, and 14% are insecure-ambivalent (*N* = 1,990; Van IJzendoorn & Kroonenberg, 1988).

After a decade of research with the Strange Situation Procedure, a fourth category was added to the three categories of secure, avoidant, and ambivalent attachment: *insecure-disorganized* (D) attachment (Main & Solomon, 1990). Main noted that some children could not be classified according to Ainsworth et al.'s (1978) coding system, and that these children had one thing in common: a momentary absence or breakdown of their strategy in an otherwise organized pattern of (in)secure attachment. For example, these children suddenly stilled or froze all movements, or they reacted with expressions of fear when their mother returned after the separation in the Strange Situation Procedure. According to Main (1999), disorganized children experience "fright without solution": they want their mother for comfort, but they cannot approach her because she is at the same time a source of fear. Main and Hesse (1990) hypothesized that parental frightening and frightened behavior may be related to children's disorganized attachment. Indeed, several studies confirmed and replicated the association between parental frightening/frightened behavior and children's disorganized attachment (Abrams, 2000; Abrams, Rifkin, & Hesse, 2006; Lyons-Ruth, Bronfman, & Parsons, 1999; Schuengel, Bakermans-Kranenburg, & Van IJzendoorn, 1999; True, Pisani, & Oumar, 2001; see Hesse & Main, 2006). In nonclinical populations about 15% of the children are classified as disorganized attached, but in clinical, at-risk samples the number of disorganized children is much higher (Van IJzendoorn, Schuengel, & Bakermans-Kranenburg, 1999).

Parental sensitivity

Ainsworth documented that children's individual differences shown in the Strange Situation Procedure are associated with their interaction history with their mother in the first year of life (Ainsworth et al., 1978). Securely attached children had sensitive mothers, who accurately perceived their child's signals of distress and responded to these signals in a prompt and adequate way (Ainsworth, Bell, & Stayton, 1974). Insecure-avoidant children had mothers who consistently reacted insensitively and unresponsively by ignoring or rejecting their child's expressions of distress and negative emotions. Finally, insecure-ambivalent children had mothers who were inconsistently responsive, sometimes responding to their child's needs but at other times not responding at all. Several studies confirmed the relation between parental sensitivity and children's attachment security (De Wolff & Van IJzendoorn, 1997; Goldsmith & Alansky, 1987).

Parents' mental representations of attachment

Empirical studies also confirmed relations between parental (in)sensitive or frightening behavior and children's attachment security and disorganization. In addition, parental (in)secure mental representations of attachment were found to be associated with parental (in)sensitivity and with insecure infant-parent attachment relationships (Main, Kaplan, & Cassidy, 1985; Van IJzendoorn, 1995). On the basis of the Adult Attachment Interview (George, Kaplan, & Main, 1985; Hesse, 1999; Main & Goldwyn, 1994), the following mental representations of attachment can be distinguished: secure or autonomous representations, insecure-dismissing, insecure-preoccupied, and insecure-unresolved representations. In contrast to *secure, autonomous* (F) parents who are able to reflect on positive or negative childhood experiences in a coherent way, *insecure-dismissing* (Ds) parents idealize their childhood experiences or devalue the importance of attachment relationships for their own lives. *Insecure-preoccupied* (E) parents, who are still angrily or passively involved with their past relationships, seem mentally entangled with their parents. Finally, *insecure-unresolved* (U) parents struggle with memories of loss or trauma, shown by momentary lapses in the monitoring of their discourse or reasoning. There is empirical evidence that attachment patterns are transmitted from one generation to the following generation: Autonomous parents usually have secure children and insecure parents usually have insecure children (for a meta-analysis, see Van IJzendoorn, 1995; Waters, Vaughn, Posada, & Kondo-Ikemura, 1995).

Interventions directed at the behavioral and representational level

Central to early attachment-based intervention is the assumption that a secure attachment relationship is an important basis for future development, especially in domains closely related to attachment, such as social development. Secure attachment involves the mental representation of others as available, responsive, and trustworthy, and the mental representation of the self as worthy of love, respect, and care (Bowlby, 1969; Jacobsen & Hofmann, 1997). Secure children tend to trust others, show adequate self-esteem in social interaction, make friends, and experience social support. Empirical studies have shown significant relations between early childhood attachment security and later favorable social

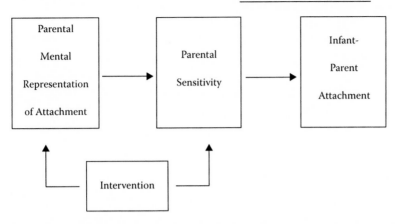

Figure 1.1   A model of interventions in attachment. (From Van IJzendoorn, Juffer, & Duyvesteyn, 1995, p. 227.)

development and competence (Fagot, 1997; Kerns, 1994; Schneider, Atkinson, & Tardif, 2001; Stams et al., 2002; Sroufe et al., 2005; Thompson, 1999).

As parents' mental representations of attachment as well as their sensitivity are empirically derived determinants of child attachment security, intervention efforts may be directed at the *representational level*, addressing parental attachment representations in order to pave the way for subsequent behavioral changes, and at the *behavioral level*, addressing parental sensitivity (see Figure 1.1).

In this volume both types of interventions are introduced, reviewed, and analyzed: VIPP, a behavioral intervention, aimed at promoting sensitivity, and VIPP-R, VIPP with a representational component, with the additional aim of promoting a secure mental representation of attachment.

Autonomy and behavior problems

In the most optimal scenario of child development, the first attachment relationships of one-year-old children serve as a secure base, enabling them to explore the world freely and to get comfort whenever they experience setbacks. When these securely attached children grow older, they develop — like all children in their second year of life — an increasing need for autonomy. However, their needs to behave independently of the parent (for example, eating, walking, talking) develop in relative harmony with the parent. Although not all interactions may be perfectly harmonious, securely attached children are more compliant, show more positive affect, and are more cooperative than insecurely attached children (Sroufe et al., 2005). In the same vein, attachment insecurity and parental lack of warmth in early childhood are associated with children's behavior problems in early and later childhood and in adolescence (e.g., Belsky, Woodsworth, & Crnic, 1996; Erickson, Sroufe, & Egeland, 1985; Greenberg, Speltz, DeKlyen, & Endriga, 1991; Olson, Bates, Sandy, & Lanthier, 2000; Van IJzendoorn et al., 1999). Consequently, in many families parents may struggle with difficult and challenging child behaviors, such as noncompliance and oppositional behaviors.

Therefore, in attachment-based interventions parents may be supported not only to interact with their children in a sensitive way, but also to cope with the (emerging) difficult behaviors of their children. We thus designed an additional intervention module, aimed at promoting parents' sensitive discipline behavior (VIPP-SD). This intervention module is based on the integration of attachment theory and coercion theory. Coercion theory departs from the social learning perspective and focuses on ineffective parental discipline resulting in increasingly difficult and challenging child behavior (Patterson, 1982). Children's behavior problems are believed to more likely occur and continue to exist when a child is reinforced for responding with negative, noncompliant behavior to parental requests or demands (see Chapter 11 for a more extensive discussion of coercion theory). In VIPP-SD parents are supported to use adequate discipline strategies in a sensitive way.

Overview of the volume

In this volume we focus on attachment-based interventions for parents and caregivers, using three perspectives. First, we introduce the VIPP methods. Second, we paint a picture of the broader field by reviewing existing attachment-based interventions. Third, we continue with the detailed descriptions and case reports of several intervention studies based on the VIPP programs designed at Leiden University in the Netherlands and adapted for different cultures, settings, and (clinical) families.

Chapter 2 provides the protocol with a detailed description of the intervention methods used in the VIPP programs: VIPP, VIPP-SD, and VIPP-R. Chapter 3 provides a case study and process evaluations to illustrate the intervention processes of VIPP and VIPP-R.

In Chapter 4 a narrative review of attachment-based interventions is presented to provide the reader with a broader framework to understand and evaluate the current state of the art of attachment-based intervention research. In Chapter 5 this review is complemented with a series of meta-analyses. Based on our meta-analyses we may conclude what works for whom; for example, do attachment-based interventions work better with nonclinical samples than with clinical groups? Also, the meta-analytic approach allows for conclusions about several intervention characteristics, such as the focus of the intervention, the number of sessions, and the best time to start an intervention.

Chapters 6 and 7 focus on how intervention may work for parents of highly reactive, preterm, or sick infants. In these studies the VIPP program, including VIPP-R, was used. In Chapter 6 our Leiden intervention study with VIPP and VIPP-R is described. For the first time the differential susceptibility of children, the propensity of some children to be more receptive to environmental influences than other children, is studied in an experimental design. Positive intervention effects were most pronounced for highly reactive, susceptible infants and their mothers. Chapter 7 describes how the VIPP-R program was adapted for and tested in a clinical group of Italian families with preterm and sick dermatitis infants and their mothers. Due to their preterm or ill condition, these babies may trigger less touch and cuddling from their mothers, leading to decreased sensitivity and attachment security.

Chapters 8 and 9 describe studies using the VIPP program (without additional intervention modules). Chapter 8 gives a detailed description of how the VIPP program is used in a clinical group of English families with postnatal eating disordered mothers and their infants. Mothers with eating disorders have difficulties feeding their baby in a relaxed way, and mother-infant conflict easily disturbs smooth mother-child interactions. An intervention program with video feedback might help these parents better attune to the needs of their children. In the same vein, adoptive parents may encounter difficulties attuning to their genetically unrelated adopted children. In Chapter 9 video feedback is tested in a sample of adoptive families. This chapter describes how a preliminary version of the VIPP program improved maternal sensitivity and reduced attachment disorganization in mothers and their internationally adopted children. Additionally, the long-term consequences of the early parent-child relationships and the long-term intervention effects are discussed.

Chapters 10 and 11 describe new extensions of the VIPP program. In Chapter 10 an adaptation of VIPP for childcare providers and results from a pilot study with professional caregivers in childcare are presented. Because many children are cared for in childcare settings and develop attachment relationships not only with their parents but also with their childcare providers, it is imperative that the caregivers in these settings respond sensitively to the children in their care. The chapter describes how the program Tuning In, based on VIPP, was implemented in an American childcare setting. In Chapter 11 we present another extension of VIPP. In this program the additional focus is on VIPP-SD, based on both attachment theory and coercion theory (Patterson, 1982). The program is tested in three age groups of children with externalizing behavior problems: one-year-olds, two-year-olds, and three-year-olds. Thus, the VIPP-SD program can be seen as an extension of VIPP not only with respect to its theoretical background but also with respect to the ages of the children, since infants as well as toddlers and preschoolers are involved.

Finally, in Chapter 12 we recapitulate the content and effectiveness of the VIPP program and its adaptations and extensions. The evidence for focused and relatively brief interventions such as VIPP is summarized, including their potential to prevent disorganized attachment. We also try to explain *why* sensitivity-focused interventions such as the VIPP program are effective. The role of fathers as intervention participants is discussed, and we address the issue of behavioral change versus representational continuity, one of the issues emerging in several chapters.

Conclusions

In this chapter we discussed the theoretical background of attachment-based interventions and presented an overview of this volume's contents. According to Bowlby, founding father of attachment theory, infants are biologically predisposed to use their parents as a haven of safety to provide protection when they are distressed, and as a secure base from which they can explore the world. Ainsworth discovered that children vary in their quality of attachment security, and she designed a paradigm to assess these differences: the Strange Situation Procedure. Based on their behavior in this observational procedure, children can be classified as secure or insecure. Ainsworth also documented that children's individual differences in attachment behavior are related to the interaction history with their parent in the first year of life, in particular to parental sensitivity. Several studies confirmed the association between parental sensitivity and children's attachment security. In addition, parental mental representations of attachment were found to be associated with parental sensitivity and infant-parent attachment relationships.

Central to attachment-based intervention is the assumption that a secure attachment relationship is an important basis for children's future development. Secure attachment involves the mental representation of others as available and trustworthy and the mental representation of the self as worthy of love and care. Secure children tend to trust others, show adequate self-esteem, and make friends. As parents' mental representations of attachment as well as their sensitivity are empirically derived determinants of child attachment security, intervention efforts may be directed at the *representational level*, addressing parental attachment representations, and at the *behavioral level*, addressing parental sensitivity. In this volume both types of interventions are discussed and introduced: VIPP, a behavioral intervention, aimed at promoting sensitivity, and VIPP-R,

VIPP with a representational component, with the additional aim of promoting a secure mental representation of attachment. In attachment-based interventions parents may be supported not only to interact with their children in a sensitive way, but also to cope with difficult child behavior. We thus designed an additional intervention module, aimed at promoting parents' sensitive discipline behavior (VIPP-SD). This intervention module is based on the integration of attachment theory and coercion theory. Patterson's coercion theory departs from the social learning perspective and focuses on ineffective parental discipline resulting in increasingly difficult child behavior.

In this volume we focus on attachment-based interventions for parents and caregivers, using three perspectives. First, we introduce the VIPP methods. Second, we review and analyze existing attachment-based interventions. Third, we provide detailed descriptions of several intervention studies based on the VIPP programs designed at Leiden University in the Netherlands and adapted for different cultures, settings, and (clinical) families.

2

Methods of the video-feedback programs to promote positive parenting alone, with sensitive discipline, and with representational attachment discussions

Femmie Juffer, Marian J.
Bakermans-Kranenburg, and
Marinus H. van IJzendoorn
*Centre for Child and Family Studies,
Leiden University, the Netherlands*

This chapter presents the protocol of the VIPP programs, including a description of the intervention methods: the video feedback, the intervention themes, the (optional) written information, and the attachment discussions. In the VIPP programs parents are offered short-term behaviorally focused (VIPP and VIPP-SD) or combined behaviorally and representationally focused (VIPP-R) interventions aimed at enhancing parental sensitivity and positive parent-child interactions. The programs are standardized and individualized, meaning that the intervener works from a general protocol but attunes the specific themes and guidelines to the individual parent-child dyad.

All VIPP programs utilize videotaped interactions of the parent and child involved and video feedback: watching and discussing the videotape together with the parent. This technique is comparable with the interaction guidance method developed by McDonough (2004) and the guided self-observation through video feedback developed by Erickson (Egeland & Erickson, 2004;

Erickson & Kurz-Riemer, 1999). Video feedback is, however, different from using videotaped model behavior to teach parents new behavior, for example, baby massage (Scholz & Samuels, 1992). A problem with videotaped model behavior may be that the parent does not identify with the model parent or child on the videotape (Lambermon & Van IJzendoorn, 1989). The VIPP approach is also different from holding and other so-called attachment regression therapies (Chaffin et al., 2006; O'Connor & Nilsen, 2005), as it capitalizes on the current strengths of the parent-child dyad and aims at enhancing parents' sensitive reactions to child behavior.

The actual behaviors of the child and parent on the videotape are the starting point of the VIPP programs, and not retrospective memories that may be biased by the parent's own childhood experiences or by negative feelings about the child. The video-feedback intervention offers opportunities to practice observational skills by watching child behavior together with the parent and opportunities to reinforce the sensitive behaviors, fleeting as they may be, that the parent sometimes does show. Although actual child and parent behaviors are the focus of VIPP, the intervener may also offer (written) information about child development during the video-feedback sessions. To evaluate the intervention processes of the VIPP programs, interveners may use logbooks to note their personal impressions after each session and an evaluation questionnaire to be completed by the parent(s) involved after the end of the intervention (see Chapter 3 for illustrations).

Outline of the VIPP programs

Video-feedback Intervention to promote Positive Parenting (VIPP) aims at enhancing parental sensitive behavior through providing personal video feedback, possibly combined with written information (in brochures, booklets, a personal book, or an individual album) on sensitive responding in daily situations. VIPP-SD (VIPP combined with sensitive discipline) includes an additional focus on the use of sensitive discipline in challenging parent-child interactions. VIPP-R (VIPP combined with representational efforts) includes additional discussions about past and present attachment relationships, aimed at affecting the parent's mental representation of attachment. The VIPP programs are usually directed at parents of infants (see Chapters 6 to 9), although VIPP and VIPP-SD have been successfully used with toddlers and preschool children too (see Chapters 10 and 11).

The VIPP programs are home based and short-term: The interventions are implemented in the home of the family in a modest number of sessions (usually four to eight). The effectiveness of interventions of relatively short duration and with a modest number of sessions has been meta-analytically documented

(Bakermans-Kranenburg, Van IJzendoorn, & Juffer, 2003; see Chapter 5). Building a supporting relationship between the intervener and the parent(s) (Bowlby, 1988) is considered a crucial element of all VIPP programs. The VIPP interventions are usually implemented by female interveners with a master's degree or doctoral degree in (developmental) psychology, education, or child/family studies. In the VIPP interventions each session has a specific theme (see below). In Chapter 3 VIPP and VIPP-R are further elaborated through a case study and first evaluation of VIPP and VIPP-R. In Chapter 11 several aspects of VIPP-SD are described, including the adaptation of the intervention for different age groups (one- to three-year-old children).

Video-feedback intervention to promote positive parenting (VIPP)

Background

A first attempt at enhancing parental sensitivity through an attachment-based videotaped model of sensitive parenting appeared to be ineffective (Lambermon & Van IJzendoorn, 1989). A problem with videotaped model behavior is that parents may not identify with the specific model of a parent-child dyad on the videotape, and they remain focused on superficial differences in outlook and appearances of the dyad involved compared with their own situation. Parents apparently need a mirror of their own daily interactions with their child to change their behavior. Based on attachment theory (Ainsworth, Blehar, Waters, & Wall, 1978; Bowlby, 1982), a preliminary version of the current video-feedback intervention program was developed in a study of families with adopted children (Juffer, 1993). This program was the first to use *in vivo* video feedback as a systematic means to enhance parental sensitivity and infant attachment security. The intervention consisted of three sessions and appeared to be successful in promoting maternal sensitivity, secure infant-mother attachment, and the prevention of disorganized attachment (see Chapter 9; Juffer, Bakermans-Kranenburg, & Van IJzendoorn, 2005b). This video-feedback intervention was further developed and elaborated at the Centre for Child and Family Studies (Leiden University, the Netherlands) into the current Video-feedback Intervention to promote Positive Parenting (VIPP), consisting of four sessions organized into structured stages according to a detailed protocol.

Intervention methods

Video feedback

In the VIPP program, mother and infant are videotaped during daily situations at their home (for example, playing together, bathing the baby, mealtime) during short episodes of 10 to 30 minutes. During the filming the intervener is not actively involved in the parent-child interaction; her role is restricted to inviting the mother to be filmed with her child in a specific situation and the actual filming. The filming should be done discreetly to enable a more natural parent-child interaction and to prevent the child's attention being attracted to the camera or the filmer rather than to the mother and the planned activity. This nonintrusive role also implies that the intervener does not give any advice, tips, or comments during the filming, nor does she intervene when the child is distressed or frustrated. This nonintrusive role is explained to the mother before the filming starts. Also, the intervener explains that she will continue with filming when a child is distressed or crying, because this behavior is part of the child's behavior repertoire and thus interesting to film, watch, and discuss. Mothers are encouraged to react to their children the way they normally react. At this point the intervener may comment that the filming is not quite comparable with making private home videos, such as filming the child's birthday party. Whereas in private home videos the aim is to record memorable events for the future, the aim of video feedback is to record the whole range of children's behavior during daily interactions for later close observation and discussion.

For some mothers, the first filming may be an awkward situation, because of their uncertainty or insecurity (see Chapters 3 and 6) or because of their body shape (Chapter 8). Therefore, the intervener starts with a first (short) episode of filming child behavior, for example, videotaping the child's playing with a newly introduced toy provided by the intervener. Moreover, the intervener may share with the parent that almost all parents feel awkward when they are videotaped for the first time. The mother is reassured that most parents get used to it quite quickly, also because young children act normally after a few moments of accommodation.

In the period between the home visit and the first intervention session, the intervener reviews the videotape and prepares her comments on the child's behavior or the mother's reactions to the child as shown on the videotape. To ease the process of connecting the comments to the pictures, a videotape with time recording is used. The intervener writes down her comments, directed by the guidelines of the intervention protocol and at the same time screening the videotape for suitable fragments to review with the mother during the intervention session. For example, when according to the guidelines the theme of exploration versus attachment behavior (see below) will be discussed in the next home visit, the intervener screens the tape, searching for fragments illustrating the theme. Thus, fragments of the child making eye contact or seeking proximity are used to illustrate the child's attachment behavior, whereas fragments of the child's conscientious play behavior are used to illustrate the child's exploratory behavior. During the preparation of the intervention the intervener connects the chosen fragments to the general messages or theme of that particular session. For example, while showing the child's attachment and exploratory behavior, the intervener may explain that these behaviors ask for differential parental reactions: Children's attachment signals should be met with prompt, adequate reactions, whereas parents should not interfere in children's exploration activities. The intervener may also comment that exploration is important for children because they learn a lot by manipulating toys. At the same time, playing *together* provides children with an extra dimension compared to playing *alone*: Their overtures are responded to, making them feel understood, and moments of joy can be shared. Or, as one intervener commented on a cheerful interaction fragment: "A rattle does not smile back, but *you* do!"

During the next visit the videotape is shown to the mother, and the intervener reviews the whole videotape with her, repeating and discussing the selected fragments, using the comments prepared earlier. Positive and successful interaction moments shown on the videotape are used in the intervention. Focusing on these (sometimes rather scarce) positive interactions serves the goal of showing the parent that she is able to act as a sensitive, competent parent, fulfilling her child's attachment and exploration needs. To focus the mother's attention on positive interaction moments, the videotape is stilled at several moments and the mother is shown a picture of a successful interaction or a happy child. By repeating positive fragments important messages of the intervention are emphasized and more negative interaction moments are counterbalanced. In case of insensitive parental behavior, the parent is encouraged to use more sensitive behaviors, preferably behaviors she displayed at other moments on the videotape. Video feedback provides the opportunity to focus on the baby's videotaped signals and expressions, thereby stimulating the mother's observational skills and empathy for her child. It also enables positive reinforcement of the parent's moments of sensitive behavior shown on the videotape. In this sense the parent is her own model for the intervention. Video feedback thus enables the intervener to focus on both parts of Ainsworth's definition of sensitivity: accurately *perceiving* child signals and adequately *responding* to them (Ainsworth et al., 1978).

Intervention themes

VIPP consists of four themes (Table 2.1) that are elaborated successively during four home visits: (1) exploration versus attachment behavior — showing the difference between the child's contact-seeking behavior and play and explaining the differential responses needed from the parent; (2) "speaking for the child" — promoting the accurate perception of children's (subtle) signals by verbalizing their facial expressions and nonverbal cues shown on the videotape; (3) "sensitivity chain" — explaining the relevance of prompt and adequate responding to the baby's signals (chain: child signal → parental response → reaction of the child); and (4) sharing emotions — showing and encouraging parents' affective

Table 2.1   Themes of the VIPP programs for each session

Session	Sensitivity	Discipline	Representation
1.	Exploration versus attachment behavior	Inductive discipline and distraction	Separations: past and present
2.	Speaking for the child	Positive reinforcement	Parenting: past and present
3.	Sensitivity chain	Sensitive time-out	Defining adult relationships
4.	Sharing emotions	Empathy for the child	Child of my parents, parent of my child

attunement to the positive and negative emotions of their child (see Chapter 3 for a case study illustrating these themes). For example, in the third session a chain of sensitivity is highlighted: a video fragment that shows a signal of the child followed by a sensitive response of the mother and completed by a positive reaction of the child. The chain illustrates and proves that the mother is competent to respond sensitively to her child's positive (looking, smiling, reaching for a toy) or negative (crying, fussing) signals. The mother's sensitive reactions (e.g., smiling back, helping, or comforting) are acknowledged in the intervention, and the relevance of these behaviors is explained. By getting adequate answers to their needs, children feel understood. They learn to trust their parent, expecting similar positive responses in the future. The last part of the chain, the positive reaction of the child, is highlighted in the intervention too. These positive child behaviors, for instance, a happy smile or stopping crying, are pointed out to the mother as evidence that her reactions were adequate and appreciated by her child. The chain also shows how important the mother is for the well-being of her child: As a consequence of her actions the child is now satisfied, reassured, or in a happy mood. Finally, it is explained to the mother that from a successful sensitivity chain both interaction partners profit in terms of shared happy moments, joy, and positive affect.

By explicitly acknowledging the mother as an expert on her own child, she is encouraged to actively participate in the discussion. For example, when in the second intervention session the intervener attempts to "speak for the child" (Carter, Osofsky, & Hann, 1991), the mother is invited to take part and to provide "subtitles" for the baby's signals and behavior as shown on the videotape. For example, the intervener may ask how the mother would interpret the child's facial expression or gestures during a specific video fragment. Or, alternatively, the intervener may ask the mother whether she agrees that her child looks, for instance, curious or fascinated while playing with this toy, whether she also noticed a triumphant look in her child's eyes after a difficult accomplishment, or whether she agrees that her child's gestures point to the wish to be physically close to her, and so forth.

The themes are chosen in a way that the first two intervention sessions focus on child behavior (e.g., by actively speaking for the child). The following two intervention sessions are (also) directed at parental behavior, for example, by discussing parental behavior in a sensitivity chain. This specific order — starting with child behavior before the focus is on parental behavior — is part of the VIPP intervention: Showing and discussing parental behavior is postponed until the parent and the intervener have had more time to build a working relationship.

Written information (Optional)

Several studies showed positive effects of attachment-based interventions using written information (e.g., Lambermon & Van IJzendoorn, 1989; Riksen-Walraven, 1978). In the VIPP programs written information may be included in the intervention. During one or more intervention sessions the parent may receive brochures on sensitive parenting and on sensitive responding in daily situations, for example, about crying and comforting or about playing together (see Chapters 3 and 6), tips for sensitive discipline (Chapter 11), or a personal book or individual album (Chapters 8 and 9). In brochures or books, information may be found about child development in a particular (clinical) group of children, parenting tips, or suggestions for personal observations.

VIPP with an additional focus on sensitive discipline (VIPP-SD)

Background

After their first birthday toddlers increasingly express their autonomy needs by acting independently, sometimes against the wishes and demands of their parent(s). Whereas secure children generally are cooperative and compliant, children's insecurity and parental lack of sensitivity are associated with children's behavior problems (e.g., Erickson, Sroufe, & Egeland, 1985). To support parents who have to cope with challenging child problem behaviors, VIPP with an additional focus on sensitive discipline (VIPP-SD) was developed.

VIPP-SD is based on the integration of both attachment theory (Ainsworth et al., 1978; Bowlby, 1969; see Chapter 1) and coercion theory (Patterson, 1982, 2002; see Chapter 11 for an extensive discussion of this theory). Coercion theory describes how ineffective parental discipline results in increasingly difficult and challenging child behavior (Patterson, 1982). VIPP-SD can be characterized as a behaviorally oriented intervention using video feedback to promote parental sensitivity as well as adequate discipline strategies during parent-child interactions (see Chapter 11; Van Zeijl, Mesman, Van IJzendoorn et al., 2006).

Intervention methods

Video feedback

In this intervention modality, the video feedback aims at promoting sensitive parenting and sensitive discipline in parent-child interactions. Each of the four intervention sessions follows the video feedback using the VIPP themes and guidelines (described above), integrating video feedback directed at sensitive discipline. The whole VIPP procedure of filming, reviewing, preparing comments, and showing and discussing fragments with the mother applies to the video feedback in the sensitive discipline component. However, additional guidelines and intervention themes are used for the discipline part of the intervention.

Intervention themes

The video feedback focusing on sensitive discipline (VIPP-SD) consists of four additional themes (see Table 2.1) that are elaborated during the four intervention sessions (for a more detailed description, see Chapter 11): (1) inductive discipline and distraction — recommending induction and distraction as non-coercive responses to difficult child behavior or potentially conflict evoking situations; (2) positive reinforcement — praising the child for positive behavior and ignoring negative attention seeking; (3) the use of a sensitive time-out to sensitively de-escalate temper tantrums; and (4) empathy for the child, in particular in consistent discipline and clear limit setting. For example, in the first session the mother is encouraged to distract her child in case of challenging behavior and direct the child's attention to objects or situations that are allowed, thus creating the opportunity for positive behaviors and interactions. At the same time, the mother is encouraged to use induction; that is, the reasons for a prohibition or parental intervention are made explicit (Eisenberg, 1992; Hoffman, 1984, 2000), thus helping the child to (gradually) understand the background of parental rules and empathize with other people's interests. In the Leiden VIPP-SD intervention study two extra "booster" home visits (intervention sessions 5 and 6) were used to review all feedback and information from the first four intervention sessions (see Chapter 11).

Written information (Optional)

In the VIPP-SD program, parents may be offered additional written information. In the Leiden VIPP-SD study parents received a booklet including tips on sensitive discipline. For example, following the theme of intervention session 2 (positive reinforcement) one of the tips encouraged parents to double their daily compliments to the child.

VIPP with additional representational discussions (VIPP-R)

Background

Parental (in)secure mental representations of attachment are associated with parental (in)sensitivity and (in)secure infant-parent attachment relationships (Main, Kaplan, & Cassidy, 1985; Van IJzendoorn, 1995; see also Chapter 1). Therefore, intervention efforts may also be directed at the *representational level*, addressing parental attachment representations, in order to pave the way for subsequent behavioral changes. In particular in specific risk groups, such as parents with insecure representations of attachment (Chapters 3 and 6), a representational intervention component may be highly relevant. In the VIPP program with an additional representational focus (VIPP-R) attachment discussions are used as an intervention modality. Discussions about past and present attachments may enable parents to reconsider their childhood experiences and explore the links between those experiences and the developing relationship with their baby (Fraiberg, Adelson, & Shapiro, 1975).

Intervention methods

Attachment discussions

In this intervention modality, the video feedback and brochures used in VIPP (described above) are followed by discussions about the mother's attachment experiences in her own childhood, and their possible influences on her present parenting behavior. Each of the four intervention sessions thus starts with video feedback and continues with the discussion part.

As a starting point, the intervention makes use of various materials, designed to encourage and stimulate an open discussion about past and present attachment relationships. The mother is invited to reflect on her own childhood experiences through short questionnaires or projective material, followed by a discussion about a specific theme. For example, during one visit the mother is invited to read three fictional attachment biographies and elaborate on these stories and her own experiences with her parents. The material and discussion themes are based on attachment theory (Bowlby, 1982, 1988) and inspired by the biographies of "earned secure" persons (Pearson, Cohn, Cowan, & Cowan, 1994). Persons with earned-secure representations of attachment report having had a hard or unloving childhood, but they nevertheless succeeded in restructuring their thoughts and feelings about these negative experiences. Ultimately, they appear to be able to reflect on their childhood experiences coherently, thus showing a secure representation of their attachment biography (Main & Goldwyn, 1994).

The central focus of the representational part of the intervention is on the parent's representation of her attachment biography, that is, her thoughts and feelings about attachment-related childhood and current parenting experiences. The intervener tries to connect parental representations to the parent's actual parenting behavior and to explore together with the parent how past experiences may influence current interactions with the child. The intervener offers a supporting relationship by listening to the mother's memories of the past and her thoughts and feelings concerning her parents or her own child. Also, the parent is provided with support, understanding, and opportunities to explore difficult memories of the past, without criticizing possible negative feelings. By exploring and acknowledging difficult childhood experiences the parent is encouraged to reflect on the influence of these past experiences on her parenting behavior. She is supported and stimulated to consider or practice new behaviors that are more sensitively attuned to her child's needs.

Intervention themes

In the VIPP-R attachment discussions four themes are passed in review (Table 2.1) and elaborated during the four intervention sessions (for a case study, see Chapter 3): (1) separations in the past, experienced as a child, and separations from the baby in the present; (2) parenting in the past, experienced as a child, and parenting in the present, experienced as a mother; (3) defining adult relationships — the process of breaking away during adolescence and defining adult relationships with the parents, including the mother's own experiences with her parents, as well as her expectations of the future relationship with her child; and (4) child of my parents, parent of my child — the explicit link between "being the child of my mother" and "being the mother of my child," exploring which childhood experiences the mother wants to transmit or not to transmit to her child. For example, in the fourth session the mother is provided with cards containing positive messages (e.g., "Come and sit on my lap") and negative messages (e.g., "If you don't stop crying, I'll leave you here") (this task was adapted from Erickson, Korfmacher, & Egeland, 1992). The mother is asked to choose those messages that she had heard herself as a young child and also to choose messages to pass on to her own child. During the discussions the intervener tries to address how in general children's feelings of sadness or anger can be aroused by negative messages from their parents, and how sad or angry the mother must have felt when she got negative comments from her parents. Also, the possible feelings of the baby are brought forward in case the mother chooses negative messages to communicate to her own child.

In general, the discussion part of the VIPP-R intervention takes about an hour, during which the infant may or may not be present. For infants the preceding parts of the intervention session/home visit may have been so tiring that the parent prefers to put the child to bed before the discussion takes place. Thus, VIPP-R home visits tend to last about two and a half hours, but longer visits are not uncommon.

Conclusions

In this chapter we presented the Video-feedback Intervention to promote Positive Parenting (VIPP) programs, including a description of the intervention methods. All VIPP programs utilize videotaped interactions of the parent and child involved and video feedback — watching and discussing the videotape together with the parent. The video feedback offers opportunities to practice observational skills by watching child behavior together with the parent, and it provides opportunities to reinforce the parent's sensitive behavior.

Three VIPP modalities were presented: VIPP, VIPP-SD, and VIPP-R. VIPP aims at enhancing parental sensitive behavior through providing personal video feedback, possibly combined with written information (e.g., brochures, booklets) on sensitive responding in daily situations. VIPP-SD (VIPP combined with sensitive discipline) includes an additional focus on the use of sensitive discipline in challenging parent-child interactions. VIPP-R (VIPP combined with representational efforts) includes additional discussions about past and present attachment relationships, aimed at affecting the parent's mental representation of attachment. The VIPP programs are usually directed at parents of infants, although VIPP and VIPP-SD have been successfully used with toddlers and preschool children. The VIPP programs are home based and short-term: The interventions are implemented in the home of the family in a modest number of sessions, usually four to eight.

3

A case study and process evaluation of video feedback to promote positive parenting alone and with representational attachment discussions

Mariska Klein Velderman, Femmie Juffer, Marian J. Bakermans-Kranenburg, and Marinus H. van IJzendoorn

Centre for Child and Family Studies, Leiden University, the Netherlands

The case study of Sarah and her daughter Linda described in this chapter offers an example of the implementation of four sessions of VIPP and VIPP-R in the Leiden intervention study. The intervention aimed at enhancing sensitive parenting and infant security and restructuring maternal insecure mental representations of attachment. Sarah's participation in the intervention resulted in positive effects on her sensitivity as well as on her daughter's attachment security. Overall, meta-analytic results demonstrate that short-term interventions focusing on sensitive parenting are most effective (Bakermans-Kranenburg, Van IJzendoorn, & Juffer, 2003; see Chapter 5). Positive effects on parental sensitivity were accompanied by positive, albeit somewhat smaller effects on attachment security. Because of the diverging outcomes of intervention studies, there is need to look more closely at the processes leading to successes in enhancing sensitive parenting and preventing or altering insecure attachment in young children. By examining the program implementations and process evaluations of more and less successful interventions (e.g., Lambermon, 1991; Lieberman, Weston,

& Pawl, 1991), we may gain more insight into effective components of interventions and into the process of intergenerational transmission of attachment.

In this chapter we take a closer look at the processes of the intervention programs VIPP and VIPP-R as implemented in the Leiden intervention study ($N =$ 81; see Chapter 6 for a description of the intervention effects). First, a case study is provided of a mother who successfully participated in VIPP-R. Second, the home visitors' experiences during the home visits in the intervention groups are described. The home visitors noted their impressions of the intervention sessions in semistructured logbooks. Last, we present the results of a questionnaire handed to the mothers after the intervention, evaluating the intervention as experienced by the participating mothers.

Case study

Sarah participated in VIPP-R in the Leiden intervention study. In this study, mothers were selected on the basis of their insecure mental representation of attachment, measured with the Adult Attachment Interview (AAI; George, Kaplan, & Main, 1985; Hesse, 1999). These mothers were therefore at risk for insensitive parenting behavior and for transmitting their own insecure attachment to their children. The VIPP-R focused on enhancing Sarah's sensitive parenting and her child's security by providing her with four sessions of video feedback and four parenting brochures, and additionally aimed at restructuring Sarah's insecure mental representation of attachment by discussing her past and present attachment experiences (representational focus).

When she entered the study, Sarah was 28 years old. In her childhood, her parents divorced, and from the age of 7 Sarah grew up with her mother, living on welfare. Sarah's mother had been hospitalized several times, and Sarah had therefore lived with her grandmother for some time too. At the time of the intervention, Sarah had finished general senior secondary education and worked as an administrative employee for 20 hours per week. Sarah was classified as insecure-dismissing on the Adult Attachment Interview (George et al., 1985; Hesse, 1999; Main & Goldwyn, 1994; see Chapter 1). She idealized the negative experiences in her childhood and denied the influence of these experiences on her own personality. Sarah was married to John, and they had a 6-month-old daughter, Linda. Linda scored 2.8 on overall reactivity as measured on the Infant Behavior Questionnaire (IBQ; Rothbart, 1981) at the pretest, and with that score she belonged to the 20% most reactive infants participating in our study (see Chapter 6). The IBQ assesses temperament by asking caregivers about particular behaviors of infants, such as refusing unknown or new food during meals. Highly reactive infants can be characterized as the more negative emotional infants who respond easily distressed to limitations. In our study, intervention effects were experimentally tested (see Chapter 6): The intervention and control groups were compared on measures of pre- and post-test maternal sensitivity (Ainsworth, Bell, & Stayton, 1974) and infant-mother attachment as observed in the Strange Situation Procedure (Ainsworth, Blehar, Waters, & Wall, 1978).

Pretest

At the pretest, Sarah was friendly and easygoing, but superficial in her contact with the home visitor. Sarah acknowledged a few times that she was not used to playing with Linda: "At this age they don't play, they only put things in their mouths." The home visitor had the impression that the video recording was therefore very difficult for Sarah. The home visitor noted that there was hardly any mother-child interaction or communication. Moreover, little physical contact seemed to exist. Linda was very unresponsive during this first home visit. Eye contact between mother and child was almost absent.

For playing with Linda in a 10-minute free-play episode with toys, Sarah was given a score of 3.5 on the Ainsworth sensitivity scale (Ainsworth et al., 1974), scoring below the mean of our sample: 4.23 ($SD = 1.27$; $N = 81$). Sarah's reactions to Linda's signals were mostly not prompt or adequate. Sarah found it hard to adapt to Linda's behavior. She moved Linda several times, was intrusive, and did not offer any structure. Still, Linda also got some time to explore the unfamiliar toys. Linda seemed overwhelmed by the situation.

After the pretest, the home visitor was not yet sure how to rate working with Sarah. The home visitor rated her chances to change Sarah's parenting behavior as reasonable. There were some openings: Sarah was curious about how other mothers handled things (e.g., playing together). When the home visitor said that she had seen many children, Sarah remarked that she did not know much about child development, for example, she wondered when children start crawling.

Video feedback

At the first intervention session, Sarah made some remarks before the video intervention started. It seemed that the preceding recordings had triggered her thinking. Sarah thought she "stuck her nose in" too often. She pointed it out on the videotape: She should not have given a book while Linda was still playing with the rattle. When Sarah explained why she moved Linda, "to be able to see what she thinks of it," the home visitor acknowledged that it is not just important for a mother to see her child, but also for a child to see his or her mother.

The goal of this session's video feedback was to highlight the difference between the child's attachment behavior (e.g., contact seeking) and exploratory behavior (e.g., playing). Sarah stated that she found it important for Linda to get a lot of space to play by herself. The home visitor acknowledged the mother's view, but she also stressed the importance of contact and playing *together*, and she illustrated this with a short video fragment of a playful moment including reciprocal eye contact. She explained to Sarah how important a mother is for a young, dependent child such as Linda. Sarah seemed flattered. During this intervention two brochures about children's crying behavior were handed to Sarah.

In the second intervention session, Sarah was really interested and actively joined the home visitor when the video fragments from the previous home visit were shown. The home visitor used the technique of "speaking for the baby" (Carter, Osofsky, & Hann, 1991) to draw Sarah's attention to Linda's more subtle signals and expressions. She identified when Linda showed pleasure or distress. During the previous visit, Sarah had dropped Linda on her head on a small pillow. Sarah commented on that and showed sympathy when this particular fragment was shown on the videotape. During this session, Linda was communicating a bit more and Sarah responded to Linda's utterances and seemed to enjoy it. She also seemed to be proud of her child. The home visitor felt that Sarah had learned from the first session and noted in the logbook: "There is more eye contact between mother and child. Sarah recognizes it when Linda is looking and reacts with watching, smiling, or talking. A lot has happened!" It seemed that Sarah was learning how to respond to the positive signals of her child. In this session, Sarah was offered a brochure about the relevance of sensitive parenting for children's development.

At the third session, Sarah spontaneously noticed that the interaction looked different this time, and she ascribed this to Linda being more capable because of her age. Adequate and prompt reactions were central to this session's video feedback. The home visitor emphasized that Linda's behavior was related to Sarah's own behavior. She used "interaction chains" — consisting of a signal from Linda, Sarah's sensitive response, and Linda's positive reaction to this response — to highlight adequate responses. During play, for example, Linda showed that she liked riding a horse on her mother's lap, Sarah in turn repeated it, and Linda made some noises of appreciation. The home visitor also complimented Sarah on the way she played with Linda using toys. Sarah gave Linda time and space to explore. Eye contact and a pleasant "being together" atmosphere were also confirmed by the home visitor. Sarah said that she did not want a child who always needed her. The video made her see that this was not the case. Linda could do a lot by herself and every now and then looked for her. The home visitor recognized a substantial difference between the first and present video recordings. Sarah was less interfering and her reactions were more contingent and warm. She sympathized with negative signals and was "very proud of her child." The home visitor appreciated the contact with Sarah and noted in the logbook: "It is nice to see how she enjoys her child now!" During the third home visit a brochure about playing together was handed to Sarah.

During the fourth intervention session, Sarah's reaction to the video fragments was positive — she smiled a lot. While watching the tape, she acknowledged that Linda had changed, she (again) thought because of her age. The message central to this fourth session was sharing emotions. The information seemed to get across to Sarah. The videotape was instructive: When Linda was tired and whimpering, her mother comforted her. The video then showed a peaceful "together" atmosphere, and Linda and Sarah had fun together. According to the home visitor, Sarah was more capable of seeing things from Linda's perspective by the time of the fourth intervention session. She often interacted sensitively and involved. Nevertheless, there were still moments that she did not feel like it, put into words as "I am not in the mood for playing," or that she teased Linda. The home visitor hoped that she made Linda's needs sufficiently clear to Sarah.

Attachment discussions

In each of the four home visits, the video-feedback intervention was followed by an attachment discussion. The discussions started off a bit stiff at the first intervention session. Sarah adopted a somewhat reserved and closed attitude during the discussions. She would have rather not talked about her past: "I never think about it anymore, it is the past." Sarah felt that when she was young, she could never become angry, because she expected her mother to have a heart attack if she did. This resulted in Sarah bottling up her emotions and then finally having an extreme outburst. Sarah's worries were possibly related to the frequent hospitalizations of Sarah's mother during Sarah's youth. The subjects of the discussion in this session were separations in childhood and in the present. The discussion started when a picture of the Separation Anxiety Test (Hansburg, 1980) of a girl who was going to live with her grandmother, separated from her parents, came into sight. During her childhood, Sarah had actually lived with her grandmother. When the home visitor asked Sarah if she found it hard to talk about this, she said no, but she acted as if she had meant the opposite. In this part of the discussion, Sarah acknowledged the negative aspects of her past, but she denied the effects on her own development.

The discourse of the discussion in the second intervention session went well, smoother than in the first session. In contrast to the previous session, Sarah was cooperative and more open. The way Sarah was brought up was central to this session's representational intervention. The home visitor used a questionnaire with propositions about the past to initiate the discussion. For example, Sarah was asked to rate "My mum helped me if I needed her" on a 4-point scale from "never" to "always." Sarah liked to depict her mother positively, with sometimes minimal proof. She idealized the past with her mother and seemed to lack an emotional response. She was nevertheless capable of giving a concrete example of Sarah's mother showing her love for Sarah: When Sarah was ill during carnival, her mother painted her face and placed her in front of the window when her school class came by. This way Sarah could join her classmates in the celebrations. Later in the discussion, it turned out that Sarah had felt very much misunderstood when her mother sent her to boarding school when she was 12 years old. Before this age, Sarah had had to miss her mother a lot because her mother had been in the hospital several times. According to Sarah, her mother could not help that, but she could have kept Sarah out of boarding school, which she did not. The home visitor agreed with Sarah that a child needs her mother and has to be understood in this need.

Sarah spoke of her father as a stranger instead of a father. She could only remember material things. She reproached her father for not taking care of his daughter and exposing her to bad or dangerous circumstances. Her father drank and had driven around with Sarah in his car while he was drunk, ending up at the police station. The home visitor sympathized with Sarah's difficulties with her father. The home visitor also linked the discussion to the present situation: Linda did have a father present. Sarah reacted that at first she had found it difficult to allow Linda's father, John, to do rearing tasks by commenting "I can do it by myself," but now she was happy that her child had a mother as well as a father.

At the third session, Sarah's attitude was again friendly, open, and quite accepting. Sarah and the home visitor talked about the past, breaking away from this past, and the influence of the past on the present. Sarah showed anger when she talked about the day she gave birth to Linda. Sarah had told her mother that she hoped to do better than her mother had done. Sarah's mother had been upset by this remark. The home visitor acknowledged that it was indeed a very hard message, although she could also understand Sarah's feelings.

After the fourth intervention session, the home visitor assigned high ratings for a good and smooth discourse, and she rated Sarah's behavior as friendly and cooperative. In the discussion part of this session, the home visitor helped Sarah focus on the link between being the daughter of her parents and being the mother of Linda. The home visitor provided Sarah with messages she might have heard from her parents. She was asked to select the messages she remembered hearing and she was also encouraged to choose messages that she wished she had heard. During her youth, Sarah had missed her mother saying to her that she could always count on her. Her mother had told Sarah: "Find yourself another mother." The home visitor supported Sarah and acknowledged that this was a very difficult message because her mother was all Sarah had at that time. Next, the discussion was brought round to the present situation. According to Sarah, something her mother did not say to her and she did say to Linda now was the suggestion "Shall we play together?" This was especially remarkable, taking into consideration Sarah's remarks at the pretest that she was not used to playing with Linda.

The home visitor characterized Sarah as angry about her past and attachment figures, whereas she also idealized her past experiences. Over the last sessions, the home visitor had helped Sarah explore her past and present and had been supportive of her. They had worked on recognition and consciousness of negative experiences from Sarah's childhood. The home visitor had tried to let Sarah relive her painful feelings from the past and work toward acknowledgment of the influence of youthful experiences on her personal development and current parenting behavior. At the end of the fourth session, the home visitor noted that she had reached a depth in the discussions with Sarah that had not been possible in discussions with many other mothers. The home visitor had found it very satisfactory to work with Sarah during the intervention sessions.

Posttest

On the posttest, Sarah scored 5.25 on the Ainsworth sensitivity scale (Ainsworth et al., 1974). A score of 5 on this scale equals inconsistent sensitivity. Although Sarah had shown a remarkable increase of almost two scale points, she was still not always consistent in her prompt and adequate responses. In the Strange Situation Procedure (Ainsworth et al., 1978) Linda was assigned a secure B2 classification.

In the evaluation questionnaire, Sarah was one of the seven mothers who were of the opinion that the intervention took a lot of time. However, she was satisfied with the number of home visits (four visits) and with the parenting brochures. Sarah was very positive about the video feedback. She felt that she had learned a lot from this part of the intervention. She evaluated the filming as nice, not disturbing, and interesting. She liked watching the video fragments with the home visitor. Sarah was less enthusiastic about the attachment discussions. She thought talking about the past was not pleasant, but at the same time neither hard nor inconvenient. Sarah's comment at the end of the questionnaire was that she had liked participating in this study. She found it hard in the beginning, but later not anymore. She felt that she had benefited from the video feedback as well as from the discussion part of the intervention.

Process evaluation

In the next section the experiences of the home visitors who conducted the intervention sessions are described. After that the focus is on the evaluation of the intervention by the participating mothers. To differentiate between mothers who gained more or less in sensitivity in the course of the intervention, standardized residuals were computed for sensitivity from 6 months of age (pretest) to the mean of maternal sensitivity at 11 and 13 months of the child's age (posttest; see also Chapter 6). Mothers with increases in sensitivity scores at or above the median (.04) were considered to have participated in *more successful interventions* ($n = 27$), and mothers with gains below the median were considered to have been involved in *less successful interventions* ($n = 27$). In the process evaluation below, experiences of home visitors as well as participating mothers are compared for more and less successful interventions.

Home visitors' experiences

After the pretest and after each of the four intervention sessions, home visitors noted their impression of the sessions in five semistructured logbooks. For example, they rated how much they liked working with the mother involved and whether they thought it was possible to change the mother's behavior or her mental representation of attachment. These logbooks were used in staff discussions about the intervention and as feedback for the home visitors when they prepared for the next intervention sessions. In this chapter, the first two closed-ended questions in the logbook are examined: two general questions about the intervention process. Logbook information was available for all intervention mothers ($n = 54$), with the exception of the last intervention session for which one logbook was missing.

The first closed-ended question was about how satisfactory home visitors considered it working with the mother involved. This question was answered on a 5-point scale ranging from (1) *very unsatisfactory* to (5) *very satisfactory*. On the second closed-ended question, home visitors noted to what extent they thought the mothers could be influenced. They scored this on a scale from (1) *very difficult* to (5) *very well*. At the pretest, home visitors were in many cases not yet convinced of a certain score for how open to advice the mother was, resulting in a large number of missing values. Therefore, the developmental pattern of scores on this item from intervention session 1 to 4 was examined.

During the pretest, home visitors found it moderately satisfactory to work with the mothers involved. They gave an average score of 3.9 ($SD = 0.7$) on a 1 (*very unsatisfactory*) to 5 (*very satisfactory*) scale. At the time of the last home visit, the mean score was 4.2 (SD = 0.8). There was no significant rise in experienced satisfaction in working with the mothers over time, $F(4, 45)$ = 2.11, not significant (n.s.), and no significant differences in scores over time between the mothers in more and less successful interventions, $F(4, 45)$ = 0.32, n.s. There was a substantial correlation (r = .60) between satisfaction scores and ratings of possible influence at the first home visit. A higher estimation of the potential for change was related to working more satisfactorily with the mother during the first home visit. On average, home visitors estimated the possibility of influencing the mothers as fairly good. The mean score at the first session was 3.6 (SD = 0.6) on a 5-point scale, with 1 being *very difficult* and 5 being *very good*. These scores also did not differ for mothers in more and less successful interventions, $t(49)$ = 0.22, n.s., d = 0.05, and did not change significantly over the four home visits, $F(3, 44)$ = 0.86, n.s. On average, the home visitors estimated the possibility of affecting the mothers in the VIPP group as higher than in the VIPP-R group, $t(37.70)$ = 2.29, p = .03, d = 0.63.

Although the home visitors' satisfaction in working with the mothers did not differentiate between mothers in more and less successful interventions, the home visitors' satisfaction score during the first personal contact appeared to predict mothers' increase in sensitivity. The satisfaction score at the pretest significantly predicted the standardized residual of maternal sensitivity from pretest to the posttest, $F(1, 26)$ = 7.22, p = .01. Satisfaction experienced by the home visitor during the pretest explained 18.7% of variance in increase of sensitive caregiving behavior. The correlation between the score for working satisfactorily with the mother and the increase of maternal sensitivity was significant, r = .32. This result was home visitor independent: Controlling for type of intervention (VIPP or VIPP-R), no differences among the three home visitors were found in experienced satisfaction, $F(2, 47)$ = 1.30, n.s., or in sensitivity increases, $F(2, 48)$ = 0.18, n.s.

Mothers' evaluation of the intervention

During the last intervention session, the mothers in the Leiden intervention study were handed an evaluation questionnaire that consisted of 18 questions. Sixteen questions were closed-ended and two were open-ended. The first questions evaluated the time the intervention took, for example: What did the mother think of the number of home visits? Several questions concerned the brochures provided during the intervention. In a similar vein, mothers answered questions about the video-feedback intervention and the attachment discussions. For example: Had they applied the tips and advice they received during the video feedback? Were the attachment discussions helpful and did the mother talk about these sessions with her family or friends? A total of 51 intervention mothers completed the questionnaire. A few mothers refrained from answering one or some questions, resulting in a differing n. Questions about the attachment discussions were answered by all 26 mothers of the VIPP-R group.

Time involved in the intervention

Most mothers (87%) appreciated the number of home visits and scored the intervention as taking the right amount of time (84%). Two mothers would have liked more visits, and five mothers would have preferred fewer visits. No significant differences were found between mothers in more and less successful interventions, or between VIPP and VIPP-R mothers.

Brochures

Most mothers found the information provided in the brochures (somewhat) instructive (94%), clear (98%), and (partly) interesting (98%). Most mothers did not regard the brochures as dull (72%) or redundant (80%). VIPP mothers evaluated the brochures just as positively as the VIPP-R mothers. Half (55%) of the mothers evaluated this part of the intervention as helpful: They reported that they had learned something from the brochure information. The distribution of mothers who said that they had (56%) or had not (44%) applied the information was comparable. Information about playing with infants was appreciated most (36%), followed by the brochure about the relevance of sensitive parenting (29%). The two brochures about crying were named by the smallest number of mothers (16% and 18%) as most favorite.

Video-feedback intervention

As Figure 3.1 shows, the majority of mothers were positive about the video intervention. They regarded the filming as nice (98%), interesting (81%), and not disturbing (100%). Watching the video fragments and talking them over was thought of as instructive. For 38 of 48 mothers (79%) the video feedback was (somewhat) thrilling, but only 2 of 37 (5%) mothers experienced it as a bit hard to discuss and watch the video fragments selected by the home visitor. No differences in these evaluations were found between mothers of the VIPP group and mothers in the VIPP-R group.

According to the mothers, video feedback was more useful than the brochures with written information about sensitive parenting. Forty-eight of 52 mothers (92%) reported that the video feedback taught them something. Most mothers

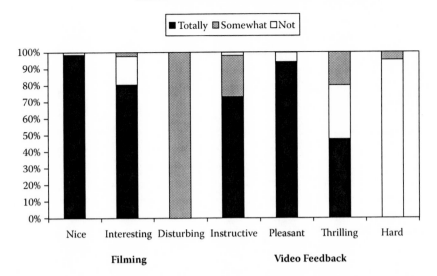

Figure 3.1   Mothers' evaluation of the video-feedback intervention as coded on 3-point scales, with (1) *totally*, (2) *somewhat*, and (3) *not* for the categories nice, interesting, disturbing (for the filming), and instructive, pleasant, thrilling, and hard (for the video feedback).

(73%) reported having applied the suggestions and advice after the intervention sessions had taken place.

Attachment discussions

The 26 mothers in the VIPP-R group were less positive about the attachment discussion than about the video-feedback intervention. About half of these mothers found it hard (58%) or partly inconvenient (48%) to talk about their memories of the past. Seven mothers judged the attachment discussions as not pleasant. Still, 6 mothers found it pleasant to talk about the past, and 10 mothers considered the discussions instructive. No significant differences in evaluations of the brochures, video feedback, or attachment discussions between mothers in more and less successful interventions were found.

Conclusions

The aim of this chapter was to illustrate the intervention process of the VIPP and VIPP-R programs in the Leiden intervention study through a case study and a first process evaluation by the home visitors and the mothers involved. Although the intervention programs were highly structured in an intervention protocol, they were also implemented in accordance with the individual concerns and needs of the mothers involved. More insight in this implementation was provided by means of a case study. Sarah and her daughter, Linda, successfully participated in the intervention, with Sarah gaining remarkably in sensitive parenting and Linda showing a secure attachment relationship with her mother at the posttest.

To get more insight in the impressions of the home visitors, their semistructured logbooks were evaluated. These logbooks showed that the home visitors found it on average reasonably satisfying to work with the mothers, and they considered it quite likely that they could influence the mothers. The satisfaction experienced during the first home visit turned out to be a significant predictor of increases in mothers' sensitive caregiving behavior between the pre- and posttest. In the 1940s, Solomon Asch (1946) recognized the significance of first impressions: "We look at a person and immediately a certain impression of his character forms itself in us. A glance, a few spoken words are sufficient to tell us a story about a highly complex matter" (p. 258). Vonk (1998) described how prominent first impressions are and how the interpretation of later attributes is influenced by the image that has been formed. The home visitors' first impressions in our study may have evoked certain expectations and behaviors in the home visitors. In turn, these may have resulted in higher increases in maternal sensitivity. This corresponds to the Pygmalion effect Rosenthal (1963) described. Teachers' expectations appeared to be very important determinants of children's intellectual performance (Rosenthal & Jacobson, 1966). Children in whom intellectual growth was expected showed greater intellectual gains than control children did. The majority of 479 replication studies in the area of interpersonal expectations found similar relations between expectations and actual behavior (Rosenthal, 2002). In a meta-analysis of 18 teacher expectancy experiments, Raudenbush (1984) showed that only first impressions count. It was difficult to persuade teachers to alter their expectations for children whom they had already known for months.

In a counseling setting, Brown (1970) found an index of counselor personal liking for the client to be significantly related to counselor satisfaction with client progress, his or her techniques, and perception of client satisfaction. Counselors liked clients whom they saw as having the most potential for change. A comparable relation was found in the present study. To our knowledge, no previous research has addressed the influence of home visitors' first impressions on the results of attachment-based interventions. More needs to be learned about the correlation between personal liking and estimates of potential for change. Furthermore, differences in first impressions of the same respondent between different home visitors should be studied. If differences exist, the first impression may be an important factor to consider when assigning certain home visitors to specific respondents.

Alternatively, it may be important to discuss home visitors' first impressions in staff discussions about the implementation and intervention process.

In our study mothers evaluated the different elements of the interventions by means of an evaluation questionnaire. They were satisfied by the intensity of the intervention and on average assigned positive scores to the written information and in particular the video-feedback intervention. They appeared least positive about the attachment discussions, although the majority of mothers still evaluated this part of the intervention in the positive range. We did not find significant differences between mothers in the VIPP and VIPP-R groups, or between mothers who participated in more and less successful interventions, that is, mothers scoring above or below the median for change in sensitivity between the pretest and posttest.

Limitations of the current study pertain to the modest sample size and to the absence of information in logbooks or questionnaires about the control group. In future intervention studies it would be interesting to compare process evaluations of intervention and control mothers. Finally, the influence of home visitors' first impressions should be an issue of further investigation.

In sum, through this case study and process evaluation some important insights were gained into the processes leading to more sensitive parenting. Two findings may be especially important for future interventions. First, most evaluations of home visitors and mothers who had participated in successful interventions did not differ from those of home visitors and mothers who had participated in less successful interventions. That is, neither mothers nor home visitors seem to be capable of foreseeing the effectiveness of the intervention. Intervention effectiveness can only be shown through external observations of behavioral or representational change. "Consumer satisfaction" was shown to be neither a necessary nor a sufficient condition for a successful intervention. Second, the results showed that the first impression of the home visitor was the most important predictor of intervention success in the sense of mothers' increase in sensitive parenting. This is a remarkable outcome, because of the fragile basis of this first experience, although it is in line with findings from social psychology of first encounters and the creation of first impressions that serve as self-fulfilling prophecies. On the basis of our findings, we concluded that the home visitors' feelings about the first home visit should at least be part of the agenda in staff discussions.

Acknowledgments

The authors thank all parents and children who participated in the study and gratefully acknowledge the assistance of Marja Duyvesteyn, Lina Kalinauskiene,

Hesther van Leeuwen, Paulette Steenblok, and Martine Terstegen in collecting and coding data.

4
Attachment-based interventions in early childhood

An overview

Femmie Juffer, Marinus H. van IJzendoorn, and Marian J. Bakermans-Kranenburg
Centre for Child and Family Studies,
Leiden University, the Netherlands

In the past, new parents often relied on the memories of their childhood experiences, using their parents and other family members as role models to plan their own parenting behavior, thus coaching or training programs aiming at support and guidance of parents with young children were largely absent. In contrast, numerous intervention programs are offered to families with young children today. Many parents in isolated or disadvantaged settings apparently need extra information and support from professionals to enhance their parenting skills.

In this chapter intervention programs that focus on parental sensitivity and child-parent attachment relationships are discussed. Based on John Bowlby's and Mary Ainsworth's legacy of attachment theory, many attachment-based research and clinical interventions have been designed and some have even been tested. An overview of these interventions is presented, illustrated with examples of programs and intervention methods.

Attachment theory suggests that children's current and later development is most optimal when they trust their parent(s) as the secure base from which they can explore the world and to which they can return for comfort and protection (Ainsworth, 1989; Bowlby, 1982). Empirical studies show that secure attachment in infancy is associated with positive outcomes in preschool years and later childhood (Atkinson et al., 2000; Fagot, 1997; Sroufe, Egeland, Carlson, & Collins, 2005; Stams, Juffer, & Van IJzendoorn, 2002), whereas insecure and disorganized infant attachment (Main & Solomon, 1990) predicts problematic stress management and behavior problems (Van IJzendoorn, Schuengel, & Bakermans-Kranenburg, 1999). Given the favorable child outcomes of secure attachment relationships, many interventions aim at promoting children's attachment security by trying to improve parental sensitivity, the generally recognized determinant of secure attachment.

Attachment-based interventions should be distinguished from enrichment programs directed at disabled or disadvantaged children's educational and cognitive development (Farran, 1990, 2000). Also, attachment-based interventions are different from parent training aimed to treat children with conduct problems (Webster-Stratton, Reid, & Hammond, 2004) or Parent Management Training (PMT) based on Patterson's coercion theory (e.g., DeGarmo, Patterson, & Forgatch, 2004), although one of our intervention programs includes principles from both attachment theory and coercion theory (see Chapters 2 and 11). Attachment-based interventions that have not been tested yet (e.g., the Attachment and Biobehavioral Catch-up Intervention [Dozier, Lindhiem, & Ackerman, 2005], the Circle of Security Intervention [Marvin, Cooper, Hoffman, & Powell, 2002]) are not included in this chapter. Neither are attachment or holding therapies used in clinical practice (for a discussion of these treatments, see the special issue of the journal *Attachment and Human Development*, O'Connor & Zeanah, 2003; Steele, 2003; and see the report on attachment therapy, reactive attachment disorder, and attachment problems by Chaffin et al., 2006).

The results of attachment-based intervention programs may shed light on both theoretical and clinical issues. Attachment-based interventions are *theoretically* relevant because of their potential contribution to testing and refining attachment theory. By manipulating and enhancing parental sensitivity through intervention programs it can be experimentally tested whether the predicted outcome, a higher percentage of securely attached children, is actually found. The association between parental sensitivity and infant-parent attachment assumed in attachment theory (Ainsworth, Blehar, Waters, & Wall, 1978; Bowlby, 1982), and empirically established in meta-analyses of correlational studies (Atkinson et al., 2000; De Wolff & Van IJzendoorn, 1997; Goldsmith & Alansky, 1987), can thus be tested with respect to its causal nature.

Attachment-based interventions are *clinically* and practically relevant as well, as many parents struggle with challenging disruptive child behaviors and inadequate family functioning (Bronfenbrenner, 1974), thus urging professionals to design intervention programs that may meet these needs. From a clinical perspective, it is important to know whether an intervention that proved to be effective in research can be generalized outside the experimental setting and implemented in a similar group of families needing support.

In the next section, a large set of attachment-based intervention studies conducted in the past are described. The narrative outcomes of these studies and the meta-analytic findings described in the next chapter may assist future researchers and clinicians in the design and implementation of effective and methodologically valid attachment-based interventions. Furthermore, the qualitative and quantitative description of intervention studies reported in the current and next chapter is meant to provide the reader with a broader theoretical and empirical framework toward understanding of the VIPP programs.

Review of intervention studies

Seventy published studies were collected presenting 88 intervention effects on parental sensitivity or infant attachment security that matched our criteria (see Bakermans-Kranenburg, Van IJzendoorn, & Juffer, 2003; Juffer, Bakermans-Kranenburg, & Van IJzendoorn, 2005a; and Chapter 5 for the meta-analytic results). Pertinent studies were collected systematically, using at least three different search strategies (Mullen, 1989; Rosenthal, 1991). First, PsycLIT, *Dissertation Abstracts International*, and MEDLINE were searched with the key words *attachment, sensitivity* (or related terms such as *responsiveness*), and *intervention* (or related terms such as *preventive* or *therapeutic*). Combinations of terms were *attachment and intervention**; *attachment and prevent**; *attachment and therapeut**; *sensitiv** and *parent** (or *mother** or *father**) combined with *intervention** or *prevent** or *therapeut**. (An asterisk indicates that the search contained but was not limited to that word or word fragment.) Second, the references of the collected articles, books, and book chapters were searched for relevant intervention studies. Third, experts in the field suggested intervention studies related to sensitivity or attachment. Interventions that started before children's mean age of 54 months were selected. Brief postnatal interventions with the Brazelton Neonatal Behavioral Assessment Scale were excluded (see Das Eiden & Reifman, 1996, for a meta-analysis of this type of intervention). Case studies were excluded as well, as were unpublished studies or interventions that were reported only at meetings or conferences.

In Table 4.1 several characteristics of the intervention studies are depicted: sample and sample size, start of the intervention and intervention intensity, intervention method or approach, and the reported positive outcomes on parent-child interaction. These studies are discussed with the objective to highlight some general trends rather than to review each separate study thoroughly. Quantitative evaluations of the interventions will not be described in this chapter, but

Table 4.1 Characteristics of early intervention programs aiming to promote positive parent-child interaction

Study	Sample (N)	Start intervention	No. of sessions or duration	Intervention method/approach	Positive outcomes on parent-child interaction
Anisfeld et al. (1990)	Low-SES mothers (N = 49)	Birth	During 8.5 months	Soft baby carrier (promoting physical contact with the baby)	-Maternal sensitivity -Infant-mother attachment -Infants cried less/looked more
Armstrong et al. (1999)	Multirisk mothers (N = 174)	Birth	6 sessions	Support from home visitor	-Maternal sensitivity and involvement
Bakermans-Kranenburg et al. (1998)	Low-SES, insecure mothers (N = 30)	7 months	4 sessions	1. Brochures/video feedback (VIPP)[a] in home visits 2. Plus discussions (VIPP-R)	-1 and 2. Maternal sensitivity
Barnard et al. (1988)	Multiproblem, low support (N = 95)	Pregnancy	>1 year	Home visits: general support	-Sensitivity
Barnett et al. (1987)	Highly anxious mothers (N = 80)	Birth	1 year	1. Support, anti-anxiety measures 2. Support, practical help	-No positive effects
Barrera et al. (1986)	Preterm infants (N = 43)	4 months	1 year	Home visits: promoting parent-infant interaction	-Maternal responsivity and involvement
Beckwith (1988)	Low-SES, sick preterms (N = 70)	Birth	1 year	Home visits: supportive relationship, sensitivity	-Maternal sensitivity -Reciprocal interaction
Benoit et al. (2001)	Infants with feeding problems (N = 28)	18 months	5 sessions	Video feedback (modified interaction guidance)	-Decrease of maternal atypical behavior and disrupted communication
Black & Teti (1997)	Adolescent mothers (N = 59)	6 months	1 session	Videotape (mothers saw tape, M = 4,5 times)	-Mealtime communication (maternal sensitivity)
Brinker et al. (1994)	Minority mothers, high-risk infants (N = 16)	8.5 months	52 sessions	Center-based parent education and therapy	-Maternal sensitivity -Child involvement

Study	Sample	Age at start	Sessions	Intervention	Outcomes
Brophy (1997)	Adolescent mothers (N = 46)	Birth	12 visits	Home visits: teaching, reinforcing, discussion	-No positive effects
Bustan & Sagi (1984)	Preterm infants (N = 16)	Birth	3 sessions	Information, demonstration, and prematurity manual	-Maternal sensitivity; infants cried less, vocalized more
Cicchetti et al. (1999)	Depressed mothers (N = 63)	20 months	46 sessions	Toddler-parent psychotherapy	-Shift to secure attachment (as assessed by the mothers)
Cohen et al. (1999)	Clinically referred infants (N = 67)	10–30 months	1. 14 sessions 2. 15 sessions	1. Infant-led psychotherapy (WWW)[b] 2. Mother-child psychotherapy	-1. Shift to secure or organized attachment 1 and 2. Decline of maternal intrusiveness
Constantino et al. (2001)	Low-SES mothers, stressed (N = 148)	3–18 months	10 sessions	Group sessions with parent education, support, and practical experience	-Trend for improvement in maternal capacity to interpret infant emotional cues
Cooper & Murray (1997)	Clinically depressed mothers (N = 172)	2 months	1. 15 sessions 2. 10 sessions 3. 10 sessions	1. Nondirective counseling 2. Dynamic psychotherapy 3. Interaction guidance	-No positive effects
Dickie & Gerber (1980)	Middle-class parents (N = 19 couples)	8 months	8 sessions	Parent education: lectures, discussions, demonstration	-Parental sensitivity -Infant responsiveness
Egeland & Erickson (1993), Egeland et al. (2000)	Low-SES, multiproblem mothers; firstborns (N = 135)	Pregnancy	1 year	Support, video feedback, mother-child psychotherapy (STEEP)[c]	-Sensitivity

(continued)

Table 4.1 (continued) Characteristics of early intervention programs aiming to promote positive parent-child interaction

Study	Sample (n)	Start intervention	No. of sessions or duration	Intervention method/approach	Positive outcomes on parent-child interaction
Field et al. (1998)	Drug-using adolescent mothers; drug-exposed infants (N = 126)	Birth	4 months: weekly	Parenting class: including interaction coaching	-Mother and infant: more optimal interaction
Field et al. (1980)	Preterm infants, low-SES adolescent mothers (N = 52)	Birth	16 visits	Home visits: education, fostering harmonious mother-child interaction	-Sensitivity -More optimal dyadic face-to-face interaction
Fleming et al. (1992)	Depressed mothers (N = 127)	6–8 weeks	8 sessions	Group meetings: social support	-Maternal affectionate contact
Gelfland et al. (1996)	Clinically depressed mothers (N = 73)	7 months	29 visits	Home visits: demonstration, instruction, support	-No increase in maternal punitive behavior (in contrast to controls)
Gowen & Nebrig (1997)	Multiproblem mothers (N = 32)	<6 months	Weekly (1 year)	Home visits: relationship approach	-Infant-mother attachment
Hamilton (1972)	Disadvantaged, poor minority mothers (N = 16)	<3 years	10 weeks (training, 3 hours a week)	Paid participation of the mother as a teacher's aide; in-service training	-Emotional climate -Child's personal-social development
Heinicke et al. (1999)	Multiproblem mothers; firstborns (N = 64)	Pregnancy	2 years	Home visits: supportive relationship with intervener, weekly mother-infant group	-Maternal sensitivity -Mother-child synchrony -Infant-mother attachment -Child more compliant
Huxley & Warner (1993)	High-risk families (N = 40)	Pregnancy–6 months	Not reported	Home visits: parent education, video feedback (CIP)[d]	-Emotional and verbal sensitivity

Study	Sample	Start	Sessions	Intervention	Outcomes
Jacobson & Frye (1991)	Low SES, low support; firstborns (N = 46)	Pregnancy	>1 year	Home visits: support, information on child development	-Infant-mother attachment
Juffer (1993), Juffer et al. (1997, 2005b)	Internationally adopted infants; first children (N = 90)	6 months	3 sessions	1. Personal book (in home visit) 2. Plus video feedback	-2. Maternal sensitivity 2. Infant-mother attachment 2. Less disorganized attachment
Kang et al. (1995)	Preterm infants (N = 245) in low- or high-SES families	Birth	1–9 sessions	3 groups: home visits with education/demonstrations	-Maternal sensitivity -Infant responsiveness
Kitzman et al. (1997)	Low-SES mothers at risk (N = 743)	Pregnancy	7 before/26 after birth	Home visits: instruction, discussion, support	-Small effect on maternal emotional stimulation
Koniak-Griffin et al. (1995)	Middle-class normal mothers (N = 49)	Birth	Daily during 0–3 months	Baby massage dependent on infant cues	-No positive effects
Krupka (1995)	Adolescent mothers (N = 46)	6 months	12–16 visits	Home visits: video feedback, discussion	-Maternal sensitivity (Q-sort)
Lafreniere & Capuano (1997)	Anxious-withdrawn preschoolers (N = 42)	53 months	20 sessions (in 6 months)	Parent training with booklets, discussion, and video feedback	-Decline of maternal intrusiveness -Child cooperation
Lambermon & Van IJzendoorn (1989), Lambermon (1991)	Mothers with large or small network; firstborns (N = 32)	6 weeks	By mail: 4 times	Education on sensitive parenting with:1. Brochure 2. Videotape	-1. and 2. Maternal sensitivity
Larson (1980)	Low-SES mothers (N = 90)	1. Pregnancy 2. 6 weeks	1. 11 sessions 2. 10 sessions	Home visits: general caregiving, sensitivity, support, child development counseling	-1. Positive maternal behavior (involvement, sensitivity) 2. No positive effects

(continued)

Table 4.1 (continued)   Characteristics of early intervention programs aiming to promote positive parent-child interaction

Study	Sample (n)	Start intervention	No. of sessions or duration	Intervention method/approach	Positive outcomes on parent-child interaction
Leitch (1999)	First-time normal mothers (N = 19)	Pregnancy	Not reported	Videotape about infant communication cues	-Maternal sensitiviy
Letourneau (2000)	Adolescent mothers (N = 16)	Birth	6 sessions	Parent training about infant states and behavior (Keys)[e]	-Maternal contingent sensitivity
Lieberman et al. (1991)	Low-SES, insecure infants (N = 53)	12 months	1 year weekly	Mother-child psychotherapy	-Maternal sensitivity -Toddler more positive
Luster et al. (1996)	Low-SES adolescent mothers (N = 83)	Pregnancy	48 visits	Home visits: emotional and instrumental support	-Maternal sensitivity and involvement
Lyons-Ruth et al. (1990)	Low-SES, multiproblem mothers (N = 40/38)	5 months	47 visits	Support from home visitor	-Infant-mother attachment
Madden et al. (1984)	Low SES (N = 110)	21–33 months	74	Home visits: modeling verbal interaction (MCHP)[f]	-No positive effects
Mahoney & Powell (1988)	Mentally retarded children (N = 41)	18 months	11 months	Home visits: modeling turn taking (TRIP)[g]	-Parental sensitivity -Parents less directive
Meij (1992)	Low SES; firstborns (N = 78)	6 months	3 sessions	1. Booklet (in home visit) 2. Plus video feedback	-2. Maternal sensitivity
Metzl (1980)	Normal firstborn children (N = 60)	1.5 months	3 sessions	1. Encouraging sensitivity (ILP)[h] (mothers) 2. As in 1 (mothers + fathers)	-Home environment
Meyer et al. (1994)	Preterm infants (N = 30)	Birth	3–17 sessions	Demonstration, discussion, counseling; reinforcing positive parenting behavior	-Maternal sensitivity -Infants less negative behavior during feeding

Study	Sample	Starting age	Duration	Intervention	Outcomes
Olds et al. (1986)	Low-SES, single, adolescent mothers (N = 39)	Pregnancy	47 sessions	Home visits: parent education regarding infant development, sensitivity, support	-Avoidance of restriction and punishment
Onozawa et al. (2001)	Mothers with postnatal depression (N = 25)	9 weeks	5 sessions	Infant massage class, support	-Maternal warmth and nonintrusiveness; -Infants more attentive, happy
Palti et al. (1984)	Low-SES mothers (N = 66)	Starting in first year	14–21 sessions	Center-based promotion of interaction (PROD)[i]	-Maternal sensitivity and involvement
Parks (1983)	Adolescent mothers (N = 77)	1 month	1–6 months	Group intervention: clinical group work, education	-Home environment
Riksen-Walraven (1978)	Low SES (N = 100)	9 months	2 sessions	1. Stimulation workbook (S) 2. Responsiveness workbook (R) 3. S and R workbook	-2 and 3. Maternal contingent sensitivity
Riksen-Walraven et al. (1996)	Low-SES, cultural minority group (N = 75)	13 months	16 weekly visits	Home visits: written information on sensitivity, modeling, feedback	-Maternal support
Robert-Tissot et al. (1996)	Clinically referred infants with (behavior) problems (N = 75)	15 months	1. 6 sessions 2. 7 sessions	1. Psychodynamic therapy 2. Interaction guidance, video feedback	-1 and 2. Maternal sensitivity; 1 and 2. Child more cooperative and less unresponsive
Rosenboom (1994), Juffer et al. (2005b)	Adopted infants in families with birth children (N = 40)	6 months	3 sessions	Personal book and video feedback (in home visits)	-Maternal sensitivity; -Less attachment disorganization
Ross (1984)	Preterms in low-SES families (N = 80)	Discharge from hospital	15 sessions	Parent education on caregiving skills	-Sensitivity; -Infants more positive mood

(continued)

Table 4.1 (continued)   Characteristics of early intervention programs aiming to promote positive parent-child interaction

Study	Sample (n)	Start intervention	No. of sessions or duration	Intervention method/approach	Positive outcomes on parent-child interaction
Sajaniemi et al. (2001)	Preterm infants (N = 48)	6 months	20 sessions	Home visits: occupational therapy, encouraging parents to read infant messages	-Less attachment disorganization (atypical attachment)
Scholz & Samuels (1992)	First-time mothers (N = 32) and fathers (N = 32)	4 weeks	1 session	Home visit: videotape, demonstration baby bathing/massage brochures	-Parental warmth, caregiving, and stimulation -Infant responsiveness
Schuler et al. (2000)	Low-SES minority mothers (N = 171)	Birth	9 sessions	Home visits: support, modeling, parent education	-Maternal sensitivity
Seifer et al. (1991)	Infants with developmental disabilities (N = 40)	8 months	6 sessions (in larger program)	Interaction coaching, video feedback	-Decline of overstimulation -Maternal sensitivity -Infants less fussy
Spiker et al. (1993), Bradley et al. (1994)	Low-birth-weight preterm infants (N = 683)	Birth	3 years (first year weekly; biweekly thereafter)	Multiservice, including home visits, parent groups, and child development center attendance (IHDP)[i]	-Maternal support -Dyadic mutuality -Child cooperation
St. Pierre & Layzer (1999)	Low-SES mothers (N = 2,799)	First year of life	>2 years	Home visits: support and early childhood education (CCDP)[k]	-No positive effects
Tessier et al. (1998)	Preterm infants (N = 488)	Birth	24 hours a day until 37/38 gestational age	Kangaroo mother care (promoting skin-to-skin contact)	-Trend for maternal sensitivity

Study	Sample	Age	Sessions	Intervention	Effects
Van den Boom (1988, 1994)	Low-SES mothers; irritable firstborns (N = 100)	6 months	3 sessions	Home visits: feedback on sensitive comforting, stimulation of attunement	-Maternal sensitivity -Infant-mother attachment -Child cooperation
Wagner & Clayton (1999)	Low-SES mothers (N = 713)	Pregnancy/birth	20 sessions	1. Home visits: parent education, support (PAT)[1] 2. Case management (support) 3. PAT + case management	-No positive effects
Wasik et al. (1990)	Low SES (N = 56)	0.5 months	116 sessions	Family education (part of group, daycare)	-Pride, affection, and warmth
Weiner et al. (1994)	Low SES (N = 116); interaction problems	4 months–7 years	12–26 sessions	Video feedback	-Parental positive communication
Whitt & Casey (1982)	Low-SES mothers (N = 32)	0 months	5 sessions	Discussions and modeling within pediatric consults	-Maternal sensitivity and cooperation
Wijnroks (1994)	Preterm infants (N = 66)	6 months	3 sessions	Home visits: video feedback and booklet on sensitivity	-Maternal sensitivity
Zahr (2000)	Poor minority families; preterm infants (N = 62)	Birth	1. 11 sessions 2. 19 sessions	Support and parent education	-No sustained positive effects
Zaslow & Eldred (1998)	Poor adolescent mothers (N = 290)	12–42 months	At least 18 months	Weekly parenting classes, group and individual counseling, childcare	-Emotional support (HOME) -Lower score on harsh treatment
Ziegenhain et al. (1999)	Multiproblem adolescent mothers (N = 29)	Birth	1. and 2. 7 sessions	1. Video feedback 2. Counseling	-1. Maternal sensitivity -2. Maternal sensitivity (but smaller effect)

(continued)

Table 4.1 (continued)   Characteristics of early intervention programs aiming to promote positive parent-child interaction

a VIPP = Video-feedback Intervention to promote Positive Parenting; VIPP-R = VIPP with a representational focus.

b WWW = "Watch, Wait, and Wonder."

c STEEP = Steps Toward Effective and Enjoyable Parenting.

d CIP = Community Infant Project.

e Keys = Keys to Caregiving.

f MCHP = Mother Child Home Program.

g TRIP = TRansactional Intervention Program.

h ILP = Infant Language Program.

i PROD = Promotion of child Development.

j IHDP = Infant Health and Development Program.

k CCDP = Comprehensive Child Development Program.

l PAT = Parents as Teachers program.

can be found in Chapter 5, in which the same set of intervention studies are examined through a series of meta-analyses.

Who participated in the interventions?

In a small number of studies the intervention was directed toward *low-risk, non-clinical families* (Dickie & Gerber, 1980; Koniak-Griffin, Ludington-Hoe, & Verzemnieks, 1995; Lambermon & Van IJzendoorn, 1989; Leitch, 1999; Metzl, 1980; Scholz & Samuels, 1992). In these studies the effect of parent education through videotapes, demonstrations, or brochures was tested. For example, Dickie and Gerber (1980) provided couples with a parent training program consisting of lectures, discussions, and demonstrations designed to increase parental competence to observe, elicit, and contingently respond to infant behavior. Nineteen parent couples and their 4- to 12-month-old infants were randomly assigned to the training group or control group. The training lasted 16 hours over 8 weeks. At the posttest, trained parents reacted more appropriately to the infant's cues, and they provided more frequent verbal and nonverbal contingent responses than the control group.

In most studies the intervention was directed toward *high-risk or clinical families*, with children at risk for problematic socioemotional development, or parents in disadvantaged settings, or a combination of both. The studies involving *children at risk* for nonoptimal social and emotional development consisted of families with clinically referred children (Cohen et al., 1999; Robert-Tissot et al., 1996), infants with feeding problems (Benoit, Madigan, Lecce, Shea, & Goldberg, 2001), preterm infants (e.g., Bustan & Sagi, 1984; Meyer et al., 1994; Sajaniemi et al., 2001; Spiker, Ferguson, & Brooks-Gunn, 1993), children with developmental disabilities (Mahoney & Powell, 1988; Seifer, Clark, & Sameroff, 1991), anxious-withdrawn preschoolers (Lafreniere & Capuano, 1997), or internationally adopted infants (Juffer, Hoksbergen, Riksen-Walraven, & Kohnstamm, 1997; Rosenboom, 1994). For example, Mahoney and Powell (1988) provided home visits to parents of 41 mentally retarded children. The intervention started at the child's mean age of 18 months and lasted on average 11 months. In home visits teachers modeled turn taking and interactive match. A pretest-posttest one-group design without a (randomized) control group was used. At the posttest, parents had become more responsive and less directive compared to the pretest.

The studies involving *parents at risk* consisted of samples with low-socioeconomic status (SES) mothers (e.g., Anisfeld, Casper, Nozyce, & Cunningham, 1990), multirisk mothers (e.g., Heinicke et al., 1999), adolescent mothers (e.g., Black & Teti, 1997), depressed mothers (e.g., Cooper & Murray, 1997), insecure mothers (Bakermans-Kranenburg, Juffer, & Van IJzendoorn, 1998), and highly anxious mothers (Barnett, Blignault, Holmes, Payne, & Parker, 1987). The study of Anisfeld and colleagues (1990) elegantly illustrates the use of an attachment-based intervention in a sample of low-SES mothers. This study was designed to test the hypothesis that experimentally induced increased physical contact would promote maternal sensitivity and secure infant-mother attachment. Low-SES mothers of newborn infants were randomly assigned to an experimental group ($n = 23$) that received soft baby carriers (promoting more physical contact) or to a control group ($n = 26$) that received infant seats as a "dummy" intervention (less physical contact). At the child's age of 3.5 months, experimental mothers were more contingently responsive than control mothers, and at 13 months many more experimental (83%) than control infants (38.5%) were securely attached in the Strange Situation Procedure (Ainsworth et al., 1978).

Finally, several interventions have been directed at *parents and infants at risk*. A number of combinations were found, such as low-SES or adolescent mothers with preterm infants (e.g., Field, Widmayer, Stringer, & Ignatoff, 1980; Ross, 1984) or low-SES mothers with insecurely attached or irritable infants (Lieberman, Weston, & Pawl, 1991; Van den Boom, 1994). For example, Ross (1984) provided home intervention to 40 low-income families with preterm newborns. To assess effects of intervention, children receiving home visits were compared with a (nonrandomized) matched control group of preterm infants who were treated in the same hospital unit later in the same year ($n = 40$). During home visits mothers were taught about infant development and caregiving skills, and they were instructed how to facilitate the social development of their children. At the posttest, intervention mothers were rated higher on the HOME (Caldwell & Bradley, 1984) factor Emotional and Verbal Responsivity than mothers in the control group.

In the VIPP studies described in this volume, the intervention was directed at parents at risk (insecure mothers, see Chapters 3 and 6; eating disordered mothers, see Chapter 8), children at risk (preterm or sick babies, see Chapter 7; children with behavior problems, see Chapter 11; internationally adopted children, see Chapter 9), and normative families/children (children in childcare, see Chapter 10).

Start and frequency of the intervention

Some intervention studies started *before birth* (e.g., Barnard et al., 1988; Heinicke et al., 1999). For example, the STEEP program (Steps Toward Effective and Enjoyable Parenting) described by Egeland and Erickson (1993) started when the participants — low-SES, multiproblem mothers — were pregnant with their first child. During one year, support was provided to the mothers, combined with either video feedback or mother-child psychotherapy. At the posttest, intervention mothers were more sensitive than control mothers, but a positive effect on infant-mother attachment could not be found. Several intervention programs started *at birth* (e.g., Kang et al., 1995; Meyer et al., 1994; Zahr, 2000). For example, Ziegenhain, Wijnroks, Derksen, and Dreisörner (1999) provided an intervention of seven sessions of video feedback or counseling to multiproblem adolescent mothers, starting at birth. In the video-feedback group positive effects on maternal sensitivity were found. Finally, other intervention programs started *after birth*, ranging from 0 to 2 months (Cooper & Murray, 1997; Fleming, Klein, & Corter, 1992; Wasik, Ramey, Bryant, & Sparling, 1990) to 53 months after birth (Lafreniere & Capuano, 1997). For example, Lyons-Ruth, Connell, and Grunebaum (1990) started an intervention of home visits in multiproblem families at the mean infant age of five months. At 18 months, the home-visited infants were more often securely attached than control infants.

Not only interventions differed when the program started, but also the *number of sessions* or contacts differed widely. In a few intervention studies, only one contact was offered to the family (Black & Teti, 1997; Scholz & Samuels, 1992). Scholz and Samuels (1992) visited 32 first-time Australian families in their home at four weeks postpartum. During one intervention session, the parents were given a demonstration of baby bathing and massage and shown a videotape about this subject. At the posttest at 12 weeks postpartum, positive effects on parental warmth and infant responsiveness were reported. Other intervention studies provided parents with a moderate number of intervention sessions (2 to 15 sessions; e.g., Armstrong, Fraser, Dadds, & Morris, 1999; Letourneau, 2000; Van den Boom, 1994) or a large number of sessions (>16 sessions; e.g., Cicchetti, Toth, & Rogosch, 1999; Luster, Perlstadt, McKinney, Sims, & Juang, 1996). In Chapter 5, the number of intervention sessions is examined meta-analytically (see also Bakermans-Kranenburg et al., 2003).

In the interventions described in this volume most programs started just before or in the second half of the baby's first year of life (Chapters 3 and 6 to 9). In one program (Chapter 11) the intervention was started at the age of one, two, or three years to test whether effectiveness differs at various ages. In Chapter 10 the intervention was implemented with childcare providers and children in toddlerhood. All VIPP interventions made use of a small number of intervention sessions ranging from three (Chapter 9) to seven (Chapter 8).

Intervention methods and approaches

Not only the number of sessions, but also the intensity of the intervention methods differs widely. The intensity of intervention methods can be seen as a continuum, ranging from nonintensive, nonpersonal to highly intensive and very personal. A few intervention programs made use of a nonintensive, rather nonpersonal intervention program, such as the provision of baby carriers (Anisfeld et al., 1990) or the implementation of brochures or a videotape, personally or by mail (Black & Teti, 1997; Lambermon & Van IJzendoorn, 1989). The study by Riksen-Walraven (1978) represents an illustration of a nonintensive program, providing low-SES mothers with a "workbook for parents." A randomized pretest-posttest control group design (N = 100) was used to evaluate the effects of the intervention. The workbook that aimed at enhancing maternal sensitivity was successful: At the posttest, at the infant's age of 12 months, intervention mothers were more contingently responsive toward their infants than control mothers.

Further on the continuum in the direction of more intensive and personal interventions the following programs can be found: programs providing parent groups or parenting classes (e.g., Field et al., 1998; Fleming et al., 1992), home visits (e.g., Beckwith, 1988; Jacobson & Frye, 1991), video feedback (e.g., Krupka, 1995), attachment discussions (Bakermans-Kranenburg et al., 1998), and mother-child psychotherapy (Egeland & Erickson, 1993; Lieberman et al., 1991).

The VIPP studies described in this volume made use of rather personal and intensive methods: video feedback (all studies) and in some studies attachment discussions (Chapters 3, 6, and 7). In several cases, brochures (Chapters 3, 6, and 11), personal books (Chapters 8 and 9), or handouts (Chapter 10) were added to the intervention.

Focus of the intervention

Following Egeland, Weinfield, Bosquet, and Cheng (2000), interventions may be distinguished in the following way: programs that are directed at the parent's sensitivity, programs that focus on the parent's mental representation, and intervention efforts that attempt to stimulate or provide social support for parents. In many intervention programs the parent's *sensitive behavior* toward the child is the focus of the intervention. Ainsworth et al. (1978) defined sensitivity as the ability to perceive the child's signals correctly and to react to these signals promptly and adequately. Some programs start at the most basic level of parental sensitivity: To make parents "better perceivers" they are taught observational skills. This goal can be reached in several ways, for example, through stimulating parents to fill in a workbook about their child's behavior (Riksen-Walraven, 1978) or by encouraging parents to engage in "speaking for the baby" (verbalizing children's facial expressions and nonverbal cues; Bakermans-Kranenburg et al., 1998; Carter, Osofsky, & Hann, 1991). Other programs that focus on parental sensitivity seem to concentrate more on the second part of Ainsworth's definition. In this case, the intervener teaches or demonstrates prompt and adequate responding to children's signals, for example, through discussing parenting brochures or by modeling the desired behaviors (e.g., Mahoney & Powell, 1988). Another strategy is reinforcing parents' sensitive behaviors demonstrated in the interaction with their child, for instance, with video feedback (e.g., Bakermans-Kranenburg et al., 1998; Seifer et al., 1991; Ziegenhain et al., 1999).

In the second type of intervention, efforts are directed toward the parent's *representation of attachment*, and the focus of change is the parent's representational model or working model of attachment (Bowlby, 1982). In this type of intervention programs, parents are involved in discussions about their past and present attachment experiences and feelings (Bakermans-Kranenburg et al., 1998), in child-parent psychotherapy (e.g., Cohen et al., 1999; Lieberman et al., 1991), or in psychodynamic therapy (e.g., Robert-Tissot et al., 1996). These discussions or therapy sessions aim at restructuring the parent's mental representation of attachment toward a more secure and balanced view of relationships.

Stimulating or providing *social support* to parents is included in the third type of intervention. Several programs provide support, sometimes by giving practical help and advice (Barnett et al., 1987) or individualized services (Gowen & Nebrig, 1997), by giving information about community services (Luster et al., 1996), or by stimulating parents to extend their social network. Other programs combine social support with another focus of intervention, for example, by aiming to promote parental sensitivity as well as providing general support (e.g., Barnard et al., 1988; Gelfland, Teti, Seiner, & Jameson, 1996). Still other interventions combine social support with both a behavioral and a representational approach. For example, in project STEEP (Egeland & Erickson, 1993, 2004; Egeland et al., 2000), mothers receive not only practical support and advice, but also video feedback to increase sensitive parenting and counseling to examine and discuss their own childhood attachment experiences.

The VIPP and VIPP-SD programs explicitly focus on parental sensitive behavior, whereas the VIPP-R intervention combines a behavioral and representational approach. In none of the intervention studies described in this volume was the explicit encouragement or provision of social support a goal of intervention, although the parent may experience the relationship with the intervener as supportive. In the next section, two intervention programs briefly illustrate two different perspectives — a program with a representational focus and a program directed at providing social support.

Intervention programs: examples of representational focus and social support

Child-parent psychotherapy

Lieberman designed child-parent psychotherapy as a relationship-based treatment approach for young children who are experiencing mental health problems (Lieberman, 1992, 2004; Lieberman et al., 1991). This type of treatment is based on Fraiberg's intervention work in which she addressed mental health problems in infants (Fraiberg, Adelson, & Shapiro, 1975). The primary focus involves the uncovering of unconscious links between the parent's psychological conflicts and her parenting behaviors that are mistuned to the child's needs and interfere with his or her development (Lieberman, 2004). In this representational approach, the parent's enduring conflicts have the role of Fraiberg's "ghosts in the nursery" that must be exorcised to free the child from their malignant influence (Lieberman, 2004, pp. 98–99). Child-parent psychotherapy usually takes place during weekly sessions lasting between 60 and 90 minutes with the parent, the child, and the psychotherapist. The duration of the treatment may range from a few months to one or two years. The sessions may take place in the home, a clinic-based playroom, or a community center (e.g., childcare center) (Lieberman, 2004). In Lieberman et al.'s study (1991) included in our narrative and meta-analytic review, visits took place mostly in the home and lasted 1.5 hours.

Child-parent psychotherapy uses several "ports of entry," roads that lead to the target of the intervention (as said above, uncovering unconcious links between parent's internal conflicts and actual parenting behavior), for example, the child's play or the parent's behavior (Lieberman, 2004). The choice of a port of entry is guided by the therapist's clinical judgment of what needs attention in the moment. Lieberman (2004) describes the following vignette of child-parent psychotherapy. During play a three-year-old boy is talking about monsters scaring him. The therapist addresses this issue, discussing it with the mother. The mother informs the therapist that she keeps telling her child that monsters do not exist, but her son does not seem to believe her. The therapist explains that many children of her son's age believe in monsters, and she asks the mother to reassure her son that she will make sure that the monsters will not come close to him. After some hesitation and encouragement from the therapist, the mother tells her son that she will scare away the monsters. After some discussion, the child is clearly satisfied that his mother will take effective action to protect him (Lieberman, 2004, p. 115). In this case, the therapist addressed the mental representations of the child (as endangered) and the mother (as refusing to take her child's fear seriously and promise protection) through behavior. The therapist stayed at the concrete level of monsters and used developmental guidance to explain children's development in general. In other cases, the therapist could have addressed through verbal interpretations the possible symbolic meanings of the monsters for the child's mental representation, or the psychodynamic meaning of the mother's initial refusal to offer protection (Lieberman, 2004).

Contrasting this intervention with the VIPP programs highlights several differences. For example, the VIPP approach is usually more restricted in time. Moreover, children are not addressed directly in the VIPP intervention, as contrasted with Lieberman's psychotherapy where the child participates actively in discussions. The representational part of Lieberman's approach is partly comparable with VIPP-R insofar as the representations are addressed through behavior or discussion, but differs from VIPP-R when interpretations or symbolic meanings of psychodynamic processes are provided by the therapist.

Home-visiting family support services

Lyons-Ruth and colleagues (1990) described a program that primarily focused on providing and stimulating social support, combined with an additonal focus of encouraging positive mother-child interaction. Their intervention study was designed to examine whether highly stressed families with infants could benefit from home-based intervention services when offered by experienced staff with determined outreach and intensive attention to family health and social service needs (Lyons-Ruth et al., 1990, p. 86). A home-visiting program with a strong social support service component was provided to 31 mothers and their infants at high social risk due to the combined effects of poverty, maternal depression, and caregiving inadequacy. The intervention was implemented during weekly home visits and lasted for almost one year. The home visitors had strong working relationships with a variety of community programs (e.g., Head Start).

The four central goals of the program were (1) providing an accepting and trustworthy relationship; (2) increasing the family's competence in accessing resources to meet basic needs, including social, financial, legal, health, and educational services; (3) modeling and reinforcing more positive mother-infant interactions; and (4) decreasing social isolation from other mothers through encouraging weekly participation in parenting groups or monthly participation in a drop-in social hour (Lyons-Ruth et al., 1990, p. 87). In the description of these goals, several ingredients of social support services can be recognized: offering practical help and advice (goals 1 and 2), providing information about community services (goal 2), and stimulating parents to extend their social network (goal 4). Encouragement of sensitivity, the additional focus of the intervention, is included in the third program goal.

Contrasting this intervention program and the VIPP programs results in some similarities (e.g., the home-visiting component, offering an accepting relationship to the mother), but also in clear differences. In the VIPP programs the provision of practical help and the encouragement of social support are not intervention goals. Furthermore, the VIPP interventions are short-term (3 to 7 sessions), whereas in this home-visiting family support program an average of 47 sessions was provided to the mothers.

Conclusions

Our review of intervention studies showed many differences and similarities of intervention programs aimed to enhance parental sensitivity and infant-parent attachment. Together, the intervention programs represent a large body of empirical and clinical evidence, providing researchers and clinicians with some first clues about what works for whom and what does not work. The strength of a narrative review is that intervention methods and approaches can be illuminated in some detail, that general trends can be summarized, and that first impressions about positive outcomes can be described. Also, gaps in our knowledge can be traced. Starting with the last issue, our review suggests that there are only a few intervention programs focusing on representations of attachment as an outcome measure, compared with more common programs focusing on parental sensitivity as an outcome variable. Furthermore, most interventions were designed for and tested in clinical and at-risk groups, whereas only a few programs were implemented in healthy, normative families. Given the fact that many well-baby clinics and community resource centers provide a lot of parenting information to new parents nowadays, it is important to test the effects of attachment-based brochures, videotapes, and so forth on normative, healthy parents as well.

From Table 4.1 some general trends regarding the success of these programs can be summarized, although it should be added that only through meta-analysis can definite outcomes be uncovered (see Chapter 5). Of the 70 studies listed in the table, 54 intervention studies reported a positive effect on parental sensitivity or a comparable construct and 3 studies reported a trend. So, according to these reports 81% of the studies were successful in enhancing positive parenting behavior. For child behavior a different picture emerges. In 11 studies positive outcomes were reported on attachment security. Moreover, in 19 studies positive effects on child behavior were reported, such as increased infant responsiveness or child cooperation. In 3 of these 19 studies, attachment security was also promoted, but in the remaining 16 studies positive child outcomes other than attachment security were found. So, according to the reports 39% of the intervention studies were successful in enhancing positive child outcomes (attachment or other behaviors; in a total of 27 studies). The discrepancy between positive parent outcomes and positive child outcomes, particularly child attachment outcomes, converges with the replicated meta-analytic finding that it is easier to promote parental sensitivity than children's attachment security (Bakermans-Kranenburg et al., 2003; Van IJzendoorn, Juffer, & Duyvesteyn, 1995).

The 16 studies that reported positive child outcomes other than attachment security all reported that their intervention successfully enhanced parental sensitivity. These findings indicate that the enhancement of parental sensitivity may be accompanied by positive child behaviors other than attachment security. For future research, it will be interesting to study intervention effects not only on attachment security, but also on a broader array of positive child behaviors (e.g., child cooperation, responsiveness, or positive mood).

Finally, narrative reviews cannot decisively inform researchers and clinicians about the effectiveness of (aspects of) intervention programs. As a next step, a meta-analysis examining the intervention programs described in this chapter may reveal more precisely the effectiveness of certain types of intervention programs for specific types of families, and examine in a quantitative way intervention features, such as the ideal number of intervention sessions or the ideal time to start an attachment-based intervention.

5

Less is more

Meta-analytic arguments for the use of sensitivity-focused interventions

Marian J. Bakermans-Kranenburg,
Marinus H. van IJzendoorn,
and Femmie Juffer

*Centre for Child and Family Studies,
Leiden University, the Netherlands*

What use is it to do meta-analyses? Many answers to that question have been formulated (Cooper, 1998; Hedges & Olkin, 1985; Hunter & Schmidt, 1996; Rosenthal, 1991), but one of the shortest may be: Meta-analyses are necessary for making policy and also for planning new research (Borenstein, Rothstein, & Cohen, 2000). They also help to get a grip on a certain research field, to find out which studies exist and what they have produced. In the case of preventive interventions, the number of studies has been increasing exponentially in the last decades. The idea that early interventions may be most effective in preventing less optimal or even deviant developmental pathways has led to an increase in efforts to shape and evaluate preventive interventions in the first few years of life, and even before the birth of the target child (e.g., Barnard et al., 1988, Huxley & Warner, 1993; Jacobson & Frye, 1991; Leitch, 1999; Luster, Perlstadt, McKinney, Sims, & Juang, 1996). In particular, the concept of a critical period of fast neuropsychological growth — as well as the possibly irreversible effects of impaired neurological development during the first three years after birth — has stimulated early interventions, although the scientific evidence for a critical period of neurological maturation is actually rather shallow (Fox, Leavitt, & Warhol, 1999; Shonkoff & Phillips, 2001).

As discussed in Chapter 4, intervention studies are important at least in two ways. First, experiments are crucial in determining whether parenting is causally related to child development or whether genetics or nonparental influences are the more powerful forces in shaping children's development (Harris, 1998; Rowe, 1994). Second, experimental interventions may indicate optimal ways of changing parental attitudes, mental representations, or behavior. Are frequent and intensive therapeutic or preventive interventions most effective, or even the only way to have an effect on parental sensitivity or the infant-parent attachment relationship? Or can shorter interventions (shorter time span, fewer sessions) be as effective as intensive programs, and are they thus more cost efficient? Parent training and family interventions are shaped anywhere on a continuum between the provision of a 15-minute videotape on reciprocal mealtime communication (Black & Teti, 1997) to intensive and weekly individual meetings with the troubled family during the first three years after a child's birth (Wasik, Ramey, Bryant, & Sparling, 1990). What effects do these different approaches produce?

Narrative reviews and meta-analysis

Several reviews on early interventions have documented their effectiveness in enhancing parental child-rearing attitudes and practices and children's socioemotional development (Beckwith, 2000; Benasich, Brooks-Gunn, & Clewell, 1992; Bradley, 1993; Egeland, Weinfield, Bosquet, & Cheng, 2000; Heinicke, Beckwith, & Thompson, 1988; Lagerberg, 2000; Lojkasek, Cohen, & Muir, 1994; MacLeod & Nelson, 2000; Van IJzendoorn, Juffer, & Duyvesteyn, 1995). Narrative reviews are very informative about the individual intervention studies. They document the intervention features of the individual studies and the type of sample that was involved, and report on which studies were effective and which studies did not find the hoped-for significant effects. However, the interventions differ in aims, methods, and types of families involved, hampering a direct comparison among the studies. Furthermore, the significance of effects is dependent on the sample size — some studies that are not significant may actually show larger effects than other studies that are significant (due to the larger sample size). That raises the question of how the effects of intervention studies may be compared, and a narrative review may end with the conclusion that some interventions were (significantly) effective, but others were not. A meta-analysis takes us one step further. In meta-analyses the unit of analysis is the empirical study. The various statistics (or the means and standard deviations provided in the study report) that are presented to describe the outcome of a study are recomputed and transformed into Cohen's d. The effect size d is the standardized difference between the means of the intervention and the control group, and d values can be compared among studies. Moreover, considering the effect size rather than the significance as the relevant outcome of a study helps us to overcome the problem of overreliance on dichotomous significance testing decisions in drawing conclusions (Rosnow & Rosenthal, 1989). For, as has been eloquently underscored by Rosnow and Rosenthal (1989, p. 1277), "God loves the .06 nearly as much as the .05."

With meta-analysis the data from multiple studies can be synthesized. When studies yield comparable effects, this effect can be reported. But in the event that the effect varies among studies, an attempt can be made to track down the source of the variation. The effect may vary with the quality of the study, the type of sample, or the timing of the intervention. The single study can only speculate about these possibilities and about the extent to which results can be generalized, but meta-analysis allows us to address these issues empirically. Meta-analysis may thus help us to come to evidence-based conclusions about what are the best intervention practices.

For example, in individual intervention studies, the best timing of interventions is difficult to evaluate because it requires the comparison of several different age cohorts. The absence of research on the timing of interventions, that is, the optimal time to begin and end the intervention efforts, is a weakness in the field of interventions, hampering the most effective implementation of intervention programs in the community (Egeland et al., 2000). Meta-analysis of extant interventions starting at different time points may address this issue and go beyond conclusions drawn from the separate studies.

Types of intervention programs

Intervention efforts vary in focus, duration, and method (see Chapter 4). What type of intervention turns out to be most effective? In their narrative review Egeland et al. (2000) concluded that long-term and frequent interventions that combined (1) behavioral feedback directed at maternal sensitivity, (2) discussions about past and present attachment experiences and their representations, and (3) providing support should be considered most effective, in particular in multirisk families. So, interventions should aim at changing many aspects of the caregiving environment and involve the parent's behavior, representation, and context. Moreover, they recommended that interventions should begin before an infant is born. This line of reasoning does not seem to lack logic — The more the better, is that not what one would expect?

In contrast, Van IJzendoorn et al. (1995) were more skeptical about long-term and more broadly focused programs. In their exploratory meta-analysis of 11 intervention studies on maternal sensitivity and of 12 intervention studies on infant-mother attachment, short-term interventions with a confined focus were relatively successful in affecting attachment (d = 0.48), whereas long-term interventions seemed to be not effective at all (d = 0.00). However, because the number of studies was small, the authors' conclusions regarding this difference were only tentative. For example, Van IJzendoorn et al. (1995) then hypothesized that short-term interventions with a narrow behavioral focus may be effective in changing parental sensitive behavior, but that they would fail to affect the more robust attachment insecurity in the infant. Furthermore, the differentiation between behavioral and representational interventions is not equivalent to the difference between short-term and long-term interventions. Although broad interventions, aimed at changes in maternal representations, are often long-term, behavioral interventions may also consist of a large number of sessions (e.g., Spiker, Ferguson, & Brooks-Gunn, 1993; Wasik et al., 1990; Zaslow & Eldred, 1998), and some representational interventions are rather brief (e.g., Bakermans-Kranenburg, Juffer, & Van IJzendoorn, 1998; Robert-Tissot et al., 1996; Ziegenhain, Wijnroks, Derksen, & Dreisörner, 1999). Last, because of the small number of studies in Van IJzendoorn et al.'s (1995) meta-analysis, it was impossible to adequately test the effectiveness of type of intervention in samples with more or less risk factors. In the larger set of studies that is available now, the effectiveness of interventions in groups with varying risk factors can also be tested. In sum, only meta-analyses of a substantial number of intervention studies with diverging intensities, samples, and intervention modalities may shed light on what type of intervention is most effective for whom.

Does sensitivity affect attachment security?

Besides their relevance for prevention, intervention studies are also crucially important for confirming or falsifying causal hypotheses (see Chapter 4). A core issue in attachment theory is the purported causal link between parental sensitivity and infant attachment security. Correlational evidence for such a link has piled up in the past decades (for a meta-analytic synthesis, see De Wolff & Van IJzendoorn, 1997), but an equally impressive amount of experimental data is still lacking. It is a replicated fact that parental sensitivity is significantly but modestly associated with infant attachment (r = .24, k = 21, N = 1,099 in nonclinical samples using the Strange Situation Procedure and observational sensitivity measures; De Wolff & Van IJzendoorn, 1997). This association, however, leaves the possibility open that infant attachment is in fact the causal determinant of parental sensitivity. Furthermore, other factors related to both sensitivity and attachment might be responsible for the (possibly spurious) correlation. The link between parental sensitivity and infant attachment is interpreted as causal, but it needs to be tested in more rigorous ways, that is, through experimental manipulation and effect evaluation. On the basis of the large set of intervention studies that has become available, we investigated for the first time meta-analytically whether changes in parental sensitivity that are brought about by preventive interventions are accompanied by corresponding changes in infant attachment security.

The set of studies

Seventy published studies were traced presenting 88 intervention effects on sensitivity ($k = 81$, $N = 7,636$) and attachment ($k = 29$, $N = 1,503$; see Bakermans-Kranenburg, Van IJzendoorn, & Juffer, 2003; and Chapter 4 for a description of the search procedure). Comparing published and unpublished data sources empirically, Rosenthal (1991) concluded that published studies are not strongly biased in their results relative to unpublished studies. However, it is possible to estimate the size of the "file drawer" problem. The so-called fail-safe number indicates the number of unretrieved studies with null results that would be needed to cancel out the combined effects found in the retrieved studies (Mullen, 1989). In the current set of meta-analyses, the fail-safe numbers for the pertinent analyses were computed.

All intervention studies reported observed sensitivity or attachment as an outcome. Because we were interested in actual changes in parenting behavior rather than parent-reported evaluations or attitudes, our search was restricted to studies that used observational measures (studies that only reported on self-reported parental attitudes at the posttest were excluded). Furthermore, the current meta-analyses were limited to parental sensitivity and children's attachment security; therefore, intervention studies that concentrated on the child's cognitive development only were not included (for reviews of cognitively oriented programs, see Farran, 1990; Zigler & Hall, 2000).

Several intervention studies used the classic Ainsworth sensitivity rating scales (Ainsworth, Bell, & Stayton, 1974); others used the Home Observation for Measurement of the Environment (HOME; Caldwell & Bradley, 1984), the Nursing Child Assessment Teaching Scale (NCATS; Barnard et al., 1988), or the Erickson rating scales for maternal sensitivity and supportiveness (Egeland, Erickson, Clemenhagen-Moon, Hiester, & Korfmacher, 1990; Erickson, Sroufe, & Egeland, 1985). In case of the HOME, the observation scale for maternal sensitivity (emotional and verbal responsivity) was selected if data on separate scales were provided. This was the case in the vast majority of the studies with HOME posttests. Also, studies were included that assessed maternal interactive behavior with measures other than the above-mentioned instruments, provided that they used observational measures of parental behavior clearly related to sensitivity (e.g., empathic responsiveness, Lieberman, Weston, & Pawl, 1991;

sensitive mealtime communication, Black & Teti, 1997). The intervention studies were not restricted to a specific population. Some samples were middle-class families with healthy infants, but studies with clinical and at-risk populations were included as well. Compared with the first meta-analysis in this area (Van IJzendoorn et al., 1995), which involved a small number of 11 interventions on sensitivity and attachment, the current meta-analyses included a much larger number of studies: 70 published intervention studies with 88 interventions directed at either sensitivity or attachment or both. The 88 interventions did not include overlapping samples. The set of retrieved studies was sufficiently large to differentiate among the different types of interventions that Egeland et al. (2000) discussed in their narrative review and to go beyond the simplified dichotomy between short-term behaviorally oriented interventions and long-term representational interventions.

Coding of the studies

Essential for doing a meta-analysis is careful coding of the studies. Not only the effect size and the exact sample size (of intervention and control groups) of the individual intervention studies must be determined, but also their values on the moderator variables must be specified (e.g., number of sessions, location of the intervention sessions, etc.). A detailed coding system was used to rate every intervention study on design, sample, and intervention characteristics. As design characteristics we coded sample size, randomization, the absence or presence of a control group, and the study's attrition rate. As sample characteristics we coded features of both the parents involved (e.g., high or middle versus low socioeconomic status (SES), adolescence, clinical reference, or at high risk because of a combination of risk factors, such as poverty, social isolation, and single parenthood) and their children (e.g., prematurity, irritability, international adoption). When reported, the percentage of insecurely attached children in the control group was included as an indicator of the risk for attachment-related problems in the sample. As intervention characteristics we coded the number of sessions, the age of the child at the start of the intervention, and the status of the intervener (professional or nonprofessional). Moreover, we coded whether the intervention took place at the parents' home and whether video feedback was used as an intervention tool. Last, we coded whether the intervention aimed at enhancing parental sensitivity, affecting the parents' mental representation, providing social support, or any of the possible combinations of these approaches.

As an example of an intervention aimed at enhancing parental sensitivity, Black and Teti (1997) provided adolescent mothers with a videotape to help them enhance their sensitivity during mealtime. An intervention aimed at affecting parents' mental representation was presented in Cicchetti, Toth, and Rogosch's (1999) study with depressed mothers. The intervention aimed at reconstructing mothers' representation of self in relation to their own parents to enable them to construct new representations of themselves in relation to their child. An intervention focused on support can be found in one of the Barnett, Blignault, Holmes, Payne, and Parker (1987) intervention programs, in which experienced mothers provided support and practical help to highly anxious mothers. Barnett et al.'s (1987) second intervention program combined the provision of social support with efforts to enhance maternal sensitivity and was thus coded in the category "sensitivity and support." Intervention studies that combined strategies directed at maternal sensitivity, representation, and support were conducted by, for example, Egeland and Erickson (1993; the STEEP project [Steps Toward Effective, Enjoyable Parenting]) and Heinicke et al. (1999).

Last, effect sizes were determined. The various statistics (or the means and standard deviations provided in the study report) expressing the outcome of a study were transformed into Cohen's d. No study or participant was counted more than once — for example, in the case of a study with two intervention groups (involved in two different interventions) and one control group (as in, e.g., Bakermans-Kranenburg et al., 1998; Ziegenhain et al., 1999) the size of the control group was divided by two, and separate effect sizes were computed for each of the interventions. In a few cases, the intervention was conducted without a control group but with a pre- and posttest design (e.g., Hamilton, 1972; Mahoney & Powell, 1988). When pertinent statistics were unavailable, effect sizes were computed on the basis of pretest and posttest means and standard deviations, using t tests for independent groups because t tests for dependent groups would require the raw data. These one-group pretest-posttest interventions were not included in the set of randomized control group studies, but they were included in the set of nonrandomized studies (see below).

Just as every primary study including maternal sensitivity or attachment security contains a check whether these variables were coded in a reliable way, a random sample of studies of our meta-analysis was double-coded to check for reliability of coding. Satisfactory intercoder reliabilities were established on this set of 10 studies (mean r = .98; range = .90 ~ 1.00; mean κ = .95; range = .78 ~ 1.00). All studies were coded independently, and two disagreements were discussed to consensus.

Two outlying effect sizes were identified in the set of sensitivity interventions on the basis of standardized z values larger than 3.3 or smaller than –3.3 ($p <$ .001; Tabachnick & Fidell, 2001). We excluded the intervention studies showing outlying z values from further analyses. The effect size of one excluded study was d = 2.62 (Van den Boom, 1994); in the other outlying intervention (a subsample of Zahr, 2000) parental sensitivity decreased substantially, that is, more than a standard deviation ($d = -1.12$).

Meta-analytic results

Random and nonrandom studies: design affects outcome

Because all studies proposed directed hypotheses predicting that the intervention would have a positive effect, the significance of the combined effect sizes was tested with one-tailed alphas set at .05 (for details about the analyses, see Bakermans-Kranenburg et al., 2003). Eighty-one studies (including 7,636 families) presented intervention effects on parental sensitivity, and the combined effect size was 0.44 ($p < .001$). This is a substantial combined effect. In a related field, for instance, Blok, Fukkink, Gebhardt, and Leseman (2005) reviewed the effectiveness of early intervention programs to stimulate children's *cognitive* development (including 19 studies). They found a combined effect size of $d = 0.32$ for effects in the cognitive domain and $d = 0.05$ for effects in the socioemotional domain.

To estimate the combined effect size in the set of studies with the strongest designs, those intervention studies with a randomized control group design were selected. Because only a small minority of the interventions aimed at both mothers and fathers (three studies: Dickie & Gerber, 1980; one of the two interventions of Metzl, 1980; and Scholz & Samuels, 1992), we selected only interventions focusing on maternal sensitivity for this set of randomized control group studies. In this set of 51 studies (including 6,282 mothers with their children), interventions were also significantly effective in enhancing maternal sensitivity ($d = 0.33$), but the combined effect size was significantly lower than the combined effect size of studies that did not use a randomized control group design ($d = 0.61$). An essential aspect of the study's design appeared to affect the outcome — nonrandomized studies seemed to run the risk of inflated effects (see Figure 5.1). Therefore, the effects of the studies with the better designs should be taken more seriously in the discussion about which interventions are most effective. The fail-safe number for the set of random intervention studies was 913. It would take more than 900 unpublished randomized intervention studies without intervention effects to cancel out the combined effect size of the randomized studies (Mullen, 1989).

Maternal sensitivity

The interventions were classified as focusing on sensitivity only; focusing on sensitivity and support; and those aiming at all levels — representation, sensitivity,

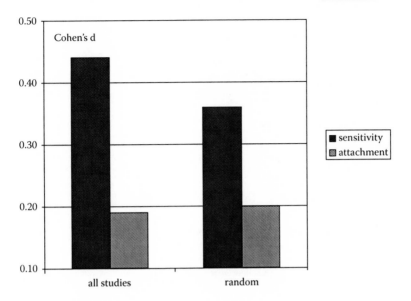

Figure 5.1 Combined effect sizes (Cohen's *d*) on sensitivity and attachment.

and support (see above). All sets of interventions showed rather substantial effect sizes: The interventions focusing on sensitivity only ($d = 0.45$); those combining sensitivity and support ($d = 0.27$); and those using all levels of influence — representation, sensitivity, and support ($d = 0.46$). Contrasting the interventions focusing on sensitivity only (20 studies) with all other categories of intervention combined (31 studies, including interventions aiming at sensitivity and support, which is a broader focus than sensitivity only), interventions focusing on sensitivity only were found to be more effective ($d = 0.45$) than all other types of interventions combined ($d = 0.27$), and this difference was significant (see Figure 5.2).

Other characteristics of the interventions appeared relevant as well. Interventions with video feedback were more effective than interventions without this method. Interventions with fewer than 5 sessions were as effective as interventions with 5 to 16 sessions, but interventions with more than 16 sessions were less effective than interventions with a smaller number of sessions. The age of the children at the start of the intervention also made a difference. Interventions starting after 6 months of infant age were more effective than interventions starting prenatally or in the first 6 months. The effect of interventions conducted at parents' homes was not significantly different from the effect of interventions conducted elsewhere.

There might be an association between the focus of the intervention and the number of intervention sessions (focused interventions might generally be

Cohen's d

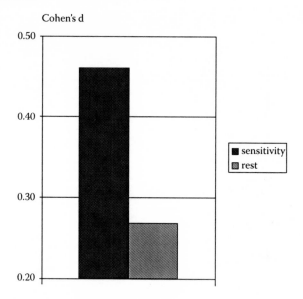

Figure 5.2   Focus of intervention.

briefer), obscuring whether large effect sizes should be ascribed to the focus of the intervention (sensitivity only), to the number of sessions (fewer than 16), or to both. Therefore, the interventions were recoded as focused on sensitivity with fewer than 16 sessions, focused on sensitivity with more than 16 sessions, other focus with fewer than 16 sessions, and other focus with more than 16 sessions. Short interventions focusing on sensitivity only were most effective.

Surprisingly, most characteristics of the samples, such as socioeconomic status (SES), prematurity, adolescent motherhood, and the presence of multiple risk factors, were not associated with significant differences in effect sizes between the studies. The only difference was between clinical and nonclinical samples: Interventions conducted with clinically referred samples were more effective than interventions with other groups.

Attrition was significantly related to effect size. In studies without attrition, the combined effect size was significantly larger than in studies in which participants were lost. Attrition may have had differential effects on the experimental and control groups, in favor of the latter, because the worst cases may disappear most readily from the control group. In that case, it would be more difficult for the experimental group to outperform the control group.

It could be argued that at-risk groups have different needs, and thus may profit from different types of interventions than relatively "normal" groups. Therefore, in a separate set of meta-analyses the influence of intervention characteristics was tested in randomized control group studies with samples suffering from multiple problems (multirisk and clinically referred; 30 studies involving 4,119 families). In this set of multiproblem samples, the interventions focusing on sensitivity only were again more effective (d = 0.48) than all other categories of intervention combined (d = 0.25). Once again the most effective interventions consisted of fewer than 16 sessions. Interventions with fewer than 5 sessions were as effective as interventions with 5 to 16 sessions, but they were both more effective than interventions with more than 16 sessions.

Certain sample characteristics or intervention characteristics that yielded differences in effect sizes might be confounded. For example, multiproblem samples might more often be involved in interventions with more sessions, and they might tend to start at an earlier age of the infant. When each of these characteristics is associated with a smaller effect of the intervention, the conclusion concerning which moderators really matter is obscured. Therefore, a multiple regression analysis was conducted. At the first step, the design characteristic "randomization" was entered to control for the influence of randomization on the size of the effects. Sample characteristics (low SES, multiproblem or clinically referred sample, adolescent mothers) were added at Step 2. Intervention characteristics — focus (sensitivity only versus other), infant age at the start of the intervention (in months), and number of sessions — were added at Step 3. Last, the interactions between focus of the intervention and number of sessions were added. The hierarchical multiple regression selected two significant predictors: focus of the intervention (b = .26, p = .03) and child's age at start of the intervention (b = .23, p = .04). Sample and design characteristics did not significantly predict effect size. The number of sessions did not significantly contribute to the regression, but it tended to be associated in the expected direction: Fewer sessions were associated with higher effect sizes. The Focus of Intervention × Number of Sessions interaction did not change the regression equation. Sensitivity-focused interventions and a later start of the intervention predicted larger effect sizes, even after controlling for characteristics of the sample.

Attachment

Twenty-nine intervention studies (involving 1,503 families) aimed at promoting attachment security. Most studies reported intervention effects on attachment security as observed in the standard Ainsworth Strange Situation Procedure (Ainsworth, Blehar, Waters, & Wall, 1978); one study used the Preschool Assessment of Attachment (Crittenden, 1992), and three studies used the Attachment Q-Sort (AQS; Vaughn & Waters, 1990) or a related outcome measure (AQS security items; Jacobson & Frye, 1991) as the only assessment of attachment. For all studies with the Strange Situation Procedure, effect sizes were computed combining the insecure groups and comparing this combined insecure group with the secure group (non-B versus B). In cases in which both three-way and four-way classifications were available, effect sizes were computed on the basis of the forced three-way classifications (the secondary A, B, or C classifications of children classified as disorganized). Intervention effects on disorganized attachment were analyzed separately (see below). The combined effect size for attachment security was small but significant ($d = 0.19$). Twenty-three studies (including 1,255 mother-infant dyads) presented randomized control group experiments, which showed a similar effect size ($d = 0.20$). The fail-safe number for the set of randomized attachment intervention studies was 191, meaning it would take more than 190 unpublished studies without intervention effects on attachment security to cancel out the combined effect size of 0.20 (Mullen, 1989).

The set of random studies with reported effects on attachment security was much smaller (23 studies) than the set with effects on maternal sensitivity; therefore, not all intervention and sample characteristics could be examined (see Bakermans-Kranenburg et al., 2003). We had to exclude tests of moderators with fewer than four studies in one of the cells (i.e., adolescence, prematurity, status of the intervener, and whether the intervention took place at the mother's home). What did the remaining contrasts show? Again, interventions focusing on sensitivity (10 studies) were significantly more effective than all other interventions combined (13 studies). For that matter, they were the only interventions that showed a significant combined effect size ($d = 0.39$). Interventions starting after the age of six months were more effective than interventions starting earlier, and interventions that did not make use of video feedback yielded significant effect sizes on infant attachment security and were significantly more effective than interventions with video feedback as an intervention means. This is remarkable in light of the larger effect size of interventions with video feedback on maternal sensitivity.

Similar to the sensitivity studies, a composite variable was constructed combining focus and number of sessions of the interventions. The contrast was significant: Again, short interventions focusing on sensitivity only were most effective ($d = 0.33$). Interventions with other foci were less effective, whether they had fewer than 16 sessions ($d = -0.06$) or more than 16 sessions ($d = 0.11$).

Most characteristics of the samples (SES, clinical referrals, and the presence of multiple risk factors) were not associated with differences in effect sizes between the studies, with one exception: More insecurity in the control groups was associated with larger effect sizes. A high percentage of insecurity may make it easier for the intervention group to outperform the control group; it prevents a ceiling effect from dampening the intervention effectiveness. Although attrition may endanger the outcomes of intervention studies (as it did in the case of sensitivity), there was no significant difference in effect sizes for attachment in studies with more or less attrition.

In the larger set of studies that included nonrandom intervention studies, similar results were found. It should be noted that the contrast between random and nonrandom studies for effects on sensitivity was not apparent for attachment: Random studies were not significantly less effective in promoting attachment security than the other studies in our data set (random studies, d = 0.20; nonrandom studies, d = 0.13).

The subset of randomized studies of multiproblem families contained 15 studies with a total of 971 families. The combined effect size (d = 0.19) was similar to the effect size in "normal" samples. Again, interventions focusing on sensitivity only appeared most effective (d = 0.34), and the difference with other interventions was significant. Furthermore, interventions with a relatively late start appeared most effective in enhancing children's attachment security, analogous to what was found in the total set of random attachment intervention studies.

Disorganized attachment

Can the emergence of attachment disorganization be prevented? Infant disorganized attachment is a major risk factor for problematic stress management and later problem behavior (for reviews see Green & Goldwyn, 2002; Lyons-Ruth & Jacobvitz, 1999; for a meta-analysis see Van IJzendoorn, Schuengel, & Bakermans-Kranenburg, 1999). Therefore, the question of whether early childhood interventions are effective in preventing attachment disorganization is highly relevant. The question of whether the emergence of attachment disorganization can be prevented has never been meta-analytically examined. In 15 studies (including 842 families) infant disorganized attachment was reported as an outcome measure. The combined effect size of these studies was not significant, d = 0.05 (see Bakermans-Kranenburg, Van IJzendoorn, & Juffer, 2005). Most effective were interventions that started after six months of infant age rather than before. The five interventions focusing on sensitivity only were significantly more effective in reducing attachment disorganization (d = 0.26) than other interventions (d = −0.08). Contrasting other intervention characteristics (the use of video feedback, the number of sessions, and where the interventions took place) did not yield significant results, or subsets of studies were too small to warrant testing the significance of the moderator. So, although parental insensitivity is supposed to be associated with organized insecurity, but not with disorganized attachment, interventions that focused on sensitivity only were most effective in reducing attachment disorganization. Studies on samples with higher percentages of disorganized attachment in the control groups were more effective than studies with lower percentages of disorganized children in the control group. In a similar vein as with insecurity, a higher percentage of attachment disorganization makes it easier for the intervention group to outperform the control group (see Chapter 12 for further discussion).

The proof of the pudding: Are changes in sensitivity related to changes in attachment?

Were successful sensitivity interventions also more effective in enhancing infant attachment security? If the answer is yes, that would be essential support for the hypothesized causal link between sensitivity and attachment. Therefore, we examined how effects on attachment related to effect sizes on sensitivity. The effect sizes for the studies' effects on sensitivity were categorized as follows: less than or equal to 0.15, between 0.16 and 0.40, and greater than or equal to 0.41. A significant difference was found among the three categories (see Figure 5.3). The studies with the largest effect sizes for sensitivity ($d > 0.40$) were also the most effective in enhancing the children's attachment security ($d = 0.45$). In fact, the only intervention studies that yielded a significant effect size on attachment security were the studies with a large effect size on sensitivity.

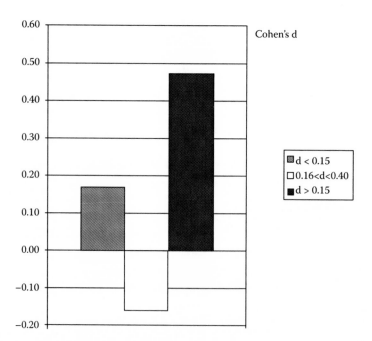

Figure 5.3 Sensitivity causes attachment.

Conclusions

This meta-analytic synthesis of studies shows that interventions can enhance maternal sensitivity and infant attachment security, but infant attachment security to a lesser extent than maternal sensitivity. In particular, interventions that only focus on sensitive maternal behavior were successful in improving insensitive parenting as well as infant attachment insecurity. Interventions with fewer intervention sessions and a start date not before six months after birth were somewhat more effective than other intervention modalities. This was the case regardless of the presence or absence of multiple problems in the family. Overall, whereas many of the intervention characteristics that were examined were significant moderators, most sample characteristics were not associated with effectiveness of the interventions. On the whole, interventions that were more effective in the total randomized set were also more effective in the subset of clinical and high-risk samples. This indicates that the effectiveness of certain types of interventions was not dependent on characteristics of the various samples. The multivariate approach underscored the effectiveness of sensitivity-focused interventions (and a later start of the intervention), even after controlling for characteristics of the sample. Although none of the studies explicitly aimed at preventing disorganized infant attachment, sensitivity-focused interventions were also the most effective type of intervention reducing attachment disorganization.

Highly intensive interventions with numerous sessions focusing on sensitivity, representations, and support show disappointingly small or even negative effect sizes on attachment security (combined $d = -0.03$). It should be noted, however, that the number of studies contributing to this combined effect size was very small. Only three studies were included in this subset (Egeland & Erickson, 1993; Heinicke et al., 1999; Lieberman et al., 1991), and they were conducted with multiproblem families. One of them, Heinicke et al.'s (1999) intervention, was effective. Long-term and broadly focused support of multiproblem families in coping with their daily hassles may be badly needed to enable the intervener to subsequently focus on sensitivity and representations. This broadband effort may, however, take too much time and energy away from a potentially effective, goal-directed intervention approach. Nevertheless, broadband interventions may have been effective on outcome measures that were not included in our analyses (e.g., parental satisfaction, perceived social support, or quality of the marital relationship).

Bradley (2004) suggested an additional reason for the effectiveness of short-term interventions. Because parenting is generally considered to be a natural competency, parents expect from themselves and from each other that they roughly know how to parent a child, whether or not these are reasonable expectations. They may thus be motivated to engage in an intervention program for a well-defined period to get some support, but less so to be tied by the bonds of a series of intervention sessions with no end in sight.

More effective sensitivity interventions were expected to also be somewhat more effective in enhancing children's attachment security. Indeed, the association between effect sizes for sensitivity and attachment confirms the hypothesis of a causal link between sensitivity and attachment security. Sensitivity interventions with rather large effect sizes were also most effective in enhancing infant attachment security. Actually, less effective sensitivity interventions did not manage to bring about any changes in attachment security.

In general, attachment insecurity is more difficult to change than maternal insensitivity, as is documented by the differences in effect sizes for sensitivity ($d = 0.33$) and attachment ($d = 0.20$ for attachment security, $d = 0.05$ for the prevention of disorganized attachment). Interventions usually aim at enhancing maternal sensitivity, but assess sensitivity and attachment outcomes at about the same time, that is, shortly after the intervention sessions. Small but significant changes in maternal sensitivity may not have had the chance to affect infant attachment security. A sleeper effect on attachment security might remain undetected. Further research on this issue of a time lag between changes in sensitivity and attachment is needed and should take this possibility of a sleeper effect into account. Long-term follow-up studies of early interventions could in principle also shed a different light on the difference in effectiveness of divergent intervention types. For the moment, however, meta-analytic evidence clearly favors short-term, behaviorally focused interventions — both for families that fare relatively well and for multiproblem families that badly need the support of a tried and tested intervention program.

6

Insecure mothers with temperamentally reactive infants

A chance for intervention

Marian J. Bakermans-Kranenburg,
Philomeen Breddels-van Baardewijk,
Femmie Juffer, Mariska Klein Velderman,
and Marinus H. van IJzendoorn
*Centre for Child and Family Studies,
Leiden University, the Netherlands*

The preceding chapters provided an overview of what has happened in the field of attachment-based interventions during the past three decades. The methodological pitfalls were described and the effectiveness of various types of intervention studies presented, with the somewhat unexpected conclusion that the most intensive, broadband interventions do not necessarily lead to the highest gains in sensitivity or attachment security.

Child characteristics were not a decisive factor in the meta-analytic results of attachment-based intervention studies (see Chapter 5), although some interventions included children with various temperamental, socioemotional, and communicative problems (e.g., anxious-withdrawn children, irritable infants). There are, however, strong, evolutionary reasons to emphasize the differential susceptibility of children to the child-rearing influences of their parents. As Belsky (2005, p. 176) argued:

> Because the future is inherently uncertain, the goals that parents have for their children, whether held consciously or unconsciously, could turn out to have huge reproductive costs if (a) realized by all their children and (b) future conditions turn out to be highly unlike those that parents, again

consciously or unconsciously, anticipate. For this reason it seems to make evolutionary sense for children, especially within a family, to vary in their susceptibility to parental rearing, with some being highly responsive and others being less responsive and perhaps not responsive at all. A growing body of evidence which is not inconsistent with this view suggests, interestingly, that it may be highly negatively emotional infants who are most susceptible to parental influence — for better (when receiving emotionally supportive care) or for worse (when receiving less supportive care).

Against the background of this hypothesis (see also Belsky, 1997, 1999a, 1999b), the potentially differential effectiveness of our intervention was tested in a group of children with high versus average to low negative reactivity. Focusing on highly reactive children may also contribute to new insights into possible mutual influences between temperament, maternal behavior, and attachment (Stevenson-Hinde, 2005). Are reactive children more affected by maternal sensitivity, and will they be more responsive to (experimentally induced) changes in their mothers' sensitivity?

The implementation of VIPP and VIPP-R in a Dutch study seems to have the features of a home game. The designers of the intervention program were involved as home visitors, sometimes as coders (that is, provided that they were unaware of characteristics of participants and never saw them live), and one was even involved as a participant in the piloting phase of the study, to try out the representational part of VIPP-R. Although this participant was pleased with the efforts of the home visitor to promote her sensitivity to the signals of her first-born child, it does not inform us about the satisfaction of other participants, let alone about the effects of the intervention. The evaluation of the intervention by mothers and home visitors of the Leiden VIPP/VIPP-R intervention study and a case study are presented in Chapter 3. The current chapter focuses on the short-term effects of the intervention (see also Klein Velderman, Bakermans-Kranenburg, Juffer, & Van IJzendoorn, 2006a; for long-term effects see Klein Velderman et al., 2006b).

Maternal attachment representation, sensitivity, and mother-infant attachment

Our intervention study aimed at promoting sensitivity and preventing insecure attachment in a group that is at risk for insensitivity and the development of an insecure attachment with the infant, namely, mothers with an insecure mental representation of attachment. The reasons for aiming at secure infant-parent attachment relationships are obvious. Secure attachment relationships have been associated with better social competence (e.g., Weinfield, Sroufe, Egeland, & Carlson, 1999) and more optimal parent and peer relationships than insecure attachments (e.g., Bretherton, 1991; Schneider, Atkinson, & Tardif, 2001; Sroufe, 1988; Sroufe, Carlson, & Shulman, 1993; Sroufe, Egeland, Carlson, & Collins, 2005). Moreover, attachment relationships have been shown to be continuous across the first two decades of life in relatively stable child-rearing circumstances (Fraley, 2002; Hamilton, 2000; Waters, Hamilton, & Weinfield, 2000; Waters, Merrick, Treboux, Crowell, & Albersheim, 2000; Waters, Weinfield, & Hamilton, 2000). Thus, the beneficial effects of secure attachments not only may be observed in more harmonious parent-child relationships and in more satisfying close friendships in the immediate years after early childhood, but also may endure in adolescence and adulthood. It is an encouraging, supportive, and stable parental figure during children's early years of life who contributes to young children's sense of attachment security and trust in significant others (Ainsworth, Blehar, Waters, & Wall, 1978; Bowlby, 1982; Cassidy, 1999; Verschueren & Marcoen, 1999).

Parental sensitivity, that is, parents' ability to perceive signals accurately and to respond to them promptly and adequately (Ainsworth, Bell, & Stayton, 1971, 1974), has been shown to be associated with the development of attachment security in a consistent, albeit modest way (Ainsworth et al., 1978; De Wolff & Van IJzendoorn, 1997; Pederson et al., 1990). Meta-analytic results (Van IJzendoorn, 1995) also demonstrated that parents' mental representations of attachment (i.e., the perception of their childhood attachment experiences and the influence on current psychosocial functioning; Hesse, 1999; Main, Kaplan, & Cassidy, 1985) partly determine their sensitivity to children's attachment signals. Parents with secure representations of attachment are on average more sensitive and frequently develop a secure attachment relationship with their child. The intergenerational transmission of attachment quality amounts to 75% (Van IJzendoorn, 1995). Parental insecure attachment representations constitute a risk factor for parental insensitivity and the development of insecure attachment relationships with offspring, and both parental sensitivity and parental attachment representations should be considered promising candidates for preventive intervention efforts (see Chapter 1).

Changing maternal attachment representations?

There is a large number of interventions that successfully enhance parental sensitivity, and prevent or alter insecure attachments in young children (e.g., Anisfeld, Casper, Nozyce, & Cunningham, 1990; Heinicke et al., 1999), but there are only a few intervention studies that implicitly or explicitly address the issue of changing parental mental representations of attachment (Brophy, 1997; Erickson, Korfmacher, & Egeland, 1992; Fraiberg, Adelson, & Shapiro, 1975; Leifer, Wax, Leventhal-Belfer, Fouchia, & Morrison, 1989; Lieberman, Weston, & Pawl,

1991; see Bakermans-Kranenburg et al., 2003, and Chapter 5 for a meta-analysis; see Chapter 4 for a review). Only one study evaluated the effects of an intervention on parental attachment representations (Egeland, Adam, Ogawa, & Korfmacher, 1995). The absence of positive changes in mothers' representations of attachment in this study may have been related to the rather high percentage of secure mothers as well as secure infants in their control group (i.e., a ceiling effect). With this state of affairs no firm conclusions regarding the effectiveness of interventions on parental attachment representations can be drawn.

Why aim at changing parental attachment representations? Fraiberg et al. (1975) pointed out how "ghosts in the nursery" can play a crucial role in daily family life across generations. Past attachment experiences may, although unnoticed, interfere with caregiving and, in some families, take over and control the lives of several generations where the past is allowed to repeat itself. According to Fraiberg and her colleagues (1975; Egeland, Weinfield, Bosquet, & Cheng, 2000; Lieberman & Pawl, 1993), parents can be freed from these ghosts by remembering and re-experiencing their childhood anxieties, reflecting on them, and thereby reconstructing the mental representations of their childhood attachment experiences.

Moreover, one could imagine that interventions enhancing parental attachment security might create more firmly rooted behavioral changes in the parent, and therefore achieve more persistent changes in children's attachment security. In interventions with a behavioral focus, mothers receive suggestions on how to respond to the attachment signals of their child at a certain age, for example, infancy. However, toddlers may use other signals to express their attachment needs than do infants, and they may require other parenting behaviors. Parents may fail to attune themselves to their growing child when their inner working model of attachment is insecure. Parents with an insecure attachment representation might, for example, have trouble combining sensitive responses to attachment signals with limit setting when the child is misbehaving. Secure attachment representations may facilitate empathy with the child's perspective, enhancing a flexible adaptation to the changing behavioral repertoire of the child and finding sensitive solutions to developmental issues that the child struggles with. Therefore, we hypothesized that a combination of attention to parental sensitivity and parental attachment representations might lead to firmer and more enduring changes in both parenting behavior and children's attachment security. In the VIPP-R program, parents were helped to restructure their current attachment representations by discussing their early attachment experiences and by exploring the link between those experiences and the developing relationship with their own child.

The Leiden VIPP and VIPP-R study

The Leiden intervention study aimed at mothers of firstborn infants with insecure mental representation of their own childhood attachment experiences, and implemented VIPP and VIPP-R in two intervention groups. Our main goal was to help these mothers prevent the transmission of their own insecure attachment to the next generation. To our knowledge, this study is the first to include mothers who had been selected on the basis of their attachment representation.

Intervention effects were expected on both maternal sensitivity and quality of the infant-mother attachment relationships. Interventions focusing on sensitivity or attachment were most effective if the intervention sessions were aimed at sensitive parenting behavior and included only a moderate number of sessions (less is more), whether or not the families involved were facing multiple problems (Bakermans-Kranenburg et al., 2003; see Chapter 5). This is one of the reasons why a behaviorally focused attachment-based intervention with a small number of intervention sessions was implemented in the current study.

Furthermore, we expected that highly reactive children would be more susceptible to their mothers' sensitivity and changes in maternal sensitivity than less reactive children, and that the mothers of children characterized by high negative reactivity would profit most from the intervention. The differential intervention effects for highly reactive children compared to less reactive children was an experimental test of Belsky's (2005) model of differential susceptibility to child-rearing influences.

Procedure

Mothers with firstborn four-month-old children were identified by using town hall records of a city in the western part of the Netherlands and by using the records of the children's health centers in five neighboring villages. Mothers with more than 8 but less than 14 years of formal education were selected. Our assumption was that parenting information and other resources were less available to these mothers than to more highly educated women (Viswanath, Kahn, Finnegan, Hertog, & Potter, 1993). Selected mothers were invited to participate in the Adult Attachment Interview (George, Kaplan, & Main, 1985; Hesse, 1999) and to complete a questionnaire on their child's temperament (Infant Behavior Questionnaire [IBQ]; Rothbart, 1981). To facilitate timely intervention, the time-consuming transcription of the Adult Attachment Interview was omitted and a tentative attachment classification was assigned on the basis of the audiotaped interview by the first or fifth author (see below). Eighty-four mothers tentatively classified as insecure were included in this study. They were coded as dismissing or preoccupied, regardless of an additional classification as unresolved (Hesse, 1999). Three mothers only participated in the pretest home visit, one because of the child's illness and two because of lack of time, leaving 81 mothers who participated in all activities.

The mothers were randomly assigned to one of three groups: (1) a *control group* (n = 27), (2) a group with personal video feedback and written information about sensitive parenting (hereafter called *VIPP group*, n = 28), and (3) a group with personal video feedback, written information about sensitive parenting, and additional discussions about early attachment experiences (hereafter *VIPP-R group*, n = 26). The mothers' mean age was 27.8 years (SD = 3.60), and their mean educational level was 2.5 (SD = 1.00) on a scale ranging from 1 to 4, with 1 = primary school or junior secondary vocational education and 4 = senior secondary general education followed by senior secondary vocational education. Control mothers were on average two years older than intervention mothers, $t(78) = 2.72, p < .01$. The two groups did not differ on educational level or intelligence (as assessed at the pretest).

The intervention

The first home visit in both the control group and the intervention groups took place at about seven months and typically lasted 1.5 hours. During this visit the home visitor introduced herself to the mother and explained the procedure. All mothers were asked to complete a "baby's diary" (St. James-Roberts, personal communication, April 1993; see also Wolke, 1993), noting the baby's behavior (sleeping, awake and satisfied, fussing, or crying) and parental activities with the baby (e.g., feeding, bathing, playing, carrying the baby around) for three consecutive days. The baby's diary was used in the first intervention session to talk about the baby's crying behavior. Finally, video observations were made of the mother-infant dyads to assess sensitivity during free play. The control mothers also completed a baby's diary, but it was not discussed with them and they did not receive any further treatment.

The first home visit and the intervention sessions were implemented by three female home visitors who knew that the respondents were selected on the basis of their insecure attachment representation, but were unaware of the mothers' type of insecurity (the tentative dismissing versus preoccupied classification) and of all other information about the mothers or infants enrolled in the intervention. The intervention sessions took place between the babies' 7th and 10th month of age. At 11 months, videorecorded observations of the mother-infant dyads at home were made by a research assistant unknown to the mother to assess the mother's sensitivity. At 13 months, infant-mother attachment and mothers' sensitivity during free play were assessed at the laboratory.

The VIPP and VIPP-R intervention programs took place during four home visits of, on average, 1.5 (in the VIPP group) to 3 (in the VIPP-R group) hours each, with intervening periods of three to four weeks. Each session started with making the videotape that would be used during the next intervention session. These videotaped mother-infant interactions were standardized in the four intervention sessions and involved playing together, the mother bathing the infant, and cuddling. The recordings were for use in the next intervention session, so that the mother-infant dyad would not be filmed immediately after the video feedback. After making the videotape, the video feedback intervention was implemented using the videotape from the previous session, followed by the attachment discussions in the VIPP-R group. The video feedback was prepared in the period between home visits, selecting specific episodes to be brought to the mother's attention (see Chapter 2). At regular intervals, intervention experiences were discussed with the fifth author, who was also blind to the specific information collected on the dyads involved in the intervention. Furthermore, brochures outlining children's need to feel understood and secure with their parents were provided.

The attachment discussions in the VIPP-R group took place after the video feedback. They were initiated by using questionnaires or projective material (as described in Chapters 2 and 3). Discussions were inspired by attachment theory (Bowlby, 1982, 1988) and by the biographies of so-called earned-secure persons (Main & Goldwyn, 1994; Pearson, Cohn, Cowan, & Cowan, 1994). Earned-secure people describe their childhoods as unloving and hard, but they have been able to restructure their thoughts and feelings regarding their childhood experiences and can coherently reflect on them, without becoming angry or confused, and without diminishing the effects of their negative experiences on their personality. After each session, the home visitors noted their impression of the session, the mother's reaction to the intervention, as well as peculiarities of the interaction of the mother and child involved. For a more detailed description of the process of each session and impressions of the home visitors, see Chapter 3.

Attachment, sensitivity, and temperament

Representation of attachment

George et al. (1985) developed the Adult Attachment Interview to measure the quality of adults' attachment representations. The interview presents the respondent with two central tasks: first, to produce and reflect on memories involving early relationships and, second, to maintain coherent, collaborative discourse (Hesse, 1999; Main, 1995). As described in Chapter 1, four categories of attachment representations are distinguished: *secure* or *autonomous* (F), *dismissing* (Ds), *preoccupied* (E), and *unresolved* (U). Several studies have shown the Adult Attachment Interview's reliability and validity (Bakermans-Kranenburg & Van IJzendoorn, 1993; Crowell et al., 1996; Sagi, Van IJzendoorn, Sharf, & Koren-Karie, 1994; for a meta-analytic validation, see Van IJzendoorn, 1995). In our study the Adult Attachment Interview was only used as a selection instrument. Mothers were selected on the basis of their insecure-dismissing or -preoccupied attachment representation, irrespective of whether they were also considered unresolved with respect to trauma or loss. The first and fifth authors, both trained by and reliable with Main and Hesse, assigned a tentative classification to the interviews on the basis of the audiotaped interviews.

Sensitivity

Maternal sensitivity is defined as the mother's ability to perceive her baby's signals accurately and to respond to them promptly and appropriately (Ainsworth et al., 1971, 1974). Sensitivity was assessed on the basis of 10 minutes of free play at home at 6 and 11 months and 10 minutes of free play at the institute when the infants were 13 months old. Mothers were instructed to play with their infants as they liked. Each mother was provided with a collection of toys brought by the researchers (e.g., a mirror, rattles). Scores for the three sessions were independently assigned, using the Ainsworth's rating scale for sensitivity (Ainsworth et al., 1974), ranging from (1) *highly insensitive* to (9) *highly sensitive*. Coders were unaware of other data concerning the respondents. Intercoder reliabilities were high (mean intraclass correlation = .84, n = 25). Posttest sensitivity scores (11 and 13 months) were significantly correlated (r = .45, p < .01); therefore, aggregated mean scores for maternal posttest sensitivity were used in the analyses.

Infant-mother attachment

Infant-mother attachment was observed in the Strange Situation Procedure (Ainsworth et al., 1978) when the children were 13 months old. The gold standard for the assessment of infant attachment involves eight episodes in which the infant is exposed to mildly stressful events: the entrance of a stranger and two separations from the parent, followed by a reunion. As described in Chapter 1, the infants' patterns of attachment behavior are classified as *secure* (B), *insecure-avoidant* (A), or *insecure-ambivalent* (C). The additional classification of *disorganized* (D) attachment is assigned when a child shows a (momentary) breakdown of a consistent strategy to cope with the stress in the Strange Situation Procedure. In our study, infants classified as disorganized were forced into an alternative classification as A, B, or C. All Strange Situation Procedures were coded by the first or fifth author. Coders were not aware of other information concerning the dyads. Intercoder reliability was adequate (92%, *kappa* = .73 for the three-way A, B, C classifications; 88%, *kappa* = .82 for the four-way A, B, C, D classifications, n = 25). Using the simplified Richters, Waters, and Vaughn (1988) algorithm, continuous scores for attachment security (Van IJzendoorn & Kroonenberg, 1990) were computed on the basis of the interactive Strange Situation Procedure scale scores for proximity seeking, contact maintaining, resistance, and avoidance. The intercoder reliability for these continuous security scores was adequate (intraclass correlation = .76, n = 14; single measure, absolute agreement).

Temperament

Temperament of the infants was assessed using the Dutch translation of the Infant Behavior Questionnaire (Rothbart, 1981). The mothers completed this questionnaire during their visit to the institute after administration of the Adult Attachment Interview, when the infants were on average 6 months old. The Infant Behavior Questionnaire was designed to assess temperament by asking caregivers about particular behaviors of infants. It consists of six subscales: Activity Level, Smiling and Laughter, Fear, Distress to Limitations, Soothability, and Vocal Activity. A seventh scale, Overall Reactivity (Rothbart, 1986), was computed by subtracting the standardized scores on Smile and Laughter (α = .73) and Activity (α = .72) from the standardized score on Distress to Limitations (α = .64).

To test the differential susceptibility hypothesis, an *a priori* split was chosen that was meant to separate the most reactive children from the children with moderate or low reactivity. In Van den Boom's (1994) intervention study among lower-class mothers and their irritable infants, 17% of six-months-old infants were found to be irritable. This is congruent with the borderline/clinical cutoff for children scoring above the 82.7th percentile as used for the Child Behavior Checklist (Achenbach, 1991). Therefore, infants with scores on Overall Reactivity at or above the 80th percentile (scores > 1.36) were considered as highly reactive (n = 17). The remaining 64 infants, scoring below the 80th percentile, were considered less reactive.

Effectiveness of the intervention

Did the intervention enhance maternal sensitivity?

At the posttest, intervention mothers in both the VIPP and VIPP-R groups were significantly more sensitive than control mothers, with an effect size of d = 0.49. Taking pretest sensitivity as a covariate into account, we found that sensitivity of intervention mothers increased significantly more than control mothers'

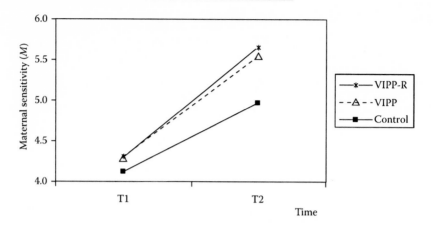

Figure 6.1   Increases in mothers' mean level of sensitivity from T_1 (6 months) to T_2 (11 to 13 months) in the VIPP, VIPP-R, and control groups. (From Klein Velderman, Bakermans-Kranenburg, Juffer, & Van IJzendoorn, 2006a, p. 270.)

sensitivity (see Figure 6.1). Post hoc analyses showed that this was also true for both posttests separately, at 11 and 13 months.

Mothers' posttest sensitivity in both intervention groups was significantly higher than in the control group. The effect size for the VIPP group was $d = 0.46$, and for the VIPP-R group the effect size was $d = 0.52$. As indicated by these effect sizes, the two types of interventions did not differ in their effectiveness on maternal sensitivity.

Were intervention children more secure?

Given that VIPP and VIPP-R were successful in enhancing maternal sensitivity, the question arises as to whether the children also showed significantly more secure attachment behaviors in the Strange Situation Procedure. The answer is no, the intervention was not significantly effective in changing children's attachment security. Although 67% of the infants in the intervention groups developed a secure attachment to their mothers, the same was true of 56% of the infants in our control group, and the difference was not significant, $d = 0.22$. In the VIPP group 71% of the children were secure ($d = 0.33$), and in the VIPP-R group 62% of the children were secure ($d = 0.12$). Again, the effectiveness of the two types of interventions did not differ.

Using the continuous attachment security score no significant intervention effect was found either. However, the infants of intervention mothers who showed more increase in sensitivity were more securely attached (using the continuous security scores). The correlation between change in pre- to posttest maternal sensitivity in the intervention group and posttest infant security was significant, $r = .25$, a medium-sized effect ($d = 0.52$).

Differential susceptibility?

To examine Belsky's differential susceptibility hypothesis, the effectiveness of the VIPP and VIPP-R interventions on sensitivity and attachment was compared for the highly reactive infants and their mothers with the intervention effects for their less reactive counterparts. Mothers of highly reactive infants profited more from the intervention than the others. At the posttest, mothers in the highly reactive intervention group were significantly more sensitive than mothers in the highly reactive control group, $d = 2.27$ (see Figure 6.2). Posttest sensitivity in the less reactive intervention group did not differ significantly from sensitivity in the less reactive control group, $d = 0.29$. The interaction was significant, $d = 0.47$.

For attachment there was no significant differential intervention effect; that is, attachment security in the highly reactive intervention group did not differ significantly from attachment security in the highly reactive control group,

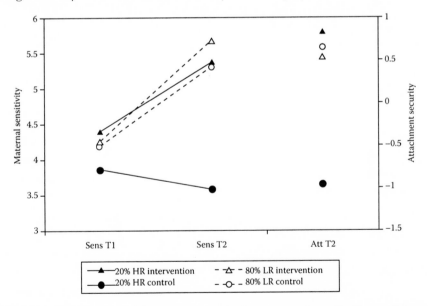

Figure 6.2   Increases in mothers' mean level of sensitivity from T_1 (6 months) to T_2 (average of 11 and 13 months), and infants' mean score on attachment security (continuous measure) at T_2 in the intervention groups ($n = 54$) and control group ($n = 27$) for the 20% highly reactive (HR) and 80% less reactive (LR) infants. (From Klein Velderman, Bakermans-Kranenburg, Juffer, & Van IJzendoorn, 2006a, p. 271.)

although the highly reactive intervention children tended to have higher scores on the continuous attachment security scale (M = 0.84 for the intervention children, M = –0.97 for the control children), d = 0.90 (see Figure 6.2). Attachment security in the less reactive intervention group (M = 0.54) did not differ from attachment security in the less reactive control group (M = 0.65). Does this result mean that it is the mothers rather than the children who are more susceptible to intervention effects? In a way this is true. However, the intervention was not aimed directly at the children, but at their mothers. Therefore, to test Belsky's differential susceptibility hypothesis, one should not test for a direct intervention effect on the children, but rather test whether highly reactive children were more susceptible to their mothers' sensitivity and more susceptible to changes in maternal sensitivity. In the group of highly reactive infants, maternal sensitivity (posttest assessment) and attachment security were significantly correlated, r = .57. In the less reactive group the correlation was r = .28. Although this points to a substantial difference in association, the difference was not statistically significant (p = .11). Infants with high reactivity, however, were significantly more susceptible to changes in maternal sensitivity. In the group of highly reactive intervention infants, attachment security and change in pre- to posttest maternal sensitivity were significantly correlated, r = .64, p < .05. In the less reactive intervention group the correlation was r = .11, not significant (n.s.). The difference in correlations was significant (p = .03). The most reactive infants were more susceptible to their mothers' change in sensitivity.

Conclusions

VIPP and VIPP-R were effective in enhancing maternal sensitivity to infants, but failed to produce a significant effect on infant attachment security. Short-term effects did not point to divergent effects of VIPP and VIPP-R. Moreover, evidence was found supporting the differential susceptibility of highly reactive infants and their mothers to changes in the (caregiving) environment.

Let us first turn to the effectiveness of VIPP and VIPP-R as intervention modalities. This study confirms the findings of our meta-analysis on attachment-based interventions, that a moderate number of sessions and a clear behavioral focus may be quite effective (see Chapter 5). Four extensive home visits with video feedback (and representational discussions) led to significant enhancement of maternal sensitivity. Our results also reflect the meta-analytic finding that it is more difficult to improve attachment security than it is to enhance maternal sensitivity; the interventions only tended to improve the attachment relationship with infants. On the other hand, support was found for the meta-analytic finding that studies with large effect sizes on maternal sensitivity were also effective in promoting infant attachment security: In our study, larger increases in maternal sensitivity were associated with more improvement in attachment security.

Experimental evidence for the differential susceptibility hypothesis

A new aspect was the experimental test of Belsky's differential susceptibility hypothesis. In the meta-analysis it was impossible to examine the difference in effectiveness of interventions including emotionally reactive children compared to interventions focusing on less reactive children, due to the small number of studies with emotionally reactive children. In the current study, we found that the mothers of highly reactive infants were more susceptible to the influence of the intervention sessions, and that highly reactive infants were more susceptible to (changes in) their mothers' sensitivity. The intervention effects for less reactive infants were much less impressive. The experimentally induced change in maternal sensitivity appeared to impact more strongly on attachment security in the highly reactive infant group. Thus, the most stringent test of the differential susceptibility hypothesis confirmed the prediction that highly reactive children are more susceptible to experimentally induced environmental change than less reactive infants. Diverging outcomes of previous intervention experiments may be related to differential susceptibility for environmental influences in the specific type of children involved. Parents of highly reactive infants may be the most rewarding targets of intervention efforts even when the number of sessions is rather small.

Previous studies showed differential susceptibility of mothers of irritable infants for the positive effects of social support (Crockenberg, 1981), the effectiveness of an attachment-based intervention on irritable infants and their low-SES mothers (Van den Boom, 1988, 1994) and on anxiously withdrawn children (LaFreniere & Capuano, 1997), as well as the larger effect of gentle parental discipline de-emphasizing power on compliance in more fearful children (Kochanska, 1995). From these and similar studies, Belsky (1997, 1999a, 1999b, 2005) derived his suggestion that it may be the highly negatively emotional infants who are most susceptible to parental influence, at least with regard to developmental outcomes related to self-control and emotion regulation, to which attachment security has been linked.

Studies that experimentally manipulate the environment for infants who differ in emotional reactivity allow for firmer conclusions. For example, in a cross-fostering experiment on rhesus monkeys Suomi (1999) found that control infants with normative patterns of reactivity displayed normal developmental patterns independent of the quality of caregiving of their foster mother. In contrast, highly reactive infants only showed normal or optimal patterns of development in cases of cross-fostering to nurturant females. Another example is derived from the Infant Health and Development Program, in which low-birth-weight, pre-term infants from economically disadvantaged homes were randomly assigned to experimental and control treatment conditions. Blair (2002) found that tem-peramentally difficult (highly negatively emotional) program infants who expe-rienced early intervention scored substantially lower on externalizing problems at three years of age than did similarly tempered control infants. In the case of other infants with less negative emotionality no such treatment effect was detectable. Similarly, highly reactive children in the present study were more susceptible to experimentally induced changes in maternal sensitivity than less reactive infants.

Moreover, the mothers of highly reactive children in the present study profited more from the intervention. Two explanations come up for discussion. First, the mothers of highly reactive infants may be more readily reinforced by their infants' positive behavioral changes in the dyadic context. The mothers' subtle increases in sensitivity may readily affect the infant's behavior, which in turn evokes more sensitive behavior from the mother. As an alternative or additional interpretation, we speculate that it is also the mothers of highly reactive chil-dren who are more susceptible to environmental influences, because — given the substantial genetic factor in explaining differences in emotional reactivity (Bokhorst et al., 2003; Bouchard & Loehlin, 2001; Goldsmith, Lemery, Buss, & Campos, 1999; Zawadski, Strelau, Oniszcenko, Riemann, & Angleitner, 2001) — these mothers are more reactive themselves. The extension of the differen-tial susceptibility hypothesis to both children and their parents would broaden Belsky's evolutionary model to the dyadic level. In future research, infant and maternal reactivity should be included to build on our findings and broaden insights into the interplay among attachment, temperament, and maternal behavior (Stevenson-Hinde, 2005). Furthermore, observational measures of negative reactivity may be used in future studies of differential susceptibility of highly reactive children. It should be noted that Bridges, Palmer, Morales, Hurtado, and Tsai (1992) found significant convergence between the IBQ and the observational Goldsmith and Rothbart Laboratory Temperament Assess-ment Battery (Goldsmith & Rothbart, 1996). Besides, Weinfield, Whaley, and Egeland (2004) hypothesized that in the context of the attachment relationship, "maternal perceptions may be just as relevant as the child's actual behavior, because maternal perceptions may influence how she interacts with her child" (p. 90). Nevertheless, observational measures may lead to stronger results, with less error variance.

Attachment representations, VIPP, and VIPP-R

Our study aimed at a sample that was at risk for insensitivity and the development of an insecure attachment with the infant because of an insecure mental representation of attachment. The selection of the mothers on the basis of the Adult Attachment Interview from audiotape may not have led to a sample with 100% insecure mothers. In fact, the percentage of securely attached control infants was rather high (56%), which may have led to a ceiling effect for our intervention (actually, the effect size for the intervention effect on attachment in our study was $d = 0.22$, which equals the effect size of $d = 0.24$ for random intervention studies of less than five sessions in at-risk samples in the meta-analysis). In a completely insecure sample the possibility of an improvement in maternal sensitivity and infant attachment security would have been larger. Assigning classifications to Adult Attachment Interviews from tape instead of transcript may not be sufficiently valid, although in mitigation, coding more than 250 interviews after transcription would, given the time available between interview and start of the intervention, have been an impossible task to complete. However, the selection of participants on the basis of audiotaped interviews also means that conclusions cannot be drawn regarding the potentially differential effectiveness of VIPP and VIPP-R for mothers with, in order, insecure-dismissing and insecure-preoccupied representations of attachment. In a subsample of our study, with classifications based on Adult Attachment Interview transcripts, insecure-dismissing mothers were found to have profited most from VIPP, whereas insecure-preoccupied mothers gained most from VIPP-R (Bakermans-Kranenburg, Juffer, & Van IJzendoorn, 1998). Intervention efforts combining a representational and behavioral focus might work particularly well for preoccupied mothers, who still feel angry toward their parents or still struggle with past attachment experiences.

Differences between VIPP and VIPP-R may also become apparent in the long run. It may be that the VIPP-R intervention will produce more lasting intervention effects, as changes in sensitivity might be accompanied by changes in the mothers' attachment representations. A secure mother is sensitive to her child's emotions and needs (Van IJzendoorn, 1995). If security of maternal attachment representations and maternal sensitivity are not consonant with each other, because only sensitivity has been enhanced (the intervention target in VIPP), intervention effects on sensitivity may fade, because in the next developmental stage the child may require different parenting behaviors. It is expected that parents who have developed more positive and coherent views of their past attachment experiences will be more capable of perceiving their children's signals accurately even if these signals are negative and emotionally disturbing (Hesse, 1999; Van IJzendoorn, 1995). However, the results of a follow-up study have to be awaited to obtain more insight into the long-term effects of the two intervention modalities.

In the meantime, our study shows the implications of differential susceptibility for attachment-based intervention studies. Even with a modest number of sessions, parents of highly reactive infants may be very rewarding targets of intervention efforts.

Acknowledgments

The authors thank all families who participated in the study and gratefully acknowledge the assistance of Marja Duyvesteyn, Lina Kalinauskiene, Hesther van Leeuwen, Paulette Steenblok, and Martine Terstegen in collecting and coding data.

7

Supporting families with preterm children and children suffering from dermatitis

Rosalinda Cassibba,[1] Marinus H. van IJzendoorn,[2] Gabrielle Coppola,[1] Simone Bruno,[1] Alessandro Costantini,[1] Sergio Gatto,[1] Lucia Elia,[1] and Alessia Tota[1]

[1]*University of Bari, Italy*
[2]*Centre for Child and Family Studies, Leiden University, the Netherlands*

With the birth of a new baby, families have to cope with new rhythms and routines and a new organization of time. The stress resulting from these changes is generally temporary, but if a baby is diagnosed with (chronic) illness, the stress can become conspicuous and interfere with the development of the mother-child relationship. The parents' concerns for the baby's health condition, the fatigue of taking care of a sick baby, and the depressive feelings that the parents may experience, together with the interaction difficulties due to the baby's illness, may lead to reduced sensitivity in perceiving and reacting to the baby's signals. These conditions can constitute a risk factor for the development of a secure infant-parent attachment relationship.

Many studies of children from clinical samples have shown high levels of stress in their parents, together with feelings of loneliness and depression (Minde, 1999). Also, studies of attachment in samples of sick children affected by specific chronic illnesses (for example, cystic fibrosis, heart disease, Down syndrome, asthma) have reported higher incidences of both insecure and disorganized attachments compared to healthy children (e.g., Fisher-Fay, Goldberg, Simmons, & Levison, 1988; Ievers, Drotar, Dahms, Doershuk, & Stern, 1994).

Moreover, Goldberg, Gotowiec, and Simmons (1995) found that the incidence of insecure attachment in a sample of babies affected by heart disease from birth, but already resolved through medical surgery before the beginning of the study, was the same as in a sample of children currently affected by cystic fibrosis. This finding suggests that the quality of the mother-child relationship may be influenced by the early characteristics and behaviors of the baby and by the mother's thoughts, fears, and concerns. It may reflect parents' incapacity to adjust dynamically their own mental representation about the vulnerable child to the characteristics of the real child after recovery from illness or surgery; in other words, there may be a "vulnerable child syndrome" (Minde, 2000), a condition in which the parent persists in taking care of the child as if she or he is fragile and ill, even though this condition is no longer present. This situation has been found particularly in the parents of preterm children (Fava Vizziello, 2003; Minde, 2000).

In this chapter we first review the impact of the child's diagnosis on the parents; then we describe characteristics of both the sick child and her or his relationship with the parent. Subsequently we discuss attachment studies involving children with different types of diseases to determine if the distributions of attachment patterns differ significantly from healthy samples. Last, we discuss the planning of interventions aimed at promoting the security of attachment in those parent-child dyads who have to cope with the problem of a child's (chronic) illness. The last section of the chapter presents the first results of the application of the VIPP-R intervention in two samples of families forced to cope with their child's health problems: families with preterm and dermatitis infants. These dyads are considered at risk for insecure attachment; in fact, impairments in the children's communicative behaviors may make their signals less readable, and they may interfere with the "good enough" sensitivity that their mothers would display under normal conditions. Moreover, frequent hospitalizations may jeopardize the efforts of parents to remain focused on the child's attachment behaviors and needs.

The impact of the child's illness on the parents

The reaction of family members to a child's diagnosis may depend on many factors. It is reasonable to suppose that the parents' reactions to the baby's diagnosis at birth, when the relationship with the child still needs time to develop, may be different from those of parents who are confronted with illness when the child is older and the relationship has been consolidated (Goldberg, Washington, Morris, Fisher-Fay, & Simmons, 1990b). Moreover, the impact of the diagnosis on the parents depends on many other factors, such as the severity of the illness, the types of medical treatment required, the probability of recovery, and the possible disabling outcomes (Pless & Pinkerton, 1975). Goldberg, Morris, Simmons, Fowler, and Levinson (1990a), studying three different samples (children with cystic fibrosis, children with heart disease, and healthy children), showed that parents with children affected by chronic disease suffered higher levels of stress in comparison with parents of healthy children. Moreover, they reported more depressive symptoms, and they felt less confident of their own parental skills. It is worth noting that all mothers were assessed shortly after their children were diagnosed. This shows how rapidly the child's illness can affect the parents' well-being. In many cases, the parents need to wait for months to know a "definite" diagnosis, and this waiting period may prepare the ground for feelings of depression and discouragement. For parents, children's hospitalization also can be an experience of separation and loss with respect to the familiar environment of their homes, their own daily life routines, and their intimate relationships. Indeed, hospitalization can be a depersonalizing experience: There may not be any private rooms, patients are frequently identified only on the basis of their illness or ID number, and loneliness and boredom may arise. All these experiences may activate hostility and isolation on the part of the children as well as their parents (Capurso, 2001).

Furthermore, the family's network of normal social relationships is at risk. The continuous concern for the child's health condition and the difficulties that occur in organizing family life can lead parents to give up almost all free-time activity and other occasions to relax or meet friends.

The psychological implications of this situation may vary in terms of severity and length, depending on the psychological resources and social support parents have access to. Sheeran, Marvin, and Pianta (1997), examining the relation between maternal resolution of a child's diagnosis of chronic illness and several self-report measures, found that effective resolution of diagnosis was related to lower parenting stress, higher levels of social support, and higher marital satisfaction. Similar findings were obtained by Hobfoll and Lerman (1988) in a longitudinal study of parents' reactions to their child's illness: They found that the more social support the parents received, the lower their psychological distress was. Moreover, the perceived inadequacy of support appeared to have substantial predictive power for the subsequent onset of parents' minor psychiatric symptoms (West, Livesley, Reiffer, & Sheldon, 1986). Parental effective resolution of the child's diagnosis was also strongly associated with secure versus insecure child-parent attachment assessed using the Strange Situation Procedure (Marvin & Pianta, 1996), as well as the caregiver's attachment-related representations of the self and others (Williamson, Walters, & Shaffer, 2002).

The child's illness as a risk factor for attachment

Ainsworth, Blehar, Waters, and Wall (1978) showed that parents who correctly perceive children's signals and who respond to them in a prompt, appropriate, and contingent way are more likely to have a secure attachment relationship with their child. In contrast, insensitive parents, who are unable to adequately respond to their children's signals, are more likely to establish an insecure attachment relationship. In several experimental intervention studies a causal relation between maternal sensitivity and the child's attachment security has been confirmed (for a meta-analysis, see Chapter 5).

Under normal conditions, the construction of an attachment relationship is eased by the presence of species-specific behaviors that have emerged from a process of natural selection (Bowlby, 1973). The interaction with the child may, however, be limited or distorted due to the illness, and the parents' preoccupation with their child's condition may interfere with the development of a secure attachment relationship. Although child health problems may be compensated for by parental sensitivity (Van IJzendoorn, Goldberg, Kroonenberg, & Frenkel, 1992), in case of children suffering from dermatitis, physical contact — which is an essential ingredient of the emergent attachment relationship — is impaired (Field, 2002) and parental compensation may be more problematic.

A child with health problems may well present behaviors or developmental trends different from those presented by a healthy child. Health problems may require that parents modify their expectations and their way of responding to the child's signals. It has been shown, for example, that the spectrographic characteristics of sick children's crying are different from those of healthy children and that such differences are clearly perceived by parents (Lester & Zeskind, 1979). These conditions, especially when they are associated with the feeling of having been unable to give birth to a healthy child, may lead parents to see their own child as a baby who behaves and develops in deviant ways. In this case, parents may not be able to use the well-established and consolidated schemas (being also the result of one's own childhood attachment experiences; see below) of how to interact with a child.

Children affected by atopic dermatitis illustrate how parents have to find alternative ways to communicate (Zangheri, Cassibba, Ferriani, & Fabrici, 2002). Because the skin is the privileged means for newborns through which they are learning about themselves and the surrounding world, the presence of eczema may alter their perception of physical contact and may affect the quantity and quality of contact between the adult and the baby. A child affected by dermatitis may, for example, experience physical contact with the parent as unpleasant and hurtful rather than pleasant and consoling. In turn, parents may be induced to avoid physical contact with their child, for fear of irritating the child's skin, or because it is not pleasant for themselves. In such cases, therefore, the only physical contact that the baby experiences with the parent may be left to the uncomfortable moments of changing cream or bandages to prevent the skin from itching. These experiences may have serious repercussions for the emerging attachment bond.

Another example of how challenging the interaction between a mother and a child with specific impairments may be is provided by the preterm child. The start of a social life may be very different for the preterm child than it is for a term one. Preterm infants have not yet reached any autoregulation capacity, and they are not ready to process complex stimuli such as those of a social nature. For this reason, their first reactions lack organization and preterm newborns may tend to avoid external stimuli (Goldberg & Di Vitto, 1995). The signals that the easily overwhelmed preterm child produces may be difficult to decode because of their ambiguous nature, which may induce mothers to hardly attribute communication intention to their child (Singer et al., 2003). For their part, preterm children may respond slowly to their parents' interventions, and this deprives parents of immediate feedback about their behavior. In addition to such difficulties and preterms' less predictable rhythms (Macey, Harmon, & Easterbrooks, 1987), the consequences of illnesses and more frequent hospitalizations associated with preterm birth may make the child less responsive and attuned to parental stimuli.

A vast literature documents the difficult start of parent-preterm child interaction in the first year of life. In their interactions with the mother, preterm children are found to be more irritable and less easily comforted; they show higher shares of negative feelings; they are less attentive, sensitive, and responsive to their mothers' signals; they participate less in social interaction; and they smile and vocalize less often. These peculiarities may hamper the mother's tuning in to the child (Crnic, Ragozin, Greenberg, Robinson, Basham, 1983; Wille, 1991). Mothers may adopt an excessively active role in the interaction, sometimes even becoming intrusive, with the aim of stimulating the child in a way as to ensure visible feedback (Goldberg & Di Vitto, 1995). Hyperstimulating and intrusive maternal behavior or, on the contrary, an interaction style characterized by sporadic maternal sensitivity and low emotional involvement may increase the risk of establishing an insecure attachment relationship.

Furthermore, the child's illness may interfere with the construction of a secure mother-child attachment relationship in a more indirect way, that is, by the distress that the illness brings into family life. This, in turn, may influence parents' sensitive behavior and the quality of the relationship. From this perspective, McCallum and McKim (1999), observing children affected by chronic middle otitis (inflammation of the middle ear), suggested a complex model to explain why the disease may lead, in a more or less direct way, children to develop an insecure attachment relationship with the parent. The irritability, the apathy, the bad mood, and the sleep disorders that frequently follow otitis may cause parents to feel frustrated and incompetent because they are unable to comfort their child and to involve the child in more enjoyable interactions. This stressful situation, when extended in time, can result in parents' psychologically moving away from their child. This detachment lowers the parent's sensitivity to the child's signals and reduces the chances of appropriate emotional and affective responses, which are the base of a secure attachment relationship.

Last, the child's illness might interfere with the development of a secure attachment relationship because of specific stressful conditions the child may experience during interaction with the mother. As an example, children affected by asthmatic bronchitis may experience disruptions in the establishment of appropriate autonomy during the process of finding a balance between attachment and exploration as a result of their respiratory difficulties and multiple hospitalizations (Mrazek, Casey, & Anderson, 1987). Moreover, mothers may establish an overprotective and insecure-ambivalent attachment relationship with their child as they feel uncertain about their ability to take adequate care of the sick child. Parents may also refrain from committing themselves to a bond with their child with recurrent asthmatic bronchitis and develop an insecure-avoidant relationship as a result of their feelings of anxiety (Cassibba, Van IJzendoorn, Bruno, & Coppola, 2004).

The distribution of attachment patterns in children with health problems

Studies of security of attachment in clinical samples have focused on several specific problematic conditions; the majority included samples of preterm children (Frodi & Thompson, 1985; Goldberg, Perrotta, Minde, & Corter, 1986; Minde et al., 1989; Plunkett, Meisels, Stiefel, Pasick, & Roloff, 1986; Poehlmann & Fiese, 2001); fewer studies took into account children with physical disabilities, as, for example, cystic fibrosis, asthma, or heart disease (Cassibba et al., 2004; Fisher-Fay et al., 1988; Goldberg et al., 1990b; Goldberg, Simmons, Newman, Campbell, & Fowler, 1991; Ievers et al., 1994; Zangheri et al., 2002), or with multiple physical impairments (Wasserman, Lennon, Allen, & Shilansky, 1987). In the same way, there are very few studies of children with sensory disabilities, with Down syndrome, or autism (but see Capps, Sigman, & Mundy, 1994; Rogers, Ozonoff, & Maslin-Cole, 1991; Shapiro, Sherman, Calamari, & Coch, 1986; Vaughn et al., 1994; Willemsen-Swinkels, Bakermans-Kranenburg, Buitelaar, Van IJzendoorn, & Van Engeland, 2000).

The literature on attachment in preterm samples is controversial. This may be due to the fact that the samples across the studies differ with respect to many potentially relevant characteristics, for example, birth weight, gestational age, days of hospitalization, and presence of pathologies associated with preterm birth. In most studies, however, there are no significant differences in the distribution of insecure and secure attachment categories compared to samples of term babies. This has been found both in samples of preterm babies at relatively moderate risk, that is, babies having birth weight slightly under 2500 grams (low birth weight) and with gestational age slightly under 37 weeks (for example, Frodi & Thompson, 1985; Plunkett, Klein, & Meisels, 1988; Rode, Chang, Fish, & Sroufe, 1981), and in samples of high-risk preterms, that is, babies having birth weight around 1000 grams, gestational age around 28 weeks, and an average of 60 days of hospitalization (e.g., Cox, Hopkins, & Hans 2000; Easterbrooks, 1989; Goldberg et al., 1986; Macey et al., 1987; Pederson & Moran, 1996; Poehlmann & Fiese, 2001; Plunkett et al., 1988; Rodning, Beckwith, & Howard 1990).

Significant differences in the distribution of the attachment patterns between preterm and term children seem to be due to the concurrence of other risk factors that in combination with preterm birth may increase the probability for developing insecure attachment. Wille (1991), for example, found a higher incidence of insecure attachment in a sample of preterm babies whose families were disadvantaged from a socioeconomic point of view, compared to a sample of term babies from the same socioeconomic background. Other studies found a higher incidence of insecure attachment in preterm babies who presented medical complications, for example, respiratory diseases associated with preterm birth (Plunkett et al., 1986).

Studies investigating the impact of physical health problems on the quality of attachment suggest the similarity of the distributions of attachment categories between clinical and normal samples. Goldberg et al. (1990a) took into account three samples of children (healthy, affected by cystic fibrosis, and affected by congenital heart disease) and found no significant difference in the distribution of attachment patterns across the three samples, even though they found a higher incidence of secure attachment in the sample of healthy children.

Children with psychosomatic disorders, such as atopic dermatitis or asthma, however, show a different picture. Mrazek and colleagues (1987) found a higher incidence of insecure attachment in children affected by severe asthma than in healthy children. This result is similar to the findings of Cassibba and colleagues (2004) in a sample of children between three and five years affected by recurrent asthmatic bronchitis, a condition that generally arises before and predicts asthma. The overrepresentation of insecure attachments may be ascribed to the difficulties caused by the child's respiratory disease and by the tendency of the parents to establish an overprotective or neglectful relationship with the child (Madrid & Schwartz, 1991).

The meta-analytic study of Van IJzendoorn et al. (1992) provides an overview of the distribution of attachment categories in clinical samples, including 34 clinical samples with 1,624 children. The studies included in the meta-analysis were divided in three different groups: (1) those including children with established health problems (for example, blindness, Down syndrome, etc.), (2) those including mother-child dyads with mothers who presented a variety of different difficulties (maltreatment, psychiatric diagnosis, and so forth), and (3) those including samples not falling into the previous two categories. The data obtained from the clinical samples were compared with those of 21 samples (with 1,584 children in total) of dyads not affected by any problems. The aim of the meta-analysis was to verify (1) if the presence of problems on the mother's side or on the child's side increased the percentage of insecure or disorganized attachment, and (2) whether maternal problems played a predominant role compared to the child's problems in determining insecurity and disorganization of attachment.

From the comparison between the clinical samples and the normative data it emerged that the presence of problems on the child's side was not associated with a decrease in the percentage of secure attachment; the children affected by Down syndrome appeared to be the only exception, as for these children an increase in the percentage of disorganized attachment was found (see also Rutgers, Bakermans-Kranenburg, Van IJzendoorn, & Van Berckelaer-Onnes, 2004). Instead, maternal problems were associated with a significant decrease of secure attachment and with a significant increase of both resistant and disorganized attachment compared with the normative data.

In conclusion, children's mental or physical problems may not necessarily compromise their capacity to build secure attachment relationships, because parents may compensate for their child's problems. Nevertheless, serious problems in the child may hamper balanced communication with the parent in such a way that the risk for insecure attachments is enhanced. Dermatitis and prematurity may be such problems.

The VIPP-R intervention in Italian families with a preterm child or a child suffering from dermatitis

Parents with secure attachment representations tend to be more sensitive to their child's signals and more often establish a secure attachment relationship with their child (see Van IJzendoorn, 1995). Moreover, they tend to seek more social support that may be badly needed when parents are confronted with having a baby with a chronic disease.

When a parent does not have an internal working model with flexible, coherent, and integrated representational elements, the child's security is at risk. If parents are excessively involved in their past disappointing attachment experiences or with resolving their own attachment losses and traumas, they run the risk of failing to perceive and interpret the child's signals correctly, especially if the interpretation of the signals requires more effort than would be the case if the child was healthy. Furthermore, if parents have an insecure attachment working model, it may be more difficult to work through the child's diagnosis and to find an effective strategy to cope with the difficulties, and to accept, for example, the help and support offered by family members and friends.

The VIPP-R intervention may meet the specific needs of these dyads. The intervention aims at increasing maternal sensitivity by focusing on maternal sensitive behavior (see Chapters 2, 3, and 6). It may help mothers to improve their capacity of reading and interpreting the child's signals, especially when these signals are less effective and clear because of the child's illness. This may increase their confidence about their capacity to respond in an appropriate way to the child's signals. Moreover, the intervention aims at restructuring parental attachment representations, which may be particularly useful in the case of parents with insecure attachment models who are challenged by their sick child. The parents are enabled to reflect on their own past attachment experiences and the influence on their present attachment relationships, and they may revise and work through negative childhood experiences and thus gain a more balanced view of their own past and its role in their present life (Hesse, 1999; see Chapters 2, 3, and 6). The process of restructuring attachment representations, in other words, is the basis for all those maternal characteristics identified as protective factors that may support the construction of secure attachment relationships or protect existing secure relationships. Last, the help offered to families by the alliance with the intervener may provide the social support needed in the unknown and unpredictable situation of being the parent of a sick child (Williamson et al., 2002). Because of the illness of their child parents may be more open to process negative information and to change their perspective of the child.

Our longitudinal intervention study has a two-fold aim. First, it aims to test if the child's health problems (atopic dermatitis and preterm birth) in the first year of life are a risk factor for the development of attachment security. Both preterm birth and the presence of atopic dermatitis may be significant stress factors for the mother and the child, and therefore may interfere with the construction of a secure attachment relationship. The second aim is to test the efficacy of an intervention with video feedback and representational discussions (VIPP-R) on maternal sensitivity and infant security of attachment in a sample of children with health problems and in a control group with healthy infants. Because in a previous study the effectiveness of VIPP-R was demonstrated in a group of mothers with insecure attachment representations with nonclinical children (Bakermans-Kranenburg, Juffer, & Van IJzendoorn, 1998), we decided to test whether VIPP-R effectiveness might be different for those parents who demonstrated insecure states of mind regarding attachment compared to parents who already had a more balanced and secure state of mind.

The design and results of the intervention study

Eighty children (36 female) and their mothers participated in the study; all children were born in Italy and were reared in two-parent families. The sample was divided into four groups: The clinical subsamples were composed of 20 preterm children and 20 children affected by atopic dermatitis. The comparison groups were composed of 40 children born at term matched with the clinical subsamples on the basis of sex and age. The preterm group was composed of 20 preterm children (11 female; gestational age, $M = 29.9$ weeks, $SD = 2.6$; weight at birth, $M = 1,201$ grams, $SD = 166.2$). The criteria used for the selection of preterm children were their weight at birth (between 750 and 1500 grams) and the absence of congenital defects and serious neurological damages. The educational level of the mothers (age, $M = 33.25$, $SD = 5.12$) was average to high (years of education, $M = 11.10$, $SD = 3.56$). The comparison group for the preterms was composed of 20 term children (11 female) and their mothers (age, $M = 30.85$, $SD = 5.33$; years of education, $M = 11.35$, $SD = 4.19$), selected by matching with the preterm group with respect to sex and birthday of the children.

The dermatitis group consisted of 20 children (7 female) and their mothers (age, $M = 30.85$, $SD = 4.08$; years of education, $M = 12.35$, $SD = 4.47$). The children affected by dermatitis were selected with the cooperation of municipal pediatricians. The criteria used to diagnose atopic dermatitis included six conditions: itching presence, inflammation of the epidermis, insurgence before the second year of life, personal history of asthma or hay fever, skin dryness, and presence of flexural eczema (Williams, Burney, & Hay, 1994). The comparison group for the children with dermatitis was composed of 20 children born at term (7 female) and their mothers (age, $M = 35.15$, $SD = 4.00$; years of education, $M = 14.50$, $SD = 3.28$), selected by matching with the dermatitis group with respect to sex and age of the children.

After obtaining the written consent from both parents, a meeting was scheduled at home for the administration of the Adult Attachment Interview (Main, Kaplan, & Cassidy, 1985; see Chapter 1), to assess maternal attachment representation before the intervention. The interviews were coded for the classifications expressing the mental state with respect to attachment: secure, dismissing, and preoccupied. Second, a continuous attachment security score on the basis of the scores on the continuous Adult Attachment Interview scales for idealization, anger, derogation, and coherence of transcript was assigned using the discriminant function equation of Waters, Treboux, and Crowell (in press). The interviews were coded from transcript by two trained and reliable coders, who did not know to which subsample the participants belonged. The agreement between independent coders was Cohen's $k = .80$, computed on $n = 16$ (20%) of the interviews.

At six months of age (corrected for prematurity), two times 10 children were randomly drawn from each of the premature and dermatitis subsamples and included in the VIPP-R intervention. The same intervention was proposed to the first 20 arbitrarily contacted families in each of the two comparison groups. Thus, 40 children and their mothers were included in the intervention, 20 of whom belonged to clinical subsamples (10 children with dermatitis and 10 premature children) and 20 comparison children. The control dyads received two "dummy" visits at home during which some structured play interaction between mother and child was recorded.

At 14 months of age (corrected for prematurity), all 80 children were invited to the laboratory for the Strange Situation Procedure (Ainsworth et al., 1978; see Chapter 1) to assess the quality of the attachment relationship with the mother. The coding of the observations was based on the child's reaction to the separation from and the reunion with the mother. The child's pattern of attachment behavior was classified into one of four groups: secure, avoidant, ambivalent, and disorganized. Moreover, a continuous security score was computed on the basis of the interactive scales for Proximity Seeking, Contact Maintaining, Avoidance, and Resistance, using the discriminant function equation presented in Van IJzendoorn and Kroonenberg (1990). At the end of the Strange Situation Procedure, after a short break, the dyads were invited to play as they were used to at home for three more minutes. This situation was also videotaped and coded for maternal sensitivity with the Emotional Availability Scales (Biringen, Robinson, & Emde, 2000). The Strange Situation Procedure was coded by observers who were trained by Dr. Vaughn and blind to the attachment classifications of the mothers and the subgroup to which the children belonged. The intercoder reliability (agreements/disagreements using three-way classification) calculated in 75% of cases was .84. Furthermore, coders did not know whether the mother had received intervention. Maternal sensitivity was coded by the first author, who was unaware of all other information about the children and their mothers. The agreement between two independent observers, in 25% of cases, was rho = .80. Last, a posttest Adult

Attachment Interview was administered to obtain a measure of mother's mental representation with respect to attachment after the intervention.

The first aim of the study was to verify whether there was a higher incidence of insecure attachment in the clinical samples than in the nonclinical samples. For this purpose, in the group of children who did not receive intervention, a t test for independent groups was performed on the child's security scores, using the clinical versus nonclinical condition as a factor. The results showed lower levels of security in the clinical sample than in the control group, although the difference between the means was not statistically significant. Actually, taking into account the categorical assessments of the child's attachment, only 55% of the children of the clinical sample were classified as secure, whereas in the comparison group a significantly higher percentage (85%) of the children were found to be secure.

To test the efficacy of the intervention on infant attachment security and maternal sensitivity (the second aim of the study), a $2 \times 2 \times 2$ between-subjects multivariate analysis of variance was performed on two dependent variables: maternal sensitivity and infant attachment security. Between-subjects factors were intervention (with versus without), group (clinical versus nonclinical), and maternal representation of attachment (Adult Attachment Interview; secure versus insecure). Maternal attachment was included to test our hypothesis of potentially differential intervention effects for the secure versus insecure maternal attachment working models. Results revealed a significant interaction effect between intervention and Adult Attachment Interview security for infant attachment security. For maternal sensitivity the result was not significant, although the trend was in the predicted direction. No main or interaction effect of the group factor (clinical versus nonclinical) was found; thus, the VIPP-R effects were not dependent of the clinical status of the children (Cassibba et al., submitted). More specifically, infants of insecure mothers appeared to benefit from the intervention program, regardless of clinical status. That is, within the subgroup of infants of insecure mothers, those with intervention were significantly more secure than infants without intervention. Conversely, in the subgroup of infants of secure mothers, the intervention was ineffective, and even seemed to result in less infant attachment security. For maternal sensitivity the effect was not significant, although the trend was in the predicted direction. Insecure mothers benefited from the intervention; in fact, their sensitivity increased after taking part in the intervention. But in the case of mothers with secure representations regarding attachment, the intervention did not contribute to enhancing their sensitivity (Cassibba et al., submitted).

Case studies of interventions in families with preterm or atopic dermatitis children

Two cases are presented to illustrate the interventions that involved families with children born prematurely or affected by atopic dermatitis. Even though these families have to cope with specific problems due to the child's health condition, the original structure of the VIPP-R intervention was not modified. Nevertheless, as the cases suggest, it was necessary to focus more closely on some specific aspects of the mother-child interaction, especially during the video feedback. In the case of the dyads with atopic dermatitis, the themes more frequently discussed had to do with the importance of physical contact for the child. Actually, these mothers often expressed feeling ill at ease in physical contact with their child: Their desire to be physically close to their child was frequently overruled by their concern with irritating the child's skin. In families with a premature child, the intervener tried to focus mothers' attention mainly on the importance of refraining from overstimulating their child and giving them time to "know," "choose," and "discover" their own reality. That is, the mothers of premature children generally seemed to be heavily concerned with the need to make their child "recoup" the missing months, and to provide their child with adequate experience for competence development.

Alessia and Alba (dermatitis group)

Background

Alessia is 31 years old; she has one sister and two brothers. Her grandmother and her aunt from her father's side used to live with her family; they were both chronically ill. The household was kept mainly by her mother, who was a house-wife; her father was very busy with his job. Alessia attended university; she is married, and Alba is her first daughter. When the pediatrician reported this case, Alba was affected by a mild form of atopic dermatitis. The first diagnosis occurred when she was about three months of age. The intervention started at nine months of age, since the mother repeatedly postponed appointments. When the intervention started, the dermatitis had improved notably.

The Adult Attachment Interview before the intervention

During the first Adult Attachment Interview, Alessia started describing her family as "a normal … quite normal and large" one. She chose very positive adjectives to describe her mother, but she is unable to support them with positive episodic memories from her childhood. She says: "It was a normal life, nothing special." When the interviewer insists on asking for specific episodes, Alessia continues to say that she cannot remember, stressing that her childhood "has always been normal." She describes her father using both positive and negative adjectives, but also in this case she cannot support them with episodic memories.

From the interview, her mother seems to have been an emotionally absent figure and her father seems rejecting. With respect to illnesses, Alessia remembers her father making her feel guilty when she was sometimes sick as a child, while her mother provided her with a doll that could comfort her. When Alessia is asked about possible consequences of her childhood for her future development, she answers: "It's obvious that your parents will have influence on your life … that's normal, but there is nothing particular about it." She reasserts this idea many times. When she is asked about specific experiences that may have interfered with her development, Alessia answers: "It wasn't the relationship with my parents that affected my life, but other experiences, such as school, for example." The interview documents an insecure-dismissing mental representation with respect to attachment (Ds3/Ds1; rate U = 2). Her interview is characterized by a strong insistence on lack of memory, high idealization and normalization, and by a strikingly dismissing attitude.

The intervention

The intervention with video feedback and discussions started when the child was nine months of age. Even when the mother had agreed to start the intervention at six months of age, Alessia continuously postponed the appointments, because she was busy with her work. The mother was very volatile; sometimes she was compliant and interested in the intervention, and at other times she appeared to be intolerant to the intervener. She appreciated the video feedback of the intervention, and she took active part in it, and sometimes she even anticipated the intervener's comments, but the attachment discussions seemed to bother her.

During the first session, Alessia asked the intervener to help her understand her mistakes through the fragments of videos they watched together. From the beginning, the mother showed a good ability to perceive Alba's signals, but she had great difficulty in being emotionally tuned to her daughter. For example, while watching a video fragment in which Alba was trying to cling on to her mother, Alessia spontaneously made the comment: "Alba likes to be held, but I don't want to spoil her because I get tired of having to hold her all the time. I want her to detach from me; otherwise, she will become one of those kids who constantly cling to their moms." During the last videos, the intervener had the impression that Alessia was trying to meet her child's need for physical contact, as she accepted holding her and cuddling her more. Neither the mother nor the intervener ever referred to the child's dermatitis during the intervention sessions.

During the discussion about her past experiences, the mother never really collaborated; she used to answer superficially the intervener's questions and proposals; she seemed willing to "make her happy," more than really taking part. She also explicitly expressed her preference for the video feedback rather than the discussions.

The assessments after the intervention

The second Adult Attachment Interview was administered when the child was 14 months old, and it did not show any changes in the mother's internal working model of attachment. That is, the transcript was coded again as Ds3/Ds1. Idealization of the relationship with the parents and lack of memory were both still strongly present. With respect to the possible influences of her childhood on her personal development, she stated again: "I didn't have any problem, in the sense that it was good to have had a quiet childhood, of course with the normal problems everyone has."

In contrast to her insecure-dismissing attachment representation, Alessia's sensitivity after the intervention was high, with a score of 8.5. Also, Alba's security, assessed with the Strange Situation Procedure, appeared to be more than what could be expected on the basis of the mother's insecure attachment representation. That is, the child was classified as B1, displaying a secure pattern of attachment.

From the beginning of the intervention Alessia was willing to think about her mistakes in the actual relationship with her child, as she was explicitly asking the intervener to help her in this task by watching the videos together. She was able to understand her child's signals, even though she was not always willing or able to react to them in a proper way. Moreover, the mild dermatitis did not seem to interfere with the normal activities of either mother or child. These conditions may have enabled the mother to focus on changing her caregiving behavior toward the child, increasing her sensitivity, and building the basis for the child to develop a secure attachment relationship.

Delia and Alice (preterm group)

Background

Delia is 37 years old; at 23 she went to live on her own, after a religious conversion that according to her brought more serenity in her life. Her father died when she was 12 years old; she describes him as a charming and well-educated man, but also as very authoritarian and aloof, whereas her mother is described as very severe and authoritarian, and as extremely pessimistic. When her father died, the family broke up: Delia found her self completely alone in having to handle inheritance problems and because of other family arguments; as she says, "I found myself alone and abandoned by friends and family members." Even though her parents used to have arguments, the father's death brought an even deeper disruption in the family. Delia says she finally found some peace in her life when she had her religious conversion and when she met her husband, whom she married when she was 36 years old.

Alice is her first daughter. She was born prematurely at 33 weeks of gestation, after the couple had been married for a year. At birth Alice weighed 1,260 grams. Delia tells the story of her pregnancy and the birth of the baby with many details and great emotional involvement. She remembers being at risk of losing her baby; immediately after birth the baby had to be resuscitated. She is convinced that her and her baby's lives are miracles of God. She also remembers her sense of impotence while standing in front of the incubator during the very first days, and she felt the only thing she could do was to pray for the baby to survive.

The Adult Attachment Interview before the intervention

During the first Adult Attachment Interview, Delia speaks continuously, expanding on many details that appear irrelevant to the topic. She describes her mother in a very negative way, and she uses exaggerating speech when she explains the negative aspects of the relationship with her. For example, she remembers having lived through "really atrocious and difficult moments in tears." She describes her father with both positive and negative adjectives. She says: "He was a typically charming and well-educated man.... I idealized him by setting him on a pedestal, but he was the typical person that thought that children needed to be kissed only when they are asleep; so, consequently, from there came all his authority; that is, only a reproach of his was enough to make me cry, because it was a stab at my heart."

During the interview, Delia's speech oscillates in an unpredictable way between present and past events, showing that the conflicts with her mother are still in progress. Her speech is full of uncompleted sentences and vague and evasive words, which is typical for adults with a preoccupied state of mind with respect to attachment. The interview demonstrated an insecure-preoccupied representation with respect to attachment (E2/E1), that is, Delia describes her past negative experiences, showing she is still emotionally entangled. This involvement does not give her the possibility of analyzing and rethinking her childhood experiences in a logical and coherent way. She is still preoccupied with the past, as feelings of anger and resentment predominate her speech. The transcript also revealed a moderate level of unresolved loss of father (rate, 4.5).

The intervention

The intervention started when Alice was six months of age. Both the mother and the father were enthusiastic to take part in the research project, and they were very compliant. As the father was normally actively involved in the child's caregiving, he asked to be present during the sessions. Moreover, he took part in the bathing video, as he was the parent who was normally in charge of that routine.

The video feedback seemed to be very effective. From the first video it was clear how intrusively the mother behaved in interaction with her child. Even though in the first video-feedback session the intervener generally does not focus on the mother's behavior (see Chapter 2), Delia was very insightful in realizing how "wrong" her behavior was. In a specific fragment it was clear that the baby became more and more irritated because Delia did not give her enough time to explore a new toy but presented more toys than she could handle. Delia immediately pointed out her feelings about watching the videos, as she was "feeling guilty and suffering" from seeing her behavior and being afraid of "traumatizing her baby." It was necessary for the intervener to reassure the mother, and to think together with the mother about more positive alternative behaviors in such situations. Both mother and father were very cooperative and constructive during the video feedback. The video-feedback session was concluded in a positive way by watching nice fragments of cuddling between mother and child.

During the next video-feedback sessions, the mother seemed to become more aware of her intrusive behavior, and during the third session, there were clear episodes during which the intervener could reinforce chains of sensitivity (see Chapter 2). The mother was actually trying to follow the baby's suggestions, instead of forcing the baby to follow her. The intervener underscored that this would make it more enjoyable for the baby to share her discoveries with her, instead of trying to defend herself from mother's intrusiveness. The intervener, the mother, and the father were able to appreciate together many video fragments during which the mother was not actively interfering with Alice's exploration, and supported the baby only with verbal comments and visual contact when she was looking for such feedback. By watching a fragment in which Delia immediately told Alice that a specific toy she was exploring could not make any sounds, without letting her discover it by herself, the mother was able to explain why she continuously anticipated the child's discoveries: She wanted to protect her child from being disappointed in not finding what she was looking for. The intervener showed empathy for her concerns, but reassured her that such discoveries can be exciting for a child. On his part, the father was very involved in the discussion, as he was helping his wife to search for alternative strategies and supporting her understanding.

The last video-feedback session seemed to be very productive: While watching a fragment during which she was reacting too fast to her child, Delia said, "I can't understand how come, on one side, I do understand my mistakes, but, on the other, I end up acting with her maybe in the same way my mom used to do with me.... Couldn't this be that unconscious attitude to repeat your own mother's behavior? ... Even though ... I don't have memories of my mom being intrusive with me while I was playing." This insight may be the starting point for Delia to think about the difference between rational understanding and emotional working through past and present experiences and their linkages.

From the first representational discussions, the mother seemed strongly involved with her past and present conflicts with her mother, and she expressed involving anger during all intervention sessions in a way that made it difficult for the intervener to contain and restructure her feelings and experiences. For example, Delia said, "I was almost on the verge of suicide.... My mom lost completely reliability in my eyes.... I don't believe her any more" and "Today me and my sister could have been hysterical ... my only real psychologist was God." There were moments during which the intervener was able to help Delia to think about her childhood conflicts in a more balanced way, trying to take into account her mother's point of view. Sometimes Delia seemed able to be forgiving with her mother, even though she was oscillating. At the end of the intervention, both mother and father expressed great satisfaction about the intervention and would have been happy to continue it.

The assessments after the intervention

The second Adult Attachment Interview was administered when the child was 14 months of age. It did not show any changes in the mental state of mind with respect to attachment (E2). Delia describes both her mother and her father in a very negative way. Her speech still expresses strong emotional entanglement, passivity, and involving anger. When describing the way past experiences have influenced her adult personality, she says: "The reaction of my personality toward my mom has been of pure hysteria.... When we had arguments I never hit my mom of course, but when she really exasperated me by telling me ridiculous things, she yelled ... she is an insufferable woman, I used to get whatever, for example, an ashtray, and smashed it on the floor ... to make her understand 'Shut up! I can't stand you anymore!'"

Even though the insecure state of mind with respect to attachment persists, Delia's sensitivity is moderate after the intervention (score = 4). The child's security, assessed at 14 months of age with the Strange Situation Procedure, seems to have been positively affected by the intervention, as the child was classified a secure B1.

Delia always took active part in the video feedback, and she was concerned to find alternative parenting strategies so that she could better adapt to her child's needs; moreover, she was supported by her husband and happy to have him involved in the sessions. She could also reflect on her childhood and made connections between her past and present attachment experiences. Actually, she seemed insightful during the intervention, even though her speech during the second Adult Attachment Interview after the intervention did not radically change.

Conclusions

In this study with premature and dermatitis infants the incidence of insecure attachment is higher than in comparison samples. Clinical problems may indeed make the children's signals less readable. Both the child and the parents may experience the child's hospitalization as a traumatic separation from the familiar environment of their homes and as a disruption of their own lives and relationships. This stressful child-rearing context is already present from the first months after the diagnosis of the child's illness, and it may interfere with the parents' feelings of being in charge of the child's specific needs and treatments. In the case of dermatitis and of premature infants, the relation among the parent's representations, sensitivity of the caregiving behavior, and child's security may be mediated by many potentially interfering factors, such as the intensity and duration of the illness, the psychological resources of the partner, and the social support available to the parents (Marvin & Pianta, 1996; Williamson et al., 2002). Secure parents may become overburdened due to a lack of social support, whereas insecure parents may feel challenged by their children's illness or prematurity to draw on every possible inner or external resource to make the best of the difficult situation.

The effectiveness of VIPP-R appears to depend on the security of parental attachment representations, but the intervention program is equally effective in families with clinical or nonclinical children, although the former parents may need more support because of their children's developmental problems. An interaction effect between the mother's state of mind with respect to attachment and participating in VIPP-R was found on infant attachment and maternal sensitivity. More specifically, children of insecure mothers appeared to profit from the intervention on attachment security, whereas children of secure mothers became less secure. A similar trend could be observed for maternal sensitivity: The VIPP-R seems to enhance the sensitivity of insecure mothers, but the sensitivity of secure mothers did not improve. Intervention effects did not differ for child clinical condition, although we had expected that parents of clinical children would be more in need of intervention, and would thus profit more from its support. Parents of preterm children or children suffering from dermatitis may need more tailor-made interventions of longer duration to increase their sensitivity more drastically than in the current intervention developed in nonclinical groups. Further research should focus on variation in content and duration of VIPP or VIPP-R in families of children with severe health problems.

We speculate that our intervention was more effective with insecure mothers because a revision of a mother's mental representation of attachment may be more effective when these representations are associated with less accurate representations of the child's reality, and with doubts about the parent's own competence to cope with the child's clinical problems. In contrast, an intervention with parents who have a balanced and open working model of attachment may not only be superfluous, but even create doubts about well-established interactional patterns where the need for change is absent. A secure mother, whose mental representation is flexible and open to change, may be stimulated by VIPP-R to explore new modalities to interact with her child. In case of an optimal balance between the child's and the parent's needs, the generic approach of VIPP-R might cause iatrogenic side effects.

In conclusion, the application of the VIPP-R to families with preterm infants and infants suffering from dermatitis is encouraging and suggests the opportunity of using it for preventive purposes in both clinical and nonclinical samples, but only in those cases in which mothers do not have secure mental representations of attachment. Our findings point to potential negative side effects in the case of secure parents. In screening families for participation in the intervention, only parents at risk for insecure attachment representations should be included.

8
Video-feedback intervention with mothers with postnatal eating disorders and their infants

Helen Woolley,[1] Leezah Hertzmann,[2] and Alan Stein[1]

[1]*Warneford Hospital, University of Oxford, Section of Child and Adolescent Psychiatry, Oxford, United Kingdom*
[2]*Tavistock and Portman NHS Trust, London, United Kingdom*

This chapter describes the VIPP treatment modified and extended to help mothers with eating disorders to interact with their infants at mealtimes in a more harmonious way. The background research that informed a treatment trial, the piloting of the modified treatment package, and the treatment protocol are described. The trial itself resulted from the findings of a longitudinal observational study of mothers with eating disorders and their infants, the purpose of which was to examine the influence of maternal eating disorder psychopathology on mother-child interaction and child development, including children's feeding and growth. We start with a description of our observational study. We then describe the rationale for the development of a specific treatment, our pilot work for our trial, and details of the ways in which we modified VIPP for the purposes of helping mothers with their eating disorders and their infants. The last section contains a description of the treatment trial and the intervention outcomes.

The observational study

In our observational study, two groups of mothers and their infants were recruited: The first consisted of 34 primiparious mothers who had experienced significant eating psychopathology of the bulimic type during the postnatal year. The second consisted of a comparison group of 24 mothers who had been free from such psychopathology (see Stein, Woolley, Cooper, & Fairburn, 1994) and were balanced with the eating disorder group with respect to maternal age, social class, and the child's gender. Mothers and infants were seen at home with their infants at 12 months and videotaped during a mealtime and play.

Detailed videoanalysis (coded blind) revealed a number of significant differences between the groups (Stein et al., 1994). The mothers with eating disorders were less facilitating of their infants than the comparison mothers with their infants during play and during the feed. Maternal facilitation is a measure of sensitive responsiveness, which refers to any maternal behavior that assists infants in an activity in which they are engaged or seem ready to engage. Such facilitation requires that the mother notices what her infant is doing or wanting/attempting to do and sensitively gauges when and how assistance or encouragement is needed. Mothers with eating disorders were more verbally controlling with their infants in using a higher proportion of strong verbal directives (e.g., commands, demands, or insistence) rather than mild directives (e.g., prompts, suggestion, or guidance).

There was no group difference in how often mothers praised their infants during either feed or play, but specifically during the meal (and not during play) the mothers with eating disorders were more likely than comparison mothers to make negative or critical comments (expressed negative emotion) directed at their infants. There were no differences between the groups in terms of the amount the mothers spoke to their children or in the amount of physical warmth they showed. The mothers with eating disorders were found to be more intrusive than the comparison mothers during both feed and play. Intrusions were defined as those maternal actions that inappropriately interfere with, take over, and disrupt the infant's activity. The mothers with the eating disorders and their infants manifested significantly more mealtime conflict than comparison dyads (see also Stein, Woolley, & McPherson, 1999). Conflict was characterized by a struggle for control between mother and infant that was associated with infant distress, noncompliance, and a serious disruption in the feeding of the baby.

Infants of mothers with eating disorders were rated as showing more negative emotional tone (less happy) than the infants of the comparison mothers. The children did not differ in terms of the amount they vocalized or in terms of the amount of their activity.

In terms of infant weight, the infants in the index group were lighter than the infants in the control group, expressed as standard deviation scores from the median on standardized growth charts (Hamill, Drizd, Johnson, Reed, & Roche, 1977). While the centile weights of the control infants were normally distributed, the index infants' weights were skewed with a subgroup whose weight was low. This is noteworthy as their birth weights were very similar. Eight infants of mothers with eating disorders and one control infant had dropped to the 15th centile or below and by at least 20 centiles since birth. A ninth index infant had dropped from just above the 10th centile to below the 3rd centile. Two further index subjects had experienced substantial reductions in their weight centiles over the first year: one from the 90th to the 35th centile and another from the 65th to the 35th centile. It emerged that the strongest predictor of infant weight was the extent of mealtime conflict between mother and infant, accounting for 20% of the variance in infant weight at 1 year.

The growth of the infants of mothers with eating disorders and controls was also compared to the growth of infants whose mothers had experienced depression in the postnatal year. It was found that infants of mothers with eating disorders weighed less than both the healthy controls and the infants of mothers with postnatal depression at 1 year of age, and there were no differences between the latter two groups. This suggests that this infant growth faltering may be specific to the infants of mothers with eating disorders (Stein, Murray, Cooper, & Fairburn, 1996).

Why might conflict be important?

In addition to the potential influence of conflict on infant weight, persistent and marked conflict may impact adversely on the mother-infant interaction in other ways. Infants may come to regard and anticipate mealtimes as adverse experiences, and then develop negative associations around food. If early infant attempts to self-feed are repeatedly disrupted, their initiatives dampened and their sense of agency not acknowledged, this may be important for subsequent development where experience of successful initiative taking encourages exploratory learning and may reinforce motivation and self-confidence. It has been shown that infants appraise the affective expressions of their parents to help understand their social situation (social referencing; Campos, Barrett, Lamb, Goldsmith, & Sternberg, 1983); thus, extensive conflictual interaction and maternal negativity may adversely influence that understanding by repeatedly communicating a negative message about a particular social situation. It has also been noted clinically that some patients with eating disorders confuse emotional and somatic experience (Bruch, 1973) and have difficulty identifying and communicating feeling states. This may make for difficulty where mothers are trying to gauge their infants' hunger and satiety cues, or read their emotional state, and where the misreading of cues easily leads to disputes.

A sequential microanalysis was undertaken to identify specific classes of antecedents to those episodes and factors that mediated between antecedents and conflict outcome (Stein et al., 1999). The hope was that this inquiry might help to inform future attempts to prevent or diminish conflict. Three main antecedents to conflict episodes were identified (for some episodes more than one antecedent was identified): (1) An issue arose between mother and infant as to who fed the infant. Typically the infant indicated a wish to self-feed while the mother clearly indicated she preferred to do all the feeding. (2) The mother expressed concern over the manner in which her infant ate, typically over making a mess. (3) Persistent food refusal, where the infant refused food despite repeated offers from the mother. All tapes were re-examined to identify where such potential antecedents occurred but without leading to conflict. We then examined which factors mediated between antecedents and conflictual outcome, that is, factors that, if they occurred in the presence of an antecedent, made conflict less likely. Three were identified: (1) whether the mother recognized/acknowledged the infant cues; (2) whether the mother was able, even briefly, to set aside her expressed concern; and (3) whether the infant disengaged. This examination indicated that the comparison mothers responded in a much more child-centered way by acknowledging cues and setting aside any expressed concerns so as to put the infant needs first, indicating that the difficulties experienced by the mothers with eating disorders were specific and particularly tied to eating disorder psychopathology. The following examples illustrate the findings.

> At the start of a meal an infant seated in a high chair reaches for a plate of food that the mother holds out of his reach. The mother appears not to notice the infant's repeated attempts to reach the food (the mother does not acknowledge the infant's signal). She is wholly concentrated on repeated food offers all of which he refuses with increasing distress (persistent food refusal). The mother becomes verbally and behaviorally very insistent in her food offers. The infant lunges for the plate and screams. The mother replies, "No! You will only get it all over the place" (mess concern and refusal to allow infant to jointly feed). The mother laughs and offers more food to the protesting infant, who refuses it by burying his head in his hands. The mother leans back and murmurs, "So you've had enough then" (food refusal is read as satiety).

> In the second example a mother feeds her infant from a plate of food that she rests on the tray of the high chair in which her son is sitting. After a few minutes he reaches forward and grabs a piece of carrot in his hand. The mother's smiling facial expression suddenly freezes into a severe frown, a momentary look of dismay. Her son becomes momentarily still as he watches her face. She relaxes, sighs, and says, "Oh, Uh! Oh well, here we go! Messy time again!" She smiles at her infant, who relaxes and nibbles the carrot. The mother remarks in a resigned but gentle tone, "I suppose you have to learn somehow, don't you?" She watches him eat and says, "Well done!" He smiles at her. (The mother overrides her expressed concern about her son feeding himself and the possible ensuing mess. She is able to let his need take precedence.)

How does maternal disorder psychopathology potentially interfere with parenting?

The question is raised as to why mothers with eating disorders are more likely to experience such conflicts with their child. The core features of bulimia nervosa are pervasive and potentially disruptive of daily activities and sensitive parenting. Particularly debilitating are the intractable urges to overeat; avoidance of the fattening effect of food by episodes of extreme dieting, vomiting, exercising, and use of laxatives; and a morbid fear of becoming fat, with weight and shape being central to self-valuation. Central to the condition is loss of control over eating and a marked fear of such loss. Preoccupation with thoughts about food (and its avoidance) and with body shape and weight, and the associated compensatory behaviors, all have the potential to interfere with everyday life.

It has been argued that the extent of self-absorption and preoccupation in psychiatric illness probably affects the caregiver's ability to separate her own needs from those of her child, and hence her capacity to understand and respond to those needs (Zahn-Waxler, Ianotti, Cummings, & Denham, 1990). Sensitivity and availability of parents have long been seen as key factors in the infant attachment literature. Given the eating behaviors and attitudes of those suffering from bulimia nervosa, it follows that their ability to notice infant signals may well be interrupted by preoccupying thoughts and behaviors around food. Furthermore, the recognition and interpretation of those signals that are noticed may well be colored by the mother's own eating concerns and perceptions. An example of this would be where a small food posset, so common at the introduction of solid feeding, is interpreted in a highly critical manner by the mother as deliberate vomiting, spitting out, or rejection of food.

Potential difficulties exist for these mothers when feeding their infants. A mother who oscillates between eating large quantities of food (often very quickly) and starving herself for extended periods may find it hard to judge her infant's comfortable eating pace or hunger and satiety signals. The mother's sense of control may be threatened by her infant refusing food when she herself is very hungry yet avoiding eating. At the same time, she has to sit patiently while her infant is fed. The very presence of leftover food may trigger a binge for some women, and the anxiety that this creates may lead the mother to insist that all the food be eaten, thus missing or overriding infant satiety cues. Even throwing leftovers away can pose a major challenge. This problem is compounded if a mother mistakenly gives her infant very large quantities of food, having lost track of what a reasonable portion might be.

Feeling challenged by food refusal, by infant attempts at self-feeding, by the loss of control over the amount eaten, by the infant eating too fast or too slowly, and by the manner in which food is eaten, particularly if mess ensues, are all potential areas of difficulty that came up during video observations of mother-infant interaction. We hypothesized that the mother's need for control of the infant's behavior and her extreme concern with infant self-feeding and mess make it very difficult for her to appreciate the infant's perspectives, or to notice and recognize infant cues. In turn, this may lead to the disruption of infant initiatives, conflict, and the relative failure to address the infant needs. The infant may then internalize this experience, and the difficulties are reflected in later, less optimal social functioning. Indeed, our work suggests that by five years of age, for example, these children have more difficulty in appreciating the perspective of their peers during play than controls (Stein et al., in preparation). In particular, during a standard dressing-up play assessment at home with a chosen friend, the children of mothers with eating disorders scored significantly lower on two of the three higher-order positive interaction initiative measures, which involved sharing experiences with a peer, bringing the attention of the peer to objects or events by showing (z = 3.16, p < .01) and requesting information of the peer, particularly about the shared environment (z = 2.87, p < .01). No significant differences were found on aggressive/assertive measures.

Planning an intervention to address mealtime conflict

The next step was how best to help prevent or limit early mealtime conflict, and particularly how to help in a way that does not undermine the mother's potentially fragile self-confidence and precarious sense of control. Previous clinical experience and our own pilot work indicated that treatment of the maternal eating disorder alone did not appear to be sufficient to address the interactional problems. In this pilot study we examined whether cognitive behavior therapy (CBT) for mothers with bulimia nervosa, the treatment of choice for the disorder (Fairburn, 2002) in the postnatal year, led to improvements in the disorder and a reduction in mother-child conflict. A case group of nine mothers with bulimia nervosa was treated with full CBT in the postnatal year, and the mothers and infants were followed up when the infants were 12 months of age. Comparisons were made between this group of nine and the subgroup of mothers and infants from our original observation study cohort who had not received any treatment (n = 27). While there were significant improvements in the mother's eating disorder psychopathology, there were no significant differences in the mother-child conflict/harmony ratings (z = 0.04, p = < .97).

In our observational study the specific conflictual difficulties observed during the videotaped feeds had frequently not been alluded to by mothers despite lengthy interviews, although they had visibly created maternal anxiety and infant distress as they occurred. Away from the actual feeding situation these observed difficulties were frequently not recalled by mothers. As mentioned above, one of the reasons that mothers might not notice or pick up on their infant's communication is because psychiatric disorders are characterized by preoccupation in which a person's mind is dominated by negative thoughts that are difficult to dismiss and when dismissed tend to recur. The focus of attention is therefore on issues germane to the disorder (body shape, weight, or eating issues) rather than on other environmental cues. Thus, attention is consumed by these thoughts and feelings, leaving less attention available to other aspects of the environment. In the case of a postnatal psychiatric disorder, this would potentially result in diminished attention to the infant. This suggests that written information or other forms of psychotherapy might not be sufficient to focus the mother away from her concerns and onto the baby's communication. Videotape has the potential to enable the observers to revisit the feed and pinpoint the specifics of what was going on, and we believed that looking at the videotape with the mothers would give access to those events in a way that discussion away from the event could not do. However, given the mothers' preoccupation with their own specific feeding issues and their negative self-evaluation, we were also concerned that in reviewing the videotapes the mothers would focus on the negative aspects and that this focus would reinforce their negative feelings and cognitions. Therefore, a technique was needed that would build on the mothers' strengths, enhance their self-esteem, and enable them to re-focus on the positive aspects of their infants' communication and development, hence the idea of using VIPP.

The pilot study

Brief interventions had already been shown to be effective in improving maternal sensitivity (Van IJzendoorn, Juffer, & Duyvesteyn, 1995), and this was confirmed by a major meta-analysis (Bakermans-Kranenburg, Van IJzendoorn, & Juffer, 2003). Our aim was to adapt the video-feedback intervention developed by Juffer (Juffer, 1993; Juffer, Bakermans-Kranenburg, & Van IJzendoorn, 2005b) and extended to the VIPP method (Bakermans-Kranenburg, Juffer, & Van IJzendoorn, 1998; see Chapter 2) for use with mothers with eating disorders and their infants. Specifically, the aim of the pilot study was to test whether the modified intervention would be both feasible and effective in producing change in mother-infant interaction, and particularly in diminishing mealtime conflict.

Considerable piloting was carried out to develop the intervention with a series of mothers in the postnatal period. Formal piloting was then carried out in two stages and aimed at mothers suffering from eating disorders, mainly of the bulimic type, and their infants in their first year of life. Ten mothers (aged 19 to 37 years) were piloted, six in the first phase and four in the second. The first six were recruited through psychiatrists caring for mothers with eating disorders. Mothers and infants were seen at home on six fortnightly visits during which four infant mealtimes and play sessions were videotaped and four video-feedback sessions given. The first and final mealtime videotapes were coded on measures used in the observational study (described above) in order to record any changes affected in each case. Mothers also gave feedback on their experience of the sessions.

Improvements were recorded in five of the six mother-infant dyads in terms of better maternal facilitation, fewer intrusions, and less verbal negativity toward their infants, who in turn scored higher on emotional tone. Crucially, there were fewer conflict episodes during feeds. The sixth dyad did not show any change.

This first pilot stage tested the contents, style of delivery, and acceptability of the proposed modified VIPP program, but uncovered two areas where it was felt that further help should be offered in the forthcoming trial. The first concerned the additional provision of written and pictorial information on infant development, particularly highlighting issues around infant feeding, in an album to be assembled by the researchers using material from the observational study. The second area concerned finding a way of integrating the help offered to mothers for their eating problems within the treatment trial program so as to access more readily the way the mothers' eating disorder psychopathology impacted on their behavior with their infants during infant meals. Clinical impressions during piloting confirmed previous research findings (Stein et al., 1994, 2001) that the way mothers managed their infant feeding was influenced, at least in part, by their own eating disorder psychopathology, and in particular their eating cognitions, and so we felt it necessary to provide parallel, separate, but complementary help for mothers alongside the help with their infants to deal with their eating disorder cognitions. For this purpose it was planned to adapt guided self-help CBT programs successfully used to date for eating disorders in primary care (Carter & Fairburn, 1995; Cooper, Coker, & Fleming, 1994) for use with mothers in the postnatal period, including a brief manual.

The second stage of piloting with four mother-infant dyads (recruitment as for the treatment trial; see below) was carried out to implement the full treatment protocol and led to some practical alterations, particularly in the timing of the delivery of the three components of treatment to be used in parallel (VIPP with information album and CBT). This fine-tuning proved necessary when delivering the treatment in the context of the full treatment trial protocol and the pre- and posttest assessments.

Description of the video-feedback intervention

The treatment was conceptualized in three stages: (1) The first stage concentrated on children's perspective and focused on their signals (actions, facial expression, and vocalizations) to enhance the mother's observational skills, including infant initiatives toward the mother, exploratory behavior, signals indicating hunger, satiety, responses to new foods, tastes and textures, and early attempts at self-feeding. (2) The second stage included the mother's perspective, highlighting mother-infant initiatives, mutual responses, moments of shared emotion, and noting the success of sensitive, prompt reactions to infant cues. (3) Third, as treatment progressed the videotapes were used to help the mothers identify and address potential triggers to mealtime conflict. The VIPP fine-tuned in piloting was developed on the basis of the key work of Juffer et al. (2005b; see Chapter 2). We also supplemented with elements of other work by Carter, Osofsky, and Hann (1991) and Muir (1992), and the Touchpoints technique of Brazelton (1994).

Thus, a critical feature of the video-feedback treatment is to focus on the positive aspects of the interaction between the infant and the mother. At least initially, the therapist focuses on where the mother does respond to heighten her sense of responding, rather than on where the mother misses cues or does not respond appropriately. In this way the mother can be helped to notice her infant's cues and to respond to them while still feeling in control of her feeding.

Sensitive responding

The aim of the treatment was to prevent or reduce mother-infant conflict by enhancing the mother's recognition of and responsiveness to her infant's cues and improving her awareness of her infant's developmental needs and processes, focusing principally on mother-infant interaction during mealtimes implemented through guided video feedback. Mothers and infants were videotaped at home during the principal solid feed of the day (sometimes including play), and extracts preselected by the therapist were then shown and shared with the mother on the next video-feedback visit. This feedback was driven by the view that sensitive parenting requires differential responsiveness to two different types of infant behavior, contact- or proximity-seeking (attachment) behavior and exploratory behavior (see Chapter 2). The infant's contact seeking requires the mother to comfort, respond to visual contact, look, talk, and if necessary initiate playful interaction. The infant's exploratory behavior often calls for a relatively noninterfering and supportive attitude from the mother: When the infant's attention is directed at objects, the mother should not disturb or interfere with her or his activities if possible. She may be facilitating in her response but not intrusive or interruptive. When babies repeatedly experience their mothers as interfering by, for example, showing them "the right way," they may not get a chance to discover things by themselves and experience their own competence. This is particularly so in the case of mealtimes, and very pertinent around the second half of the first year when children's attempts at self-feeding usually begin. Mothers with eating disorders frequently find these attempts of their children challenging and difficult to cope with (see above).

Added to the infant's need to explore from a secure base is the need for adequate, prompt caregiver responses to infant signals. The mother's appropriate response to the infant's signals can be selected and shared with the mother on video replay, as can moments of affect attunement (Haft & Slade, 1989) and the sharing of emotions between the mother and her infant (see Chapter 2).

Central to these themes is the caregiver's ability to pick up, recognize, and respond to the infant's signals in a timely and congruent manner. Helping the mother to develop this ability was a primary target for treatment in the piloting given the pivotal role that missing, misreading, or countermanding infant signals plays in the evolution of conflict episodes in the context of maternal eating disorders.

We argued that missing infant cues might relate to the degree of maternal preoccupation around food, which narrows the focus of attention; that the misreading of cues was likely to be driven, at least in part, by their own eating concerns; and that the countermanding of cues may have arisen from the mothers' constant need to keep control by taking charge.

In the observational study, mothers with eating disorders had been significantly more likely than their healthy counterparts to be more strongly verbally controlling during infant feeds (see above). In fact, dietary restraint was the one feature of eating disorder psychopathology associated with the use of strong verbal control (Stein et al., 2001). The fact that at a behavioral level they were also more intrusive with their infants (see above) indicated a need to take charge behaviorally as well as verbally, irrespective of their infants' current behavior. These mothers described constantly feeling on the edge of losing control around food and eating, and this need to keep tight control is likely to be greater when the very presence of food and the concerns related to infant mealtimes trigger powerful preoccupying thoughts and feelings that distract from focusing on the infants' more subtle signals. We therefore felt that it was doubly important for these mothers, trying to establish some regularity and order in both their own and their infant's eating routine, that the style of help offered should be such as to reinforce their self-confidence and not undermine their sense of being in control — in fact, to help them find new, more appropriate ways of feeding and being in charge during infant mealtimes.

Style of video feedback

The style of video feedback to be offered was therefore collaborative with the therapist as a supporting and enabling agent, and the dialogue with mothers was essentially descriptive and curiosity driven, with the infant as the central reference point. The process of mother and therapist watching video extracts together was unlike a purely verbal discussion of a feed where both therapist and mother rely on the accuracy of recalled events filtered by memory, and where events that go unnoticed are not available for discussion. With video, the observed image on the screen is the replayed picture of the actual event, which is available for interpretation.

Viewers attribute their own meaning to what they see. The video can be watched from the infant's viewpoint ("as if" watching) and then from the mother's viewpoint, thus separating the two perspectives. Two valid pictures can be drawn, each belonging to different referents (infant and mother). Separating out the needs of the mother and infant may in effect begin here and provides the opportunity to address differing ways of meeting their separate needs (particularly if their needs appear to conflict).

Techniques to explore the infant's perspective

With these issues and processes in mind, video-feedback piloting specifically focused on preventing and reducing conflict through helping mothers to (1) recognize and respond (where appropriate) to infant cues; (2) become aware of antecedents to conflict; (3) set aside their concerns, especially about mess, where those concerns interfere with the infants' needs; and (4) foster appropriate autonomy. Focusing on the infant's signals and emotions to improve maternal responsiveness to and empathy with the infant, the therapist selects and replays extracts of the video and comments with the mother on the infant's signals and responses by verbalizing the infant's reactions and facial expressions using the descriptive curiosity-driven approach described above, and drawing on the "speaking for the child" (Carter et al., 1991; see Chapter 2), "Watch, Wait, and Wonder" (Muir, 1992), and "Touchpoints" (Brazelton, 1994) techniques as is contextually appropriate.

These three techniques offer specific ways to explore the infant's perspective. For instance, when the mother persists in food offers despite her infant's repeated refusals and turning away, the therapist might first try to elicit the mother's perception of her infant's perspective, and then she herself might add, "I think I've had enough mum" ("speaking for the infant"; see Chapter 2). Or, speaking less directly during guided video replay with the mother, the therapist might say,

"Look at his expression. I wonder what he is thinking. What do you think?" so drawing the mother into noting and interpreting her infant's expressions from a child's viewpoint.

The therapist can then extend this discussion by focusing on the *what*, *how*, and *why* around the infant's signal. For instance, when the infant reaches for the mother's feeding spoon, *what* denotes noticing that event; *how* denotes the way he does it, perhaps with eager determination and excitement (which describes the style and temperament of this particular infant); and, finally, *why* puts the action into an interactional context (with the mother) and a developmental context (he is at a stage where he wants to grasp the spoon and experiment with using it himself).

The "Watch, Wait, and Wonder" approach (Muir, 1992) provides another way into the infant perspective. It requires the parent to respond exclusively to infant initiatives in the here and now, so as to place the initial emphasis on observation and understanding what the infant is doing, feeling, indicating, and communicating. In guided video viewing this focus on infant initiatives is useful in drawing in the mother who is unavailable through being distracted, preoccupied, and missing cues. It can also refocus the attention of mothers for whom an infant's action has suddenly triggered overwhelming anxiety and a defensive intrusive response (e.g., when the infant reaches for the mother's spoon, the mother experiences sudden heightened anxiety around potential mess, and abruptly and angrily pulls the spoon away saying, "Don't be silly, you'll only make a horrible mess").

The therapist highlights any instances where the infant acknowledges and communicates with the mother, behaviors that preoccupied mothers often miss. Of particular importance is the recognition and appreciation of signals of hunger, satiety, and readiness for the next spoonful, the infant's pace of eating, and the wish to self-feed, as well as the infant's enjoyment of food. Allowing the infant to touch, hold, experiment, and play with handling food and utensils (cup, spoon, and so forth) requires acknowledgment and acceptance that some mess is likely as the infant acquires new skills and gains more autonomy. Infant signals relating to nonfood issues are also noted and commented on favorably to broaden the scope of mealtime interaction. The therapist comments positively on any instance of parental sensitivity to reinforce this behavior, and enables the mother to locate these positive interactions within the repertoire of behaviors with her infant.

As sessions progress the mother is encouraged to note her own behavior and review aspects that may be associated with her disturbance in eating habits and attitudes. The mother is helped to develop her own strategies for coping with her infant's feed and any infant mealtime behaviors that precipitate her anxiety, such as the infant feeding very slowly and refusing food, the presence of potential leftovers triggering the urge to binge, and the desire to get the meal over as soon as possible. This makes it difficult for mother to sit patiently through the meal and relate appropriately to the infant cues. For example, not infrequently the infant meal occurs when the mother herself is hungry, and therefore especially vulnerable to a breakdown of her own control over eating. Some mothers find it helpful to avoid this dilemma by having a small planned snack themselves before feeding their infant. During the meal the mother is helped to widen her focus of attention by reading the infant's expressions and signals, by talking to the infant about topics other than eating, commenting on exploratory behavior, and by recognizing the infant's enjoyment of different experiences.

Vignettes illustrating the video-feedback intervention in mothers with eating disorders

The following examples do not come from individual mothers but rather are composites of situations and themes that arose during the piloting.

> A mother is distraught because of the "battles" that increasingly occur during her attempts to introduce her five-month-old infant to solid food. During a videotaped feed he takes the initial offers of baby rice from the spoon, and each time a small thin overflow rolls onto his bottom lip, which the mother hurriedly wipes away. He seems to have a full mouth and turns his head aside at the next offer. He looks quizzically around responding to any sound or visual movement in his immediate surroundings. He sucks his hand repeatedly between food offers, and each time this happens the mother immediately pulls it out, wipes it, and eventually holds it down firmly. The mother looks increasingly tense and anxious, speeds up the by now abortive food offers, and the infant looks startled and unhappy. The feed ends with both mother and infant in distress.

Several issues arise within this short video extract: the mother's hasty and somewhat intrusive response to food overflow and hand sucking, and her apparent increasing anxiety and accelerated food offers when the infant pauses to look around and refuses those offers. As the therapist reviews the video to select extracts for feedback, she holds in mind the potential perspective of both the mother and infant, wondering how the mother herself perceives and interprets the events that precede her intrusive response. From the infant perspective there is the new experience of transition from sucking at the breast to negotiating more solid food. He is beginning to self-comfort with hand sucking, and his growing interest in the world around him perhaps provides more interest at the moment than this difficult-to-manage new food. The therapist selects extracts that highlight three themes: any exploratory behavior (in this case a particular "touchpoint" opportunity when the infant's spurt in curiosity in his immediate environment interrupts feeding), positive looks to the mother, and the finer signals that this infant gives around food offers. It is envisaged that through jointly viewing these extracts the mother's own perspective and beliefs will emerge, but with the infant as starting point and recurrent focus of attention.

At video feedback the therapist focuses on the infant's interest and alertness to his immediate surrounds (exploratory behavior), pausing the video at those moments when he looks intently at the mobile above his chair, then turns and listens to the sound of a cat meowing, and finally looks at his mother and smiles. The therapist comments on how alert and interested he seems, and the mother says that he has become much more interested in his surroundings recently and wonders whether it is this that interrupts his feeding. They talk about what it might be like learning to manage solid food after only knowing sucking at the breast (child perspective), and how for the moment it may be more interesting for her infant to look around than feed.

The therapist and the mother move on to watch and rewatch the first food offer, and the therapist pauses the picture when the spoon is nearly touching his lips and he opens his mouth wide. The therapist asks, "What do you think he might be saying here as he opens his mouth?" The mother replies that she had not noticed him opening his mouth, and together they wonder whether that is what he normally does when he is ready for a mouthful (as opposed to when he turns away slightly). At the next offer, they notice that he leans his head forward very slightly before accepting the offered food, a gesture he does not make before refusing an offer.

Focusing on the infant's behavior, the mother and therapist are able to think about what signs he gives to show his readiness for food, for the next mouthful; his need to pause a while; his growing curiosity in looking around; and his seeming to have had enough. Toward the end of the session the mother commented that there was a problem with her infant "being sick, spitting all the food out" (the mother points to the overspill on her infant's lip) and "deliberately doing so" (she points to the hand sucking). This opened the way into helping to reframe these cognitions through thinking about the likely developmental context for the infant's behavior.

By the next video feedback, the mother had slowed the pace of her food offers, more of which were being accepted. The feed was less tense, with some positive mother-infant sequences, with the mother watching and following her infant's cues more closely.

Tackling inappropriate attributions

As in the above example, the issues of overspill on an infant's lips and hand sucking posed problems for several mothers in piloting during early feeds and frequently appeared to trigger intense maternal anxiety and some intrusive responses. Overspill was frequently perceived by the mother as vomiting, and children's hand sucking as a deliberate attempt to reject food or to make themselves sick. These mothers had often themselves used vomiting as a compensatory behavior after binging. Having tapped these attributions, it was usually possible to think together about what these behaviors might mean in terms of the child's development, and so help a mother reframe her perceptions. For example, hand sucking could be understood as a self-comforting activity transferred from the comfort of sucking at the breast or bottle, or as an infant's way to pace the feed. When seen as part of a developmental process or as an example of infant agency, it poses less of a threat to the mother. However, in reviewing these situations we felt that concurrent help for these mothers with their own eating problems would have greatly helped in the process of disentangling these inappropriate cognitions, not least because of the closely guarded secrecy around eating disorder behavior, such as vomiting.

Preoccupation and missing infant cues

A further common situation is illustrated by a 10-month-old baby girl being fed a heaped bowl of pasta in her high chair. She reaches for the bowl several times but is not allowed to touch the food. The feed starts in a positive atmosphere, and the infant appears to enjoy the first mouthfuls. The mother then offers food very fast and the infant, with a mouth still full of food, repeatedly turns her head away, eventually arching her back and screaming. This then leads to an extended episode of conflictual mother-child interaction.

At video feedback, after the therapist highlighted the infant's exploratory behavior, she encouraged the mother to use the "talking for the baby" technique, and the mother commented that she was amazed at the range of her infant's signals and behaviors on video. She acknowledged that she had not noticed any of these during the actual feed. Her memory was of seeing and smelling the delicious food and how this stimulated an intractable urge to binge. It had then become crucial to her that the meal should be over as quickly as possible and all the food eaten so as to avoid the possibility of a binge triggered by leftovers. This narrowed focus of attention precluded any observations as to what her infant was doing and signaling. The fast pacing of food offers, and the very large quantity of food offered, with inevitable satiety and food refusal, had never previously occurred to her as issues to be thought about let alone influenced by watching her infant's cues.

Widening the focus of attention

> An infant feed is videoed in which an 11-month infant sits in his high chair feeding himself with a spoon, occasionally helped by his mother, who sits opposite. He has eaten most of the meal and is now losing interest in the food and starting to look around. Failing to get a slippery chunk of courgette onto his spoon, he grabs it in his hand and squeezes it. Mother's expression freezes into one of apparent horror. The infant drops the courgette and then leans over the side of the high chair and drops his spoon onto the floor, peering over the side to see where it has gone. He looks expectantly at his mother and back in search of the dropped spoon. Mother picks it up grumbling; he drops it again and this is repeated several times. Mother looks angry by this point and says with irritation, "You are just messing about and getting food all over the place." She then persistently tries to feed the remaining courgette to her son, who protests and turns away, becoming very fussy. Both mother and infant appear increasingly angry and distressed, and the infant ends up pushing the dish onto the floor in a rage.

At video feedback, mother and therapist watch the early part of the feed and note how dextrous the infant is in manipulating the food onto his spoon and into his mouth, observing how he uses one and then both hands to grasp, hold, and steady the dish and spoon to achieve this. Mother is pleasantly surprised to see her own part in instinctively helping him with this and comments, "I never noticed before how well he manages. Isn't he clever?" The point in the video at which her son begins to lose interest in the feed is then reached, and as she watches the video, the mother's mood visibly darkens. She says to the therapist, "Here's trouble. He's getting at me now. It feels like he was deliberately rejecting his favorite food that I'd specially prepared for him." Watching intently she describes the sudden rush of overwhelming anxiety she experienced when he repeatedly dropped the spoon onto the floor because this made her feel she had lost control of how much he was eating. She had then pressured him to eat the remaining food up so as to try and regain that sense of control, only to end up in a battle. Only while watching the video replay, and with the help of the therapist's commentary, does she become aware that he appeared to have had enough and had therefore refused her food offers.

Rewatching the section of video where the infant drops the spoon, the therapist represents a different perspective and encourages the mother to speak for the infant. The mother says, "Oh, where has it gone?" as she sees the infant peering at the floor. The therapist comments that it is like he is playing a game of hide-and-seek with the spoon, "like the peepo game he was playing with you when I arrived today." He is learning about whether things disappear when you cannot see them, and he looks up to his mother to see what she thinks (social referencing). He repeats this game and wants to go on playing long after mother has tired of it.

This feedback session served two purposes. It helped the mother to locate and think about the trigger points for her anxiety, that is, her son's actions during the feed, and it helped her to see those actions from a different perspective by understanding them in a developmental context and from his viewpoint. It enabled some alternative understanding of those actions that widened her focus of attention.

Using the video "Still" in reframing perception

The therapist videos a meal at the start of which a 12-month-old infant girl sits in her high chair watching her mother, who stands well back stirring and blowing a dish of newly cooked food. The mother had previously told the therapist that because of her own long-standing eating problems she "knows" that she has an entirely negative influence over her daughter around food, a belief that she insists is the case because her own mother is constantly telling her that it is so (in fact, the mother's mother telephones several times while this feed is videotaped to check on what is happening). The infant's mother has also said that she likes to stand as far away from her daughter (who tries to self-feed) as she can to "avoid causing trouble."

Now, while the mother cools the food she talks about what she is doing and names the ingredients in the dish, patiently holding her infant's attention. Her daughter watches her intently, smiling, copying her mother blowing the food, and attempting to copy words (the mother says "cheese," and she replies "eeees"). As the mother walks toward the high chair and offers the dish of food, the infant looks up into her face with an expression of beaming anticipatory excitement and exclaims "Ohooooooooo!" Mother gives her the dish and then retreats into the far corner of the room behind her daughter, who nevertheless repeatedly twists around trying to engage her mother's attention.

During video feedback the therapist stilled the moment on video that captured the infant's excited response to her mother's food offer. Together, the mother and therapist watched this episode several times highlighting the sequence of mother-infant interactions. The mother had no memory from the live interaction of this positive exchange. This stilled moment proved to be a turning point in the mother's reframing her perception of herself as a potential positive influence. She commented later that "it's like a photograph that I carry about in my head."

The mother in fact used this and similar subsequent episodes on video to identify and affirm ways she and her daughter could enjoy being together around
food. She started to reframe the way she perceived her relationship with her
infant daughter and to disentangle her own mother's negative belief about that
relationship from her own increasingly positive experience of it.

Several mothers during piloting asked for a copy of a particular video to give to their
own mothers as an affirmation of their positive interaction with their infants.

Conclusions drawn from the piloting

In this pilot study, changes related to maternal behaviors and style had been
observed, as well as changes in maternal perceptions and attributions made in
relation to their infants. In addition, some mothers had been able to connect
with previous emotional material that hitherto had been inaccessible to them. In
particular there was a reduction in conflictual mother-child interaction, intrusive behavior, and inappropriate attributions during meals. Mothers were more
facilitating, and mealtimes became more relaxed. The intervention appeared to
have accessed some mealtime difficulties, opened the door to change, and been
welcomed by the mothers themselves. A number of conclusions were drawn:

1. It had been crucially important to obtain the direct access to mother-infant
   interaction provided by video to identify and focus on what was happening
   as well as to access "live" maternal perceptions, feelings, and beliefs that
   underpinned the mothers' responses to their infants' behaviors.
2. It confirmed that some mothers had attentional difficulties that narrowed
   their focus of attention. This was assumed to be a feature of eating disorder
   preoccupation and appeared to be accessible, in part, through the guided
   video replay.
3. For a number of mothers, the early months of motherhood had re-evoked
   difficulties around past and present relationships with their own mothers
   (or other close relatives) so as to interfere with their current responses to
   their babies. Unresolved loss also posed a similar problem for some mothers. Although these problems were accessed during video feedback, we felt
   that additional discussion time (away from VIPP) might be needed in a
   minority of cases.
4. In a separate pilot study described earlier, mothers with bulimia nervosa
   who received treatment for their eating disorder alone, but not for the
   mother-child interaction, showed improvements in their eating disorder
   psychopathology, but this did not appear to have automatically translated
   into easing mother-infant mealtime conflict. Maternal perceptions and
   interpretations of infant signals and behavior still frequently appeared to

be bound up with cognitions related to the mother's own eating disorder psychopathology. For this reason, we deemed it necessary to include specific help for mothers with their eating problems alongside the VIPP during the trial. We also believed it was not ethically acceptable to identify a clinical problem and not offer treatment for it.

5. We felt that some additional information incorporating visual illustrations in booklet form on infant development through the first year of life would be of use in the trial as a reference resource, and to support the guided video feedback (Juffer et al., 2005b).

These two additional components of treatment were designed for, and fine-tuned in, the second pilot phase, which extended the 6 sessions previously offered to 13. This extension took into account the more intractable nature of some of the interactional problems linked to eating psychopathology, and also covered developmental phases particularly relating to feeding during the first year of life.

The treatment trial

The treatment program with video feedback

The final treatment package was therefore devised for a trial to give direct access to mother-infant interaction particularly during feeds (VIPP), and to make readily accessible to each mother information on infants in the first year of life (album) and to provide mothers with help for their own eating difficulties because the cognitions associated with the eating disorder interfered with parenting processes and needed to be addressed directly. This component, cognitive behavioral therapy (CBT), provided separate but complementary help for the mothers' own eating psychopathologies.

Guided self-help CBT

A guided self-help cognitive behavioral program developed for people suffering from bulimia nervosa and eating disorders not otherwise specified (EDNOS) of a bulimic type was adapted for the postnatal period from two established treatments (Carter & Fairburn, 1995; Cooper et al., 1994). This self-help manual employing a stepwise approach was given to all mothers in booklet form. Guided by the therapist, each mother was helped to implement the relevant steps. The aim was to help mothers gain control over their eating; to reduce binge eating, vomiting, use of laxatives, or other compensatory behaviors (e.g., exercise); to reduce extreme concern about shape and weight; and to provide mothers with the tools to tackle their eating problem should it recur.

Child development album

An individualized album illustrating, through photographs and the written word, aspects of infant behavior and development during the first year of life, with particular focus on mealtimes, was created, influenced by the one originally developed by Juffer, *Het eerste levensjaar* [*The First Year of Life*] (Juffer, Metman, & Andoetoe, 1986; see Chapter 9). It was designed to be used alongside video-feedback as a reference, where appropriate, and to help place infant behavior observed on video into a positive developmental context. It can also be used to help mothers anticipate infant feeding behavior as it changes at different stages. Album photographs illustrate early infant exploratory behavior such as looking, listening, reaching, and putting objects into the mouth. Sequences of stills (individual frames taken from a videotape) show infant expressions and responses to new tastes and textures from the introduction of solids onward. Early infant attempts to touch, hold, and play with food as precursors to self-feeding (finger feeding) are illustrated, as are the mother and infant using two spoons to take turns in feeding. Issues that frequently arise around feeding are aired, such as coping with mess during self-feeding, to set such issues into a developmental context. For example, the album illustrates instances where the infant drops food over the side of a high chair during the stage where the understanding of object permanence is developing, alongside a picture of an infant playing "peepo." It shows refusal of proffered food where the infant may want to do all his own feeding or where the infant is more interested in surrounding events.

The booklet includes a first explanatory page that addresses the mother directly and names her child. The album is made up of loose-leaf transparent sleeves so that any page can be removed and replaced by her own photographs of her infant, or by stills taken from the videotapes, if she so wishes. Some pages are left blank for this purpose also. This design was specifically created so that mothers can recreate the album for themselves if they so wish.

Video feedback program

The mothers and their infants were seen at home for 13 one-hour sessions, starting when the infants were between 4 and 6 months (and had started solid feeding) and finishing by 12½ months. Particular care was taken over arranging the timing of sessions to encompass the infant's routine and the mother's convenience and to enable the mother to have some uninterrupted space for both the CBT and the video-feedback components of treatment. For mothers with other children or family members at home this often needed considerable planning.

Half of each of the first eight sessions comprised the CBT guided self-help program for the treatment of the mother's eating disorder. Alternate videotaping of the infant's main solid feed of the day (occasionally including some play) and video feedback showing extracts preselected by the therapist prior to the session were undertaken during the 13 sessions, allowing for 7 video-feedback sessions. During the last five sessions some flexibility was allowed in this alternate video/video-feedback session routine to avoid too long a gap between making a video and its feedback, thus permitting videotaping and video feedback in the same session, if needed. Allowance was also made for some discussion about issues that may have arisen during the videotaping of a feed, or where it became evident that other difficulties, such as unresolved losses or problems in past or present relationships, interfered with the mother's sensitivity to her infant.

The aim was to see the mother and infant weekly within the first six to eight weeks and subsequently at two- to three-week intervals. On the first visit, the therapist introduced the CBT, video feedback, and the album with a chance to discuss any queries or concerns that the mother might have. By the end of the second visit the mother would have had a chance to look at her CBT booklet and start the program, to peruse her personalized copy of the album, and to watch the first video extracts with her therapist. Most mothers by this point had completed a "plans for change" sheet (relating to their own eating), which they reviewed and updated as CBT progressed. Most had also started on the first CBT step: written monitoring of their own daily eating. Mothers worked through the CBT steps with the guidance and support of the therapist.

Throughout the 13 sessions the style of video feedback, both collaborative and descriptive, was based on watching video extracts together, noticing and discussing alternative ways of interpreting perceived infant signals, and testing the possible fit between the observed event and the meaning being discussed and thought about.

In the early sessions, focus was on the infant's perspective without explicit discussion of the maternal role (see Chapter 2). The preselected extracts of video and stills centered on infant signals, actions, facial expressions, and vocalizations, highlighting infant initiatives toward the mother, and exploratory behavior (looking, listening, reaching), hunger and satiety cues, the pace of eating, and responses to new foods, tastes, and textures. As the infant progressed, any attempts to touch, hold, and play with food were noted and discussed and set in context as precursors to self-feeding. The therapist drew on the "speaking for the baby," "Wait, Watch, and Wonder," and "Touchpoints" techniques (see above) in an informal way to describe the infant's behavior and experience. The mother was likewise encouraged to do the same. The process of noticing signals and then wondering what they might signify, and trying to take the infant's perspective into account, was followed and developed in watching the videos.

Maternal concerns

Some mothers had concerns about seeing themselves on video and seemed initially preoccupied with their own image on screen. The initial concentration on their infants (see also Chapter 2) helped to refocus their attention so that when the intervener came on to gradually include the mothers' perspective, their preoccupation with their own image had often eased, while the infants remained center stage. The intervener moved on to the mothers' initiatives toward their infants and mutual responses. The success of sensitive and prompt reactions to infant cues were highlighted, particularly noting how these ministrations provided shared enjoyment of the infants' expanding skills and understanding. The mothers were able to see how these moments of successful ministration were part of their repertoires of interactions with their infants, providing an alternative model for times when some of their own interactions with their infants were more problematic.

As treatment using both CBT and video feedback progressed, the video was used to help identify and then address potential triggers to mealtime conflict. Typically this included maternal concern about mess and the infant's manner of eating, including playing with food and utensils; concern about having her sense of control challenged by the infant eating too slowly, too quickly, or repeatedly refusing food or attempting to self-feed; and concerns with any infant leftovers in case these triggered a binge. Other mothers saw their own infants enjoying food and discussed their ambivalence about this. The therapists were careful not to get involved in any dietary advice, which was always referred back to the health visitor.

Completing the intervention

By session 13 the therapist aimed for the mother to have utilized the steps incorporated in the CBT program relevant for managing her eating pattern and behaviors, and to have received seven full video-feedback sessions on her infant's mealtimes. The formal ending session incorporated a selection of brief video extracts from previous treatment sessions; a review of the mother's eating habits, attitudes, and behaviors regarding shape and weight; and a review of the mother's negotiation of any current or possible recurrent eating problems. Throughout treatment and at this final session the mother was given a number of photographs depicting mother-infant mutual delight or salient moments of her infant's developing skills and autonomy. Photos sometimes included video stills, which had proved to be important turning points in mother-infant interaction, thus reinforcing those moments of recognition that promoted positive change. The plan was to complete treatment when the infant was 12 months old.

The trial

This modified VIPP for mothers with eating disorders was formally tested in a treatment trial (Stein et al., 2006). The aim of the trial was to examine whether VIPP targeted specifically at mother-child interaction would diminish mealtime conflict by helping mothers to recognize, support, and respond to infant signals and initiatives, and whether it would increase infant weight and improve infant autonomy at mealtimes, compared with a control treatment in which mothers received counseling. As described above, we believed it would be difficult to improve mother-child interaction without some form of additional help directed specifically at the mothers' eating disorder cognitions and behaviors. Thus, both groups also received guided cognitive behavioral self-help (CBT) for eating disorders, which has been shown to be suitable for use in primary care settings (Carter & Fairburn, 1995).

Participants, design, and measures

Women were eligible to participate in the trials if they were between ages 18 and 45 years with infants between 4 and 6 months old. They needed to meet DSM-IV diagnostic criteria for an eating disorder — either bulimia nervosa or a similar form of eating disorder of clinical severity, that is, a bulimic subtype of eating disorder not otherwise specified. The final inclusion criteria were (1) overevaluation of body shape or weight to a degree that reached clinical severity; (2) recurrent episodes of loss of control over eating, that is, subjective or objective bulimic episodes; and (3) secondary social impairment. Mothers with severe co-morbid psychiatric disorders were excluded from the study.

In order to identify potential participants in the study, women who had infants aged between 8 and 24 weeks who were attending routine postnatal baby clinics in two areas in the United Kingdom were screened by using the Eating Disorder Examination Questionnaire (EDEQ) (Fairburn & Beglin, 1994), which had been adapted for postnatal use. These postnatal baby clinics are based in the community and provide free postnatal healthcare for all infants in the United Kingdom. Informed consent was obtained from the mothers for a two-stage screening procedure. Women who showed evidence of significant disturbance in eating habits and attitudes on the basis of their responses to the EDEQ were then invited for an interview using the Eating Disorder Examination (EDE) (Fairburn & Cooper, 1993) interview schedule. This validated structured interview schedule, which provides eating disorder diagnoses, was conducted in the mothers' homes at a time to suit them. Each woman who fulfilled eligibility criteria was then invited to participate in the trial and was visited at home by a psychiatrist, who confirmed the diagnosis by clinical interview. After a complete description of the trial, written informed consent was obtained. The study was approved by the relevant local research ethics committees (in Oxford and London). The mothers were randomly assigned to the two interventions by using block randomization with fixed blocks of size 6, which were computer generated by an independent statistician and stratified according to eating disorder diagnosis (bulimia nervosa or bulimic type of eating disorder not otherwise specified). Allocation concealment was facilitated by the use of sequentially numbered opaque sealed envelopes for consecutive and eligible study participants.

The Eating Disorder Examination Questionnaire was completed by 2,387 women, of whom 504 (21.1%) scored high and 377 (15.8%) agreed to be interviewed using the Eating Disorder Examination interview. Of these 377, 110 (29%) fulfilled the eligibility criteria. Ultimately 80 women were randomly assigned to video feedback (n = 40) or counseling (n = 40). The demographic characteristics and clinical presentation were well balanced across the treatment groups except for indications for imbalances in infant gender and weight. Of the original 80 mothers, only 3 (2 mothers from the video-feedback group and 1 from the counseling group) were not available for follow-up, leaving 38 in the video-feedback group and 39 in the counseling group. There were no differences between the groups in the mean number of sessions completed (12.1 for video-feedback group and 11.1 for the counseling group). All treatment was carried out in the mother's home. The fact that most mothers received the vast majority of their sessions suggests that the treatments were highly acceptable.

The pretreatment assessment of the groups was undertaken when the infants were four to six months old. The groups were then reassessed after treatment when the infants were 13 months of age. The mothers and infants were video-taped during the principal solid meal of the day. Considerable time was allowed to help mothers to get used to the cameras at both assessments. If in the mother's opinion the posttreatment meal was not typical, a further meal was videotaped on a separate occasion. This occurred in six cases. All videotapes were rated by independent raters blind to group assignment.

The primary outcome measure was the level of conflict during the principal meal of the day, measured every two minutes for the duration of the meal and averaged. Conflict/harmony was rated on a 1 (conflict) to 5 (harmony) scale, on which conflict was defined as a battle for control between the mother and infant, with associated infant distress, noncompliance, and invariable disruption of feeding. The key ingredients of this battle for control were refusal to allow infant self-feeding, or to allow feeding at the infant's own pace, and maternal concern about messiness. Infant behaviors such as repeated food refusal were common features of conflict. The occurrence of a significant conflict episode during the meal formed a dichotomous co-primary outcome measure. Such conflict was judged to have occurred if a conflict was at a severe or marked level of clinical concern (rating 1 or 2) for any two-minute observation period. The secondary outcome measures included (1) infant weight (standardized against population norms) and (2) measures of mother-child interaction, which included (a) maternal facilitation and (b) the number of verbal responses to infant cues (both appropriate and inappropriate). This measure was derived from the original sensitivity measures of Ainsworth (Ainsworth, Bell, & Stayton, 1974). A response was categorized as appropriate when the mother verbally responded to her infant's cue (action, facial expression, or vocalization) in a manner that was congruent with that cue. The response was classified as inappropriate when the mother responded verbally to her infant's cue in an incongruent or mismatching manner. The third outcome, appropriate nonverbal responses to infant cues, was rated on a time-sampled rating scale of 1 to 3 (1 = poor, 2 = moderate, and 3 = good). This measured the extent to which the mother nonverbally and congruently responded to her infant's cues; (c) maternal intrusiveness was rated as actions that inappropriately cut across or took over or disrupted the infant's activities.

Infant autonomy was rated as a dichotomous measure involving self-feeding initiatives indicating whether the infant did (and was allowed to) self-feed with fingers or a utensil, for example, spoon, or used and had access to his or her own food or joint plate.

Maternal eating disorder psychopathology was assessed using the Eating Disorder Examination (EDE) (Fairburn & Cooper, 1993). It is a structured and validated interview providing DSM diagnoses and assessing eating habits and attitudes and eating psychopathology. The Edinburgh Postnatal Depression Inventory (EPDS) (Cox, Holden, & Sagovsky, 1987), a widely used and validated screening questionnaire for depression, was completed by the mothers. It has a high sensitivity and specificity (Murray & Carothers, 1990). At the end of treatment mothers were also asked about their expectations of treatment, which were assessed on a 1 to 5 scale. Following treatment the mother's perceptions of the treatment benefits were assessed on an 18-item questionnaire, on which each item was rated from 1 to 5; the questionnaire comprised four subscales: practical issues, help with eating disorder, self-esteem, and feelings about self and relationship with the baby.

Characteristics of the sample

The baseline characteristics of the two groups were reasonably well balanced. Eighty percent of the video-feedback group (video group) and 82.5% of the counseling group were either married or stably co-habiting; 70% of both groups were white and 30% ethnic minority; 67.5% of the video group and 60% of the counseling group were of nonmanual occupations; the mothers' median ages at baseline were 31 (video group) and 29 (counseling group). Fifty percent of the video group and 57.5% of the counseling group were firstborn children. Thirty-eight percent of the video group and 55% of the counseling group were boys, suggesting a possible imbalance. In terms of infant weight, both groups were of reasonable weight at baseline, but with an apparent advantage in the counseling group (mean video group, 0.14; mean counseling group, 0.37).

Results

Analyses were adjusted for baseline measures where appropriate (see Stein et al., 2006). The video group exhibited significantly less conflict than the counseling group according to scores on the conflict rating scale: median of the video group, 4.67 (range, 1.71 to 5.0); median of the counseling group, 3.9 (range, 1.33 to 5.0); $p < 0.01$. When considering the dichotomous variable, that is, episodes of severe or marked conflict, these were observed for 23.7% of the video group and 53.8% of the counseling group (odds ratio = 0.27; 95% CI, 0.10 to 0.73). The video group also showed some benefit on some, but not all, of their responses to infant cues; there were no differences between the groups in terms of appropriate verbal responses to infant cues ($p = 0.76$); however, the video group scored higher on appropriate nonverbal responses to infant cues than the counseling group (video group median, 2.91 [range, 1 to 3]; counseling group median, 2.5 [range, 1 to 3]; $p = .05$). In addition, the video group also showed fewer inappropriate responses to infant cues (odds ratio = 0.38; 95% CI, 0.13 to 1.07; $p = .053$). The video group also showed more facilitation than the control group (video group median, 5.71 [range 1.2 to 7]; counseling group median, 3.75 [range 1 to 7]; $p = .02$). There were no differences between the groups in terms of maternal intrusions, although there were substantial reductions in intrusions across both groups. The video group also showed evidence of more infant autonomy than the counseling group (odds ratio = 4.75, 95% CI, 1.39 to 16.22).

There were no differences between the groups in terms of infant weight. However, it was important to note that both groups of infants maintained their weight trajectories over the postnatal year. Thus, although there were no significant between-group differences, it was reassuring that there was no fall-off in infant weight in either group. Although our previous work had indicated a relation between conflict and lower weight, in the study we did not find that poor infant weight gain was significantly associated with a conflict at 13 months ($r = 0.16$, $p = .16$). The factors that drive infant weight are complex and require further study.

Both groups of mothers showed significant improvement in terms of their maternal eating psychopathology and maternal depressive symptoms. However, there were no differences between the groups.

In terms of the mothers' perceptions of whether they were helped, both groups felt themselves to be substantially helped with the practical issues — help with the eating disorder and in terms of their self-esteem and feelings about self — and there were no differences between the groups. However, the video group felt substantially more helped in terms of their relationship with their baby than the counseling group (video group median, 4.0 [range 2.5 to 5]; counseling group mean, 2.6 [range 1 to 4.75]; $p < .001$).

The design of the treatment trial, which included guided cognitive behavioral self-help in both arms of the treatment to deal directly with the mothers' eating disorder psychopathology, made it impossible to ascertain how necessary the guided self-help cognitive behavioral therapy was in supporting video feedback in reducing conflict.

Conclusions

We have described the evolution and adaptation of a specific video-feedback treatment for mothers with eating disorders in the postnatal periods. The treatment aimed at encouraging and supporting more harmonious interactions of these mothers with their babies, especially during feedings. Empirical observational research led us to realize that a treatment that provided direct access to mother-infant interaction was needed, while at the same time not undermining the mothers or priming their negative self-schemas. Therefore, the VIPP model was used to provide video-feedback treatment that focused on the strengths of the mothers and promoted the positive aspects of interaction, while at the same time gradually and gently allowing the therapist to attend to the maternal cognitions affecting the mother-infant feeding interaction. Results from the controlled trial indicate that video feedback was successful in improving some of the key aspects of the mother-child interaction, including reducing mother-infant conflict at mealtimes. Further follow-up of such samples is required to establish the longer-term outcome of these children. We believe that if these findings are replicated, VIPP may hold promise in addressing interactional disturbances associated with other common postnatal psychiatric disorders.

Acknowledgments

The authors are grateful to all the families who participated in the studies involved in this chapter and to all the colleagues who contributed to this work:

Robert Senior, Mary Lovell, Joanna Lee, Sandra Cooper, Rebecca Wheatcroft, Fiona Challacombe, Priti Patel, Rosemary Nicol-Harper, Pia Menzies, Anna Schmidt, Edmund Juszczak, Christopher Fairburn, Anne McFadyen, Caroline McKenna, Jonathan Winterbottom, Joan Hartley, Jo Walker, Jo Garcia, Lynne Murray, Peter Cooper, Deborah Waller, Bob Blizard, Helen Doll, Colette McNeil, Femmie Juffer, Marinus van IJzendoorn, Marian Bakermans-Kranenburg, and Sara Phillips. The work was generously funded by the Wellcome Trust (050892) and the Tedworth Charitable Trust.

9

Supporting adoptive families with video-feedback intervention

Femmie Juffer, Marinus H. van IJzendoorn, and Marian J. Bakermans-Kranenburg
Centre for Child and Family Studies,
Leiden University, the Netherlands

This chapter describes the effects of two intervention programs designed to enhance adoptive parents' sensitivity and to promote secure infant-parent attachment relationships. The relatively short interventions, consisting of video feedback and a personal book, were provided during home visits to parents of internationally adopted children, placed before six months of age.

In the Netherlands adoption predominantly consists of international placements, around 1,200 annually, whereas domestic placements are rare (40 to 60 each year). Most internationally adopted children are foundlings or have been relinquished by their birth mother. Therefore, they experienced at least one major separation. Additionally, adopted children often have histories of neglect, abuse, malnourishment, and deprivation in orphanages (Johnson, 2000).

As adopted children often start their life with physical, medical, and psychological setbacks, it is expected that on average they are less well adjusted than nonadopted children. It should be noted, however, that adoption usually offers improved medical, educational, and psychological opportunities for institutionalized children, as has been shown in studies comparing adopted children with the children remaining in institutions (Van IJzendoorn & Juffer, 2005; Van IJzendoorn & Juffer, 2006; for a meta-analysis, see Van IJzendoorn, Juffer, & Klein Poelhuis, 2005). Also, research documented children's substantial recovery from deprivation after adoption in several domains: health and growth, cognitive and socioemotional development (Juffer & Van IJzendoorn, 2007; Rutter et al., 1998; Van IJzendoorn, Bakermans-Kranenburg, & Juffer, in press; Van IJzendoorn

& Juffer, 2006). Nevertheless, several studies have shown that adoptees appear to be at increased risk for behavior problems (Nickman et al., 2005; for a meta-analysis, see Juffer & Van IJzendoorn, 2005) and psychiatric problems (Tieman, Van der Ende, & Verhulst, 2005), in particular in middle childhood and adolescence (Bimmel, Juffer, Van IJzendoorn, & Bakermans-Kranenburg, 2003; Juffer, 2006; Verhulst, Althaus, & Versluis-den Bieman, 1990).

Adoption and attachment

As a result of their experiences of deprivation, adopted children's signals can be distorted, subtle, or difficult to interpret, making it harder for their adoptive parents to react to their signals in a sensitive way. Adopted children may have experienced "fright without solution" (Main, 1999), resulting from unmet attachment needs or profound lack of response in the depriving environment of an orphanage. Therefore, an elevated risk of insecurity, and in particular attachment disorganization, is suspected. Vorria et al. (2003), who studied infants in a Greek institution before being placed for adoption, found a high percentage of disorganized attachment (66%), compared to home-reared children and normative samples (15%; Van IJzendoorn, Schuengel, & Bakermans-Kranenburg, 1999). This finding was replicated by Zeanah, Smyke, Koga, and Carlson (2005), who found 67% disorganized attachment in Romanian institutionalized infants. Also, several studies found an overrepresentation of attachment disorganization in adopted and foster children. For example, Marcovitch et al. (1997) studied 44 children adopted from Romania and placed between 0 and 48 months in Canadian families. At the age of four years, 42% of the children were classified as disorganized. In a Dutch study of 55 infants adopted from five different countries (including Taiwan and China), placed in their adoptive homes before their first birthday, 20 children (36%) were classified as disorganized attached at 13 months (Van Londen, Juffer, & Van IJzendoorn, 2001). In the same vein, Dozier, Stovall, Albus, and Bates (2001) found in a sample of 50 foster children placed between 0 and 20 months that 17 children (34%) were classified as disorganized.

This chapter starts with describing our experimental intervention study in adoptive families, focusing on the short-term effects on maternal sensitivity, security of attachment, and attachment disorganization. Two vignettes are presented to illustrate the video-feedback intervention. The chapter continues with our follow-up study of the same sample in middle childhood, focusing on possible long-term intervention effects and on consequences of early childhood parent-child relationships. Finally, some practical implications are discussed.

An experimental intervention study in adoptive families

The adoptive families

Two related intervention studies in adoptive families were combined into one sample (N = 130). The first subsample consisted of 90 families with a first adopted child (Juffer, 1993; Juffer, Hoksbergen, Riksen-Walraven, & Kohnstamm, 1997), and the second subsample consisted of 40 families with birth children and a first adopted child (Rosenboom, 1994). All families were randomly recruited through adoption agencies. The parents did not receive any postadoption support, as these services were not available at the time of the study. The parents were white, and the mother was the primary caregiver in all cases. The families were predominantly from (upper-)middle-class backgrounds.

The children, 66 boys and 64 girls, were adopted from Sri Lanka (n = 78), South Korea (n = 39), and Colombia (n = 13). All children came into their adoptive homes before 6 months (M = 10 weeks, SD = 4.93, range = 2 to 23 weeks). The infants from Sri Lanka arrived at a significantly younger age (M = 6.7 weeks, SD = 2.5, n = 78) than the children from Korea (M = 14.7 weeks, SD = 3.4, n = 39) or Colombia (M = 14.4 weeks, SD = 4.5, n = 13). As the children from Korea and Colombia did not differ regarding their age on arrival, we decided to treat them as one group in the analyses. This was also justified by the fact that Korean and Colombian children shared a similar preadoption background (that is, in a children's home or foster family), which was different from the Sri Lankan infants, who stayed with their birth mother until adoptive placement.

Procedure and measures

The procedure and measures were identical in the two subsamples. Families were visited at home when the adopted infant was 5, 6, 9, and 12 months old. Mother and child came to the laboratory at 12 and 18 months. The interventions were carried out between six and nine months. In the first subsample two interventions were implemented: (1) a personal book and (2) three sessions of video feedback and the same book. In the second subsample only the most intensive intervention was implemented: video feedback and the personal book. In both samples, the control group received a booklet on adoption issues as a "dummy" intervention. The interventions were implemented by five female home visitors, thus controlling for an experimenter effect. At 6 months (pretest) and 12 months (posttest), mother-child interaction was videotaped in the home to rate the mother's sensitivity. At 12 and 18 months, infant-mother attachment was observed in the laboratory.

Background variables

Information on several background variables was collected from the family (socioeconomic status, parents' age, and so forth) and the adopted child (age and health condition on arrival, temperament, and so forth; Juffer et al., 1997; Stams, Juffer, & Van IJzendoorn, 2002).

Maternal sensitivity

Sensitivity was observed in an eight-minute free-play situation, videotaped at home at 6 and 12 months. While the baby was placed in an infant seat in front of a low table, with the mother sitting next to her or him, the researcher presented a transparent box containing 10 attractive toys. The mother was instructed to play with her child the way she normally would. Sensitivity was rated with two 9-point rating scales for Sensitivity and Cooperation (Ainsworth, Bell, & Stayton, 1974), and satisfactory intercoder reliability was established (Juffer et al., 1997). As sensitivity and cooperation were highly correlated, a standardized composite score was computed to indicate maternal sensitivity at 6 and 12 months (Juffer, Bakermans-Kranenburg, & Van IJzendoorn, 2005b).

Attachment (A, B, C, D)

The adopted children were observed in the Strange Situation Procedure (Ainsworth, Blehar, Waters, & Wall, 1978) at the laboratory and classified as secure (B), insecure-avoidant (A), or insecure-ambivalent (C) (see Chapter 1). Intercoder reliability was satisfactory (Juffer & Rosenboom, 1997). In a later stage of the study, the videotaped strange situations at 12 months were coded to assess disorganization of attachment (D; see Chapter 1). Children were classified as disorganized (D) or organized (non-D) and rated with the 9-point rating scale for Disorganization (Main & Solomon, 1990). Two coders (the second and third authors), who were extensively trained by Drs. Mary Main and Erik Hesse, scored the tapes, using the Main and Solomon (1990) coding system. The coders had not been involved in the studies at the time that the interventions were carried out, and they were unaware of the experimental group status of the dyads. Due to technical problems, two cases could not be coded. Satisfactory intercoder reliability was established (Juffer et al., 2005b).

Intervention

The two programs — the book-only intervention and the video-feedback plus book intervention (hereafter video-feedback intervention) — aimed at enhancing parental sensitivity, with the ultimate goal of promoting secure infant-parent attachment relationships (Bakermans-Kranenburg, Van IJzendoorn, & Juffer, 2003) and infant competence. The following profile was derived from attachment theory (Ainsworth et al., 1978; Bowlby, 1982) and served as the working basis for the intervention. A sensitive mother attunes her behavior to the baby in the following way:

1. She perceives and interprets her baby's signals correctly. (Is my baby looking for contact or is she or he exploring the world?)
2. She reacts to these signals promptly and adequately, that is, responding to attachment signals and not interfering in exploration activities, respectively.
3. She creates for her child opportunities to explore and discover the effects of his or her own behavior (Juffer et al., 1997, p. 1043).

The book-only program consisted of written information focusing on sensitive parenting (see also Riksen-Walraven, 1978; Lambermon & Van IJzendoorn, 1989). The written information was offered in a personalized book, that is, the name of the child was integrated in the text. The book's title was *Het eerste levensjaar* [*The First Year Of Life*] (Juffer, Metman, & Andoetoe, 1986; see also Chapter 8). The book comprised suggestions for sensitive parenting and playful interactions and was illustrated with pictures of adopted and nonadopted infants. Parents were encouraged to fill in questions and blanks with personal observations of their own adopted child.

The video-feedback group was supplied with the same personal book. In addition, this group was provided with three sessions of video feedback. The intervener showed the mother a video recording of herself interacting with her child and commented on selected fragments of the film. This intervention was implemented in two home visits at six months and one at nine months, and each intervention session lasted approximately one hour. At six months, a videotape of a previous home visit was used for the intervention, and at nine months, the intervener used the tape immediately after filming. In her comments the intervener focused on sensitivity: providing security by reacting sensitively to the child's (attachment) behavior and also offering opportunities for the child's exploration behavior. For example, the intervener verbalized the baby's reactions and (facial) expressions ("speaking for the baby"; Carter, Osofsky, & Hann, 1991; see Chapter 2), or she reinforced the mother's sensitive reactions to the child's behavior.

Effects on sensitivity and attachment

Positive effects on maternal sensitivity

First, the overall effectiveness of the intervention programs on maternal sensitivity was examined in the total sample. We conducted an ANCOVA on the composite score for sensitivity at 12 months, with experimental condition (three groups: video feedback, book only, and control) as the independent variable and pretest sensitivity (composite score) as a covariate. A significant main effect of experimental condition was found, $F (2, 126) = 4.42, p = .01$ (Juffer et al., 2005b). The analyses were continued with planned comparisons testing two *a priori* contrasts: the book-only group with the control group, and the video-feedback group with the control group. The analyses did not show a significant effect of the book-only intervention. However, a significant main effect of the video-feedback intervention emerged, $F (1, 97) = 9.62, p < .01$. Post hoc analyses confirmed that the effects of the video-feedback intervention on sensitivity had the same direction and comparable, medium to strong, effect sizes (Cohen, 1988) in the two subsamples (families without birth children, $d = .65$; families with birth children, $d = .63$) (Juffer et al., 2005b).

Inconsistent effects on organized attachment

In the first subsample (families without birth children), the book-only intervention did not increase attachment security at 12 months (80% secure children), compared with the control group of adoptive families without intervention (70% secure children). In contrast, the infants in the video-feedback group were more often securely attached: 90% secure children versus 70% in the control group, $X^2 (1) = 3.89, p < .05$ (Juffer et al., 1997). At the age of 18 months, comparable results were found with again 90% securely attached infants in the video-feedback group and 73% secure attachment in the control group (Juffer, 1993). In the second subsample (families with birth children), the intervention did not result in more secure attachment relationships at 12 months. There were 80% securely attached children in the control group and 53% secure children in the intervention group. At 18 months, the negative effect had disappeared: There were 79% securely attached children in the intervention group and 75% secure children in the control group (Rosenboom, 1994).

Positive effects on disorganized attachment

On the categorical level (classification D versus non-D), there was a significant difference in the total sample between the control and intervention groups, $X^2 (2) = 5.52, p < .05$ (Juffer et al., 2005b). The video-feedback intervention, but not the book-only intervention, was effective in preventing disorganized attachment, leading to only 3 disorganized children (of 49 children; 6.1%) in the video-feedback group versus 11 disorganized children in the control group (of 49 children; 22.4%; see Figure 9.1), $X^2 (1) = 5.33, p = .01$. Post hoc analyses confirmed that

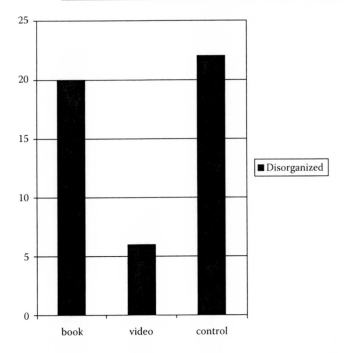

Figure 9.1   Disorganized attachment (%) in the two intervention groups and in the control group.

the direction and effect sizes were comparable in the two subsamples (families without birth children, d = .39; families with birth children, d = .62).

The continuous disorganization ratings supported these results (Juffer et al., 2005b): A significant main effect of experimental condition (three groups) was found, F (2, 125) = 4.93, p < .01. Analyses with planned comparisons for the intervention groups showed that the difference between the group with the personal book and the control group was significant, t (69, 806) = 1.76, p < .05 (unequal variances). Children in the book-only group showed lower D-scores (M = 2.62, SD = 1.79) than control children (M = 3.41, SD = 2.15). The second contrast also showed a significant difference. Converging with the effect on D classifications, children in the video-feedback intervention group showed significantly lower D-scores (M = 2.28, SD = 1.43) than control children, t (83, 492) = 3.07, p < .01 (unequal variances). Again, post hoc analyses confirmed that the effects of the video-feedback intervention on attachment disorganization were in the same direction in the two subsamples, with comparable effect sizes (families without birth children effect size, d = .64; families with birth children, d = .61).

Two vignettes

Tasnim

Tasnim, adopted from Sri Lanka at the age of six weeks, and her adoptive mother were randomly assigned to the video-feedback group. Tasnim was the first child in the family. Her adoptive parents were in their 30s when they decided to adopt because they were not able to have children of their own. Both parents travelled to Sri Lanka, where they met Tasnim's birth mother in the court. Tasnim was moderately malnourished when they got her, but she recovered quickly after her arrival in the Netherlands. The adoptive father was full-time employed as a bus driver, and the adoptive mother had a part-time job, helping elderly people.

The first videotape, of free play at six months, showed that the adoptive mother was rather uninvolved and that she did not play an active role in the interaction. With a smile on her face the mother watched her daughter playing with the toys, but she remained silent most of the time and she did not join her child's play. She did talk to the home visitor a few times, commenting on Tasnim's performances, but she did not talk to her daughter directly. Tasnim was playing on her own, exploring the toys attentively. There was no exchange of smiles or vocalizing, and there was almost no playing together. The home visitor characterized the mother-child dyad as "two islands without a bridge." When the home visitor studied the videotape more closely she noticed a short positive moment: Tasnim was playing with a little ball and when this ball accidentally went in the direction of the mother, she rolled it back to Tasnim saying: "Here it is!" Tasnim received the ball with a faint smile. After this brief moment of interaction, Tasnim played alone again.

In the first intervention session, the home visitor used this positive moment in her video-feedback intervention. She explained the difference between children's attachment and exploration behavior, and she showed and repeated the brief moment of playing together with the ball to show the mother that Tasnim enjoyed her joining in. The home visitor also paused the videotape at the moment Tasnim faintly smiled in response to her mother's action. The intervener reinforced the mother's behavior of not interfering in her daughter's play and respecting her initiatives, but also stressed the importance of reacting to her daughter's (subtle) signals of seeking (eye) contact. She explained that children feel understood when they receive an "answer" as a response to their signals of looking, reaching, or smiling, and that they then feel encouraged to send out more signals. The home visitor encouraged the mother to react to Tasnim's subtle signals of seeking contact and showed these signals on the videotape, using the "speaking for the baby" technique (see Chapter 2). During the next two intervention sessions at six and nine months, the home visitor repeated this approach and also reinforced the mother's sensitive reactions, shown on the videotape, to Tasnim's behavior.

At 12 months, there was a lively exchange of interactions when Tasnim and her mother were asked again to play together in the free-play situation at home. The mother verbalized Tasnim's behavior, and she was involved in Tasnim's play in a pleasant way. Tasnim showed toys to her mother, vocalized a lot, and smiled happily when her mother accepted a toy that she offered. The intervener had the impression that "between the two islands a bridge was built." According to unaware observers, the mother's sensitivity had improved from the pre- to the posttest (6 months, for Sensitivity a rating of 4 and for Cooperation a rating of 3; 12 months, for Sensitivity and Cooperation ratings of 6 and 5, respectively). Tasnim showed a secure attachment strategy in the Strange Situation Procedure (Ainsworth et al., 1978; see Chapter 1) (B) with only slight signs of disorganization (a low D-score of 2). At 18 months, Tasnim's attachment behavior was secure again.

Tim

Tim, adopted from South Korea at the age of three months, and his mother were also randomly assigned to the video-feedback group. Tim was the first adopted child in a family with two birth children. The parents had decided to adopt a child as they wanted to help a child in need of a home. The adoptive father (38 years) worked as an office director, and the adoptive mother (37 years) had a part-time job as a nurse. The parents met Tim for the first time at Schiphol airport in the Netherlands, where his escorts handed him over to them. Tim had been in a Korean children's home since he was found in the streets as a newborn baby. He appeared to be in good health when he arrived in the Netherlands.

When videotaped at the pretest at six months during a free-play situation, the mother immediately participated in the interaction in a cheerful, active way, testing all the new toys by herself first and subsequently offering Tim the toys that she had selected. She was rather dominantly present: talking and singing almost all the time and often addressing her son without a pause to wait for his turn. Tim, who seemed overwhelmed by her active approach, behaved in a rather passive and withdrawn way. He took all the toys the mother offered him, but he hardly played with them, and he did not reach out for a particular toy himself. When he played with a rattle in his own way — by touching and looking only — the mother immediately intervened, taking the rattle herself and demonstrating how it worked.

When the intervener studied the videotape at the institute she selected a fragment in which Tim was allowed to play on his own without interference of his mother for just a few moments. In this fragment the mother praised him, and Tim smiled and vocalized to her. The mother then stroked him on the head. In the video-feedback session the intervener highlighted the importance of children's attachment and exploration behavior. Children feel secure when their attachment signals are responded to (e.g., crying is met with comforting) and when their exploration signals are responded to as well (e.g., playing is met with watching, verbalizing, praising). The home visitor repeated the fragment showing that Tim played on his own for a few moments to explain to the mother that it is important for children to get opportunities to discover how things work and to explore toys on their own. Also, the sensitive reaction of the mother to Tim's smile was highlighted. In the second and third intervention sessions the home visitor repeated these themes, elaborating on the issue of giving children opportunities to take turns in the interaction and to show initiatives during games. These themes were illustrated with videotape fragments of Tim and his mother, thus showing the mother that she was capable of acting this way.

At 12 months, Tim and his mother were videotaped in the free-play situation again. Compared to the pretest, the mother allowed Tim much more space to explore the toys and to take turns in the interaction, although in the heat of her cheerful play she sometimes forgot to wait for Tim's turn. Also, Tim was playing more actively and his mood was more positive. The observers rated the mother's sensitivity higher than on the pretest, and in particular, her interfering behavior abated (6 months, for Sensitivity a rating of 3 and for Cooperation a rating of 2; 12 months, Sensitivity and Cooperation ratings of 4.5 and 5, respectively). Tim showed insecure attachment behavior in the Strange Situation Procedure at 12 months (C) but secure attachment (B) at 18 months. There were no signs of disorganization (D-score of 1).

Long-term intervention effects

In a follow-up study at age 7, the long-term effects of the interventions on maternal sensitivity and the adopted children's personality development, social development, and behavior problems were examined (Stams, Juffer, Van IJzendoorn, & Hoksbergen, 2001). Long-term effects on maternal sensitivity were not found. In the subsample of adoptive families with birth children positive long-term effects of the video-feedback intervention were found on ego-resiliency and optimal ego-control in girls, and on internalizing behavior problems in both girls and boys. Experimental adopted girls had significantly higher scores on ego-resiliency (the capacity to respond flexibly to changing demands; Block & Block, 1980) and optimal ego-control (adequate control of impulses and emotions) than the adopted girls in the control group. Also, adopted girls and boys in the video-feedback group had significantly fewer internalizing behavior problems than adopted children in the control group (Stams et al., 2001). However, in the subsample of adoptive families without birth children, enduring intervention effects could not be traced.

We supposed that the short-term intervention effects on maternal sensitivity and attachment disorganization in infancy predicted positive long-term intervention effects in the subsample of adoptive families with birth children at age 7. Comparable short-term and long-term intervention effects were described by Riksen-Walraven and Van Aken (1997), who found effects of an intervention program on maternal responsiveness in early childhood and girls' ego-resiliency at age 7. Van Aken and Riksen-Walraven (1992) argued that ego-resiliency should be considered in terms of competence, that is, as a general problem-solving capacity. Thus, our intervention may (also) have affected maternal sensitivity to the child's signals in the area of competence. Subsequently, this type of maternal behavior may have influenced the child's competence motivation and later personality development in terms of ego-resiliency. This explanation implies that adoptive mothers receiving intervention were encouraged to promote the adopted child's autonomy and competence. Some support for this idea was found because a post hoc analysis in this subsample revealed a significant intervention effect on maternal respect for the child's autonomy at 12 months (Stams et al., 2001). Mothers in the video-feedback group scored significantly higher on this rating scale during an instruction task (e.g., helping the child to make a puzzle) than control mothers.

Furthermore, positive effects were found on the reduction of internalizing behavior problems in boys and girls in families with birth children. Elsewhere, we reported an overrepresentation of internalizing problems in adopted children of this age (Stams, Juffer, Rispens, & Hoksbergen, 2000). Perhaps the video-feedback intervention taught the adoptive parents to react to children's sad and anxious feelings with sensitive, empathic responses, thereby preventing depressed and anxious behaviors in the long run.

There are three explanations for the absence of enduring effects in adoptive families without birth children. First, environmental instability may account for discontinuity between early attachment security and later favorable child adjustment (Sroufe, Egeland, & Kreutzer, 1990). In our study, adoptive families without birth children had to cope with more stressful life events (such as serious illness of family members) than adoptive families with birth children (Stams et al., 2001). Moreover, 15% of these families (n = 17) experienced an important family change: the birth of a biological child for the first time. Second, the absence of long-term effects of the intervention may be partly attributed to a ceiling effect because we found a relatively high rate (70%) of secure, organized child-mother attachment relationships in early childhood in the control group (Juffer et al., 1997), as well as a normative percentage (22%) of disorganized attachment (Juffer et al., 2005b). Third, a limitation of our follow-up study at age 7 is that a rather broad range of child behaviors was examined, which may have prevented the detection of more specific long-term intervention effects in the domain of child-parent attachment. Unfortunately, no suitable attachment measure for middle childhood was available at that time. In a second follow-up study at age 14 (Jaffari-Bimmel, Juffer, Van IJzendoorn, Bakermans-Kranenburg, & Mooijaart, 2006), an attachment measure is included in the study design.

Given that in the group of adoptive families without birth children the video-feedback intervention was only effective in the short run, we conclude that this type of intervention may need to be repeated in the subsequent years to establish enduring effects. Tasnim and Tim, the adopted children described in the vignettes, were both well adjusted at age 7. Tasnim's adoptive parents had divorced, and Tasnim was living with her adoptive mother and a new partner. Tasnim appeared to be a cheerful, outgoing girl who was very popular at school. She did not have behavior problems, and she was a moderate student at school. Tim was happily living with both adoptive parents and his two siblings. Although he was a bit shy, he scored in the normative range of behavior problems. He appeared to be a very bright student at school.

Consequences of early parent-child relationships for adopted children's development

In the follow-up study at age 7, adopted children's adjustment in middle childhood was examined from a broad cross-context, cross-time perspective, using different measures (observations, questionnaires, Q-sorts, and sociometric data) and multiple sources of information (mothers, teachers, and classmates) (Juffer,

Stams, & Van IJzendoorn, 2004; Stams et al., 2002). We found that maternal sensitivity in early childhood, infant attachment security, infant attachment disorganization, and early temperament each significantly predicted children's subsequent adjustment in middle childhood (Stams et al., 2002). Female adopted children were better adjusted than male adopted children, in particular in the social domain. Children's more difficult temperament in early childhood, rated by the adoptive mother, predicted lower adjustment scores at age 7 in the domains of social and cognitive development, and externalizing and internalizing behavior problems. Higher maternal sensitivity in early and middle childhood and more secure attachment in infancy predicted children's better social and cognitive development in middle childhood. Furthermore, the interaction between early temperament and infant attachment disorganization was significant. The combination of two risk factors, attachment disorganization and early difficult temperament, predicted lower levels of cognitive development, and less optimal control of impulses and emotions at age 7 (Stams et al., 2002).

Even in this genetically unrelated group of parents and their adopted children from different cultures and ethnic backgrounds, early child-parent relationship characteristics appeared to play a significant role in shaping children's adjustment in middle childhood. Based on Rosenthal's (1995) interpretation of effect sizes, the predicted variance in adjustment on the basis of earlier contextual factors was not only significant, but also substantial: This study found that half of 21% and 18% of the predicted variance in social and cognitive development, respectively, could be attributed to parenting and relationship variables (Stams et al., 2002).

Practical implications

Based on the positive outcomes of our intervention study in adoptive families, a new postadoption service has been launched in practice. Since 2000, all new adoptive families in the Netherlands are allowed to apply for up to four sessions of video-feedback, Video Interactie Begeleiding [Video Interaction Guidance], delivered nationwide by the Stichting Adoptievoorzieningen [Center for Adoption Services] in Utrecht. This postadoption service is mostly supported by the government, and the adoptive parents only have to pay a small fee. The Center for Adoption Services is also responsible for the compulsory preparation course before adoptive placement (Duinkerken & Geerts, 2000) and provides this postadoption service on request to every adoptive family in the period after the child's arrival until 2 to 2.5 years after adoptive placement, regardless of the presence of problems or the arrival age of the adopted child. (In the Netherlands, children from abroad are adopted between the ages of zero and six years.) The interveners are social workers or child psychologists who receive special training for this intervention. A formal evaluation study has not been conducted yet, but in a first report it was found that adoptive parents actively use this postadoption service and evaluate the intervention as very helpful and satisfactory (Havermans & Verheule, 2001).

Conclusions

In our prospective, longitudinal intervention study, positive short-term effects of our attachment-based video-feedback intervention were found on maternal sensitivity and insecure-disorganized infant attachment in adoptive families with and without birth children. The intervention was tested in a robust way using a randomized pretest-posttest control group design with a "dummy" intervention (a booklet on adoption) in the control group. The study controlled for any experimenter effect, and no differences were found among the five home visitors involved in this study. Furthermore, the video-feedback intervention had a narrow, behavior-oriented focus and was described in a protocol. Finally, there was no attrition between pre- and posttests. The success of the intervention cannot be explained by factors such as postadoption support, as these services were not available at the time of the study. Anecdotally, we observed that the adoptive families were open for intervention and eager to receive support (Juffer, 1993).

The intervention of three sessions of video-feedback combined with a personal book containing suggestions for sensitive parenting enhanced mothers' sensitivity and decreased the number of children classified as disorganized-attached. The outcomes for organized attachment were less consistent: The video-feedback intervention resulted in a larger number of securely attached (B) children than in the control group in the subsample of adoptive families without birth children only. The intervention with the personal book only did not lead to overall significant intervention effects, although a significant effect on disorganization ratings was found. We suggested that the intervention with the personal book only was not effective enough to lead to significant effects, as the combined intervention (video feedback plus book) resulted in significant intervention effects on parental sensitivity and infant attachment disorganization (disorganization classification as well as disorganization rating).

It is important to prevent attachment disorganization in adopted children because our follow-up study found that infant disorganized attachment in combination with difficult temperament predicted less optimal cognitive development and less optimal ego-control in middle childhood (Stams et al., 2002). Also, several studies found that disorganized attachment predicts externalizing behavior problems and psychopathology (for a meta-analysis, see Van IJzendoorn et al., 1999). In the same vein, intervention effects on maternal sensitivity and organized-secure attachment are important, as these aspects of the early parent-child relationship predicted adopted children's cognitive and social development at age 7 (Stams et al., 2002) and social development at age 14 (Jaffari-Bimmel et al., 2006). The positive short-term effects of the intervention that were revealed in the current study may (partly) explain the positive long-term effects found in one of the two subsamples: In the subsample of adoptive families with birth children, intervention children had fewer internalizing problems and girls had higher scores on ego-resiliency and optimal ego-control than the children in the control group (Stams et al., 2001). Because our study failed to show long-term intervention effects in both subsamples of adoptive families, we suggest that this type of intervention needs to be repeated (with "booster" sessions) during child development to lead to enduring effects.

A limitation of our study is that the intervention was not explicitly aimed at changing attachment disorganization. Although our intervention aimed at promoting sensitive parenting and secure attachment, the positive effect on attachment disorganization was rather unexpected. However, our intervention may have affected aspects of parenting that are important for the development of disorganized attachment, such as extremely insensitive, uninvolved, or frightening parental behavior (see Bakermans-Kranenburg, Van IJzendoorn, & Juffer, 2005; Juffer et al., 2005b; see Chapter 12 for further discussion).

In sum, our video-feedback intervention showed important positive short-term effects on the adoptive parent-child relationship and (in one subsample) positive long-term effects on adopted children's development and adjustment. Based on our intervention, a new postadoption service with video feedback was started in practice, meant for all new adoptive families. Our outcomes suggest that adoptive parents can be supported to adequately fulfill the tasks of parenting.

Acknowledgments

The authors thank the adoptive families for their participation in the study and Isolde Andoetoe, Lieke Metman, Aukje Oldeman, and Lizette Rosenboom for their dedication in implementing the intervention. Femmie Juffer is supported by Wereldkinderen, the Hague. The longitudinal adoption study was supported by grants from the Dutch Ministry of Education, Praeventiefonds, the Dutch Ministry of Welfare (early childhood study), Netherlands Organization for Scientific Research NWO (grant 575-87-701; middle childhood study), Wereldkinderen, Stichting Kind en Toekomst, and Leiden University (adolescence study).

10

Increasing the sensitivity of childcare providers

Applying the video-feedback intervention in a group care setting

James Elicker, Oana Georgescu, and Erin Bartsch

Purdue University, West Lafayette, Indiana

Most infants and toddlers in the affluent countries of the world are enrolled in out-of-home childcare with nonparental caregivers. Therefore, the quality of the childcare these children receive and its implications for their development are receiving increasing attention from researchers, policy makers, and practitioners (Oser & Cohen, 2003). In the United States, assessments of quality in infant-toddler childcare in several large-scale research studies have produced sobering results. Many children birth to three years of age receive care of only minimal quality level or below on well-validated scales (e.g., NICHD Early Child Care Research Network, 1996; Whitebook, Howes, & Phillips, 1989). Of particular concern is the low level of process quality care infants and toddlers receive, usually defined as the quality of the child's day-to-day interactions and experiences in the childcare setting. Moreover, the quality level of childcare received by very young children is consistently lower than the quality level for children three to five years old. This suggests that particular attention is needed to understand and improve childcare for infants and toddlers, with the ultimate goal of supporting optimal early development.

Whereas Bowlby (1973) and many contemporary attachment theorists and researchers have focused mainly on mother-infant relationships, there is a growing body of research that focuses on attachments between infants or toddlers and their nonparental childcare providers. In a summary of this research, Howes and Ritchie (2002) concluded that attachment relationships do in fact develop in childcare, and that the security of caregiver-child attachment relationships affects children's social-emotional development. Bowlby would probably not have taken issue with such conclusions if he was observing children in today's world, as he specifically stated that attachment relationships were not restricted to mothers, but would develop with any person who cared for a child on a regular basis for significant amounts of time (Bowlby, 1973). Although the research exploring the developmental influences of attachment with nonparental childcare providers is not extensive, there is preliminary evidence that the security of the attachment with the childcare provider is associated with child socio-emotional and cognitive functioning, both in the childcare setting and at home (Howes, 1997; Howes & Smith, 1995, Noppe, Elicker, Fortner-Wood, Shin, & Zhang, 2001; Van IJzendoorn, Sagi, & Lambermon, 1992).

Additional investigations of attachment security and its component processes within the childcare context are needed for two reasons. First, in addition to replicating the correlational studies mentioned above, more rigorous tests of theoretical hypotheses regarding the nature and implications of childcare attachments are needed. The hypothesis that consistent, sensitive, and responsive care leads to a secure attachment relationship is a key issue in childcare. The causal connection between sensitivity and attachment security originally proposed by Bowlby (1969/1982) has been established for mother-child and father-child relationships (Bakermans-Kranenburg, Van IJzendoorn, & Juffer, 2003; De Wolff & Van IJzendoorn, 1997). In addition to correlational evidence, experimental data are now available that show this causal link (Bakermans-Kranenburg et al., 2003; see Chapter 5). However, we have yet to use experimental methods and interventions to test the sensitivity hypothesis with nonparental caregivers. If in fact interveners attempt to increase the sensitivity and responsiveness of interactions between caregivers and children in childcare, using a program like Video-feedback Intervention to promote Positive Parenting (VIPP), and if this intervention leads to an increase in dyadic attachment security in childcare, this evidence would extend the reach of Bowlby's sensitivity/attachment hypothesis to nonparental caregivers.

The second reason to pursue intervention research focused on sensitivity in childcare is simply to determine if it is possible to increase the process quality of care children experience on a day-to-day basis. A number of studies have demonstrated that, when young children receive positive, sensitive childcare, they have more positive social and cognitive outcomes, both concurrently and in future assessments (e.g., Burchinal, Roberts, Nabors, & Bryant, 1996; Cost, Quality & Child Outcomes Study Team, 1995; Hausfather, Toharia, LaRoche, & Engelsmann, 1997; McCartney, 1984; NICHD Early Child Care Research

Network, 2000; Peisner-Feinberg & Burchinal, 1997). However, there is a paucity of experimental studies that would conclusively show that increasing caregiver sensitivity leads to greater attachment security, child well-being, or child social competence.

The Video-feedback Intervention to promote Positive Parenting mother-child intervention model (VIPP) and the Video-feedback Intervention to promote Positive Parenting–Representation model (VIPP-R) described in this volume were originally developed to increase the sensitivity of parent-child interactions, and thus to increase the probability that secure attachment will develop between infants and high-risk biological or adoptive parents (Bakermans-Kranenburg, Juffer, & Van IJzendoorn, 1998; Juffer, Bakermans-Kranenburg, & Van IJzendoorn, 2005b). Because the VIPP models are short-term interventions, this intervention model may be well suited to being adapted as a childcare staff development program, under conditions where staff training resources and time are necessarily limited.

This chapter describes the application of principles of attachment theory and the VIPP parent-child intervention model in a new childcare staff training program called Tuning In. First, the adaptations made to the VIPP intervention to adapt it for caregiving in a childcare context are summarized; then the basic elements of the four-week Tuning In training program are outlined. Next, the results from an exploratory study of the Tuning In intervention with four childcare providers is described, presenting observation vignettes illustrating how caregiver sensitivity changed as a result of the intervention. Finally, the chapter reviews our work currently under way to further develop and evaluate the effectiveness of the Tuning In staff training program.

Applying VIPP to childcare

How is caregiving in a childcare setting similar to or different from maternal care at home? Although the physical, social, emotional, and cognitive needs of the infant may be relatively constant across caring contexts, the provision of care in a childcare program is distinctly different from parental care in a number of ways. The typical childcare room in the United States includes 8 to 10 infants or toddlers of approximately the same age, cared for by two adult caregivers. Thus, the amount of time and attention from an adult caregiver available to each infant is significantly less than in most family homes, in which a parent may be caring for two children of different ages. Also, as suggested by Katz (2000) in an analysis of differences between parent-child and teacher-child relationships, childcare providers or early childhood teachers probably experience less emotional intensity and investment with each child, spend less total time with each child, and may strive for even distribution of caring and teaching among an entire group of children, rather than focusing exclusively on the needs and intentions of one child.

Despite these obvious differences in caregiving relationship contexts, it is also apparent that professional caregivers often have a great deal of affection for the children in their charge. When professional Early Head Start infant-toddler caregivers in the United States were interviewed about their roles and relationships with children and families, several stated that they consider themselves "substitute mothers," that they love the children, and that they strive to be partners with the parents in the care of the children (Elicker, Ruprecht, & Wittenborn, 2004). Variations in attachment security, when systematically assessed between childcare providers and children, seem to be distributed in ways not unlike security variations seen in mothers and children. For example, in our past research approximately 70% of infants and toddlers assessed with their caregivers in center-based and home-based childcare settings were judged to be securely attached (Noppe et al., 2001; see also Goossens & Van IJzendoorn, 1990). Moreover, children who entered childcare at a younger age, those who had longer durations of care with that adult, and those who were more intensely interactive with their caregiver displayed higher levels of attachment security when assessed using the observer Attachment Q-Set (Elicker, Fortner-Wood, & Noppe, 1999; Waters & Deane, 1985). This association between daily caregiver-child interaction quality and attachment security has now been found in a number of childcare studies (Howes & Ritchie, 2002). Thus, the attachment formation process hypothesized in attachment theory for parents also seems to operate in relationships between children and their professional childcare providers.

What are the basic attachment theoretical principles and VIPP intervention principles regarding caregiver sensitivity and responsiveness, and how are they applied in the Tuning In program? First, as in the VIPP interventions, the program takes as basic assumptions the attachment principles that (1) secure infant-caregiver attachment is fostered by caregiver sensitivity and (2) caregiver sensitivity and attachment security have some stability within a caregiver-child relationship, in part because they are mentally represented by both the adult caregiver and the child (see Chapters 1, 3, and 6). Second, it is assumed that caregivers' sensitivity and their capacity to form secure attachments with infants are influenced by caregiving knowledge and experience, but also by their own attachment relationship history and long-term, stable attachment representations (Bakermans-Kranenburg et al., 1998). These assumptions led us to focus on the Tuning In program on the behavioral interactions of sensitivity and responsiveness, and the caregiver's cognitive representations of sensitivity and responsiveness, as is the case in the VIPP and VIPP-R parent-child interventions.

The VIPP and VIPP-R intervention programs with parents consisted of four goals incorporated into Tuning In for childcare providers (Juffer, Bakermans-Kranenburg, & Van IJzendoorn, 2005a; see Chapter 2): (1) providing the opportunity to focus on the baby's signals and expressions, (2) stimulating the caregiver's observational skills and empathy for the child, (3) reinforcing the caregiver's positive moments of sensitive behavior shown in videotapes, and (4) engaging the caregivers in discussions about their attachment experiences in childhood and possible influences of these experiences on present caring behavior. In Tuning In the interveners parallel the home-visiting procedure of VIPP by going to the childcare center for four weekly consultation visits. Videotaped observations of group care during each visit are collected, followed by later carefully selecting and editing clips for discussion with the caregiver during the next visit. Brief handouts that explain the concepts of sensitivity and responsiveness are provided. The caregiver is allowed to self-discover examples of her sensitivity and nonsensitivity while watching the videotapes. Finally, the intervener supports the caregivers' stated intentions to change their behavior and to increase sensitivity and responsiveness with the children.

In addition to the themes and activities derived from VIPP and VIPP-R, we also thought it important to include additional elements in Tuning In to adapt it for use in childcare. Because the interveners wanted caregivers to be able to individualize care within a group of children, assessing individual temperaments and social-emotional needs was emphasized, and also how to arrange space, how to position one's self, and how to allocate time and energy to more optimally notice and respond to each child's needs. The interveners encouraged working cooperatively and collaboratively with the children's parents and with professional childcare colleagues in the childcare room.

Overview of the Tuning In program

The overall goal in the four-week Tuning In staff training program is to increase the caregiver's capacity for sensitivity, responsiveness, and effectiveness in meeting each child's needs, in the context of group childcare. Each weekly Tuning In consultation visit has several consistent elements (see Table 10.1 for an overview of the visits). First, the consultant spends approximately one hour observing and videotaping the caregiver as she or he works with children. In addition, either prior to or after the observation session, the consultant meets with the caregiver to view and discuss selected video clips from the previous week. The consultant and caregiver also complete one or two structured activities designed to help the caregiver meet Tuning In objectives. During each visit caregivers are helped to assess the sensitivity in daily caring using self-observation of the videotapes. Awareness of instances of sensitive caregiving is supported by noting

Table 10.1 Overview of the content of Tuning In consultation visits

Visits	Consistent elements	Special Activities
Visit 1 (individual session)	Introduce caregiver to the goals and objectives of Tuning In. (Discuss the videotape and how it will be used.) Discuss briefly definitions of sensitivity and responsiveness. Give caregiver overview of weekly visits. Give caregiver Childcare Staff Questionnaire to complete. Videotape the caregiver as she or he works with children for about 45 minutes.	Talking for the baby. (Introduce learning to interpret baby's feelings and thoughts.)
Visit 2 (individual session)	View and discuss selected video clips from last week's videotaped material. (Focus on awareness of child's signals, helpful or overcontrolling response, "talking for the baby" technique, anything that might have improved interactions with child.) Videotape the caregiver as she or he works with children for about 45 minutes.	Complete and discuss the Individual Temperament Checklists for two children in group.
Visit 3 (caregiving team session)	View and discuss selected video clips from last week's videotaped material. (Focus on awareness of child's signals, helpful or overcontrolling response, "talking for the baby" technique, anything that might have improved interactions with child.) Videotape the caregiver as she or he works with children for about 45 minutes	Blindfold activity. (Put caregiver in place of baby.)
Visit 4 (individual + team participation session)	View and discuss selected video clips from last week's videotaped material. (Focus on awareness of child's signals, helpful or overcontrolling response, "talking for the baby" technique, anything that might have improved interactions with child.) Evaluation of program — discuss with caregivers by providing open-ended questions.	Relationship History Questionnaire. Provide caregivers with three types of hypothetical childcare classroom situations and ask them to come up with strategies to resolve problem.

and praising instances, especially when the caregiver also notices instances of sensitivity herself. Concrete suggestions about how to provide more sensitive, responsive childcare are provided. Finally, the caregiver's stated intentions to increase his or her sensitivity and responsiveness are encouraged and supported. Overarching goals in all visits are for the consultants to be friendly and supportive to the caregiver and to encourage mutual support among the team of caregivers within the childcare room and within the childcare center. As in

VIPP home visits with mothers, the intervener strives to create an atmosphere of support and acceptance by being nondirective and nonjudgmental in the videotaped observations and discussions, by emphasizing the caregiver's competent behaviors, and by allowing the caregivers to take the lead in the consulting conversations.

Open-ended questions asked during viewing of the video clips are designed to highlight sensitivity and to stimulate the caregiver's focus on and reflection about sensitivity. After watching a video clip, the intervener asks the caregiver:

Were you *aware* of children's signals? (*sensitivity*)

Do you think you *interpreted* children's verbal and nonverbal signals accurately? (*sensitivity*)

Did you *respond* to each child in ways that were helpful, yet not overcontrolling? (*responsiveness*)

Are there some ways you might *improve* your interactions with the children? (e.g., changes in your behavior, changes in the layout of the room or furniture, changes in your physical positioning, or changes in the daily routine) (*context*)

The Tuning In program includes a number of structured activities designed to support program objectives (see Table 10.1 for an overview). The so-called blindfold activity helps caregivers to understand the importance of autonomy for infants and toddlers and to empathize with the unpleasant feeling a child might experience when a caregiver is overcontrolling. The temperament assessment focuses on two children in the caregiver's group: one who is relatively easy to care for and one who is more difficult to care for. By comparing and contrasting dimensions of temperament and the communication styles of each child, caregivers are able to think about each child in a more individualized way and think of ways to provide care more compatible with unique temperamental characteristics. In the relationship history activity, the caregiver is asked first to describe the characteristics of an important caregiver in her or his own childhood by selecting words from a checklist. Then, the caregiver is asked to describe herself or himself as a caregiver today, using the same list of descriptive words. This intergenerational comparison of caregiver qualities provokes discussion about how the caregiver is similar to or different from an early important caregiver and leads to consideration of possible connections between relationship history and current caregiving capacities, responses, and caring behaviors. The "talking for the baby" exercise (see Chapter 2) is repeated during three consultation sessions. In this activity the caregiver learns to infer and express the apparent feelings and thoughts of the child, while carefully watching the videotape. This exercise attunes caregivers to the child's signals and encourages them to interpret signals carefully. Finally, a discussion is included during the final consultation session about how to provide sensitive, individualized care for each infant when a caregiver is responsible for a group of children. The interveners support the caregiver's ideas and experiences in response to this challenging question, and they offer strategies that have been suggested by other experienced infant-toddler caregivers (see Table 10.2).

Table 10.2   List of Tuning In practical strategies for increasing caregiver sensitivity and responsiveness in group childcare for infants and toddlers

Strategies for interacting with children

Respect each child's wants and needs

Be expressive verbally and facially

Position self at child's level

Expand verbally, describing the activities the child chooses

Listen to the child's cues about enjoyment of activity

Actively reflect the child's words, feelings, and intentions

Promote positive interactions with other children

Identify each child by name, using names often

Strategies for meeting children's immediate needs when several need care at once

Take care of the child who is hurt first

Distract children who have been comforted but are still upset

Respond based on individual temperament, so that children who have more trouble waiting and disrupt the group will be attended to first

Attend to new children in the group first, so that they can build a bond of trust

Identify which caregiver works best with each child and organize a primary care system

Constant communication between staff, so that everyone knows who is doing what

Strategies for scheduling the day

Use a board for scheduling times for diapering, sleeping, and feeding

For infants: Each child's schedule is more personalized, individual

For toddlers: Each child's schedule follows the group schedule, but still with flexibility to meet individual needs

Allow enough time for routine care (changing, feeding, napping, etc.); this is a great one-on-one time

Strategies for one-on-one routine care

Talk to the children all the time during routine care (diapering, feeding, dressing, etc.)

Tell the child what is about to be done; give a choice if possible

Give the child several minutes' warning if he or she is going to have to do something he or she does not always enjoy, like having a diaper changed

Table 10.2 (continued)   List of Tuning In practical strategies for increasing caregiver sensitivity and responsiveness in group childcare for infants and toddlers

Strategies for communication with parents and co-workers

Use a logbook to communicate with parents who come early or late and cannot talk directly with their child's primary caregiver

Talk with parents one to one to find out what has been going on at home

Organize a parent-teacher conference at least once or twice a year

Empathize with parents' feelings; reflect their feelings and let them know you understand parenting is challenging and you want to support them

Use naptime to talk with co-workers about the day and care for individual children

Communicate often with co-workers about which children you are taking for routine care

Strategies to manage the physical environment

Arrange furniture in the room according to the children's development (to give them room for exploration or to see)

Arrange high chairs or tables in such a way that they allow the most visibility of all children (e.g., high chairs facing you but away from the floor where children are playing — this way you can both feed children in the high chair and supervise the ones playing on the floor)

Tuning In pilot study

The first administration of the Tuning In program took place over four to five weeks with four volunteer caregivers from the Early Head Start program. Early Head Start is a comprehensive government-funded program in the United States designed to support infant-toddler and family development, especially for families living in poverty (Love et al., 2002). Four weekly Tuning In visits were conducted with each caregiver. Content and activities in the visits followed the outline presented in Table 10.1. The Tuning In consultants were the first author and two student assistants who underwent intensive training in the Tuning In model. Videotapes were made during the four visits, approximately 45 minutes of video for each caregiver at each visit. These films provided the needed video clips for the subsequent consultation session, and the first and last sessions also were used later for independent pre- and postassessment coding of caregiver-child interactions. The coders were graduate student assistants not involved in the Tuning In program planning or consultations. Coding scales were adopted from the Caregiver Interaction Scale (Arnett, 1989) and from the parent-child video interaction scales used in the National Early Head Start Evaluation Study (Love et al., 2002).

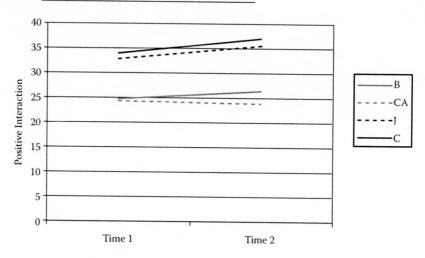

Figure 10.1   Change in four caregivers (B, CA, J, and C) in positive interaction.

Results of the pilot study were encouraging. Although some of the caregiver interaction scales did not show noticeable changes, two important interactive scales changed in the predicted direction in three of four caregivers (see Figures 10.1 and 10.2). Three caregivers increased on the Caregiver Interaction Scale Positive Interaction. This scale includes such interactive behaviors as "speaks warmly to the children" and "pays positive attention to the children as individuals." Also three of four caregivers decreased on the Early Head Start subscale Intrusiveness. This scale "reflects the degree to which the caregiver controls the child rather than recognizing and respecting the validity of the child's experience" (Love et al., 2002). It was encouraging to find improvements both in the interactions of two caregivers who started relatively high and in one caregiver who started relatively low on the interaction scales. This suggests that Tuning In has the potential to be effective for caregivers at various beginning levels of sensitivity.

Interviews with the participating caregivers in a focus group after the Tuning In pilot study confirmed that the video-feedback sessions were unique and helpful, as were the other Tuning In activities. Caregivers also suggested minor modifications for Tuning In for its future development.

Vignettes from the pilot study: changes in caregiver sensitivity

The increases in warmth and positive attention and the decreases in intrusiveness observed in the pilot study are illustrated in the following case descriptions from videotapes of one caregiver. The vignettes illustrate changes in attitudes and caregiving practices. This Early Head Start caregiver began the program

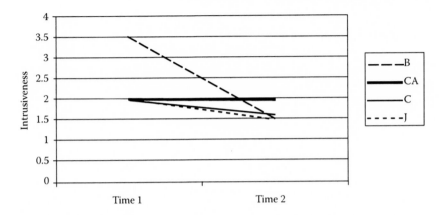

Figure 10.2   Change in four caregivers (B, CA, C, and J) in intrusiveness.

with relatively low scores on the Positive Interaction scales and relatively high scores for Intrusiveness.

First video: Feeding

The caregiver, Bonnie, is seated at a small table feeding a child with a spoon. She is seated behind the little girl, about two years in age. She is reaching around from behind with the spoon and she appears unable to see the child's facial expressions. She is pleading with the child to take another bite. The child does so while rubbing her eyes and showing a sleepy face. The child appears reluctant to eat. Bonnie praises the child for taking a bite; however, in the next second, the little girl spits the food back out on her plate. Bonnie does not seem to notice this. The girl then drinks some milk following Bonnie's pleading to do so. Bonnie does not praise the girl directly for drinking, but speaks instead to the other adult caregiver in the room, saying, "Look, Jessie, she drank her milk!" The little girl continues rubbing her eyes, but Bonnie does not seem to notice or acknowledge this.

Second video: Feeding

In a later observation, after completing two Tuning In consultation sessions, Bonnie is observed seated at the table with an older toddler and a younger toddler. This time she is positioned between the two children, seated on the floor rather than on an adult-size chair. Thus, she is able to see the children's faces clearly, and they are able to see her. She looks at each child, smiling and calling them by name when inquiring about their food. She tells one child about another child's eating, encouraging peer awareness and interaction. When praising one little boy's capable use of the spoon, she praises him directly, not by speaking to another adult caregiver. "Tyson, you are doing great using your spoon!" Because she is now able to see the children's facial expression gestures, Bonnie seems better able to observe the children and make responsive comments. For example, when a child silently motions for his cup, she says, "Oh, you are thirsty!" When a child motions for a piece of toast, but seems confused about what to do with it, Bonnie encourages her, saying, "Yes, take a bite, take a bite," and the child does so.

First video: Play

During a free play on the floor, Bonnie is rocking a little boy, age 2½ years, back and forth while holding him in her lap and within her arms. She is singing a song to him while rocking him. The child at first seems to enjoy this game and smiles briefly at the camera person who is filming him. A moment later, however, the child seems to want to get up and out of Bonnie's lap and arms. He leans and struggles a bit. But Bonnie has not finished singing the song, and she continues holding and rocking the child, even though his struggling suggests he wants to stop. During the remainder of this sequence, the child holds himself rather stiffly, with a sober look on his face, although he does not try to get away again. When Bonnie is finished rocking the boy, she does not inform him that they are done rocking and that it is another child's turn. Instead, she asks a nearby girl if she wants to be rocked. After the girl takes the boy's place and Bonnie begins to rock and sing to the girl, the boy stands nearby and watches. He seems to want to get back in Bonnie's lap, although she is now rocking another child. Bonnie notices this and stops to put both children in her lap, facing away from her. Again, after a few seconds of rocking and singing, the boy appears to want to get away, but Bonnie does not notice this and keeps rocking him.

Second video: Play

In a later observation, after completing three Tuning In consultation sessions, Bonnie is playing with a little girl on the outdoor playground. She watches the child's actions and makes comments (e.g., she counts out loud how many twigs the girl is picking up). She follows the girl's lead, commenting on things that she says and does. When another child comes over to join them, she makes sure that they know each other's names. When Bonnie moves over to play with a third child, a young toddler, she informs the girl first about what she is doing and invites her to come over and play together. As she helps the toddler walk while standing, Bonnie watches closely the expressions on his face, and the child in turn looks up at Bonnie's face. Bonnie stops and kneels down while walking the toddler, getting face to face at the child's level. When the child signals his desire to stop walking by sitting down, Bonnie stops trying to hold him up. When the child signals he is ready to walk again by reaching and straining to get up, Bonnie helps him to rise from the ground and balance. Again, Bonnie attentively watches the child's facial expressions and gestures, as he walks with her assistance. When they stop, Bonnie acknowledges his intentions. She says, "Stop!" as he stops walking, and when he starts walking again, she says, "Here we go, here we go!"

Tuning In: clinical trial evaluation and future development

The Tuning In pilot field study observed change in three of four Early Head Start caregivers in positive interaction and intrusiveness. These results suggested that the Tuning In intervention model, using the VIPP approach with video feedback and other elements, may be an effective method of staff training to increase sensitivity, responsiveness, and ultimately attachment security for children in childcare. Furthermore, because the Tuning In program is short-term and intensive, it offers promise for use in childcare programs, where longer caregiver interventions may not be practical or cost effective.

Because the Tuning In pilot study included only a few participants from a well-funded, high-quality early intervention program, further evaluations of Tuning In are needed. The next phase of development of the Tuning In program, currently under way, consists of a randomized control group, pretest-posttest experimental evaluation. This rigorous evaluation includes 20 Tuning In caregivers and 20 control caregivers, randomly assigned to conditions by center. Measures of caregiving outcomes used in the pre- and postassessments include subscales from the Caregiver Interaction Scale (Arnett, 1989) and from observation scales used in the Early Head Start National Evaluation Study (Love et al., 2002).

Prior to beginning the experimental evaluation of Tuning In, the pilot study participants were consulted to guide us in making modifications to improve the program. First, a small participant observation study was conducted with two caregivers who displayed the highest levels of sensitivity in the pilot study. Each caregiver was visited, and several hours were spent observing and assisting with the care of the infants or toddlers. The caregivers were interviewed to understand better how these caregivers conceptualized caring and how they organized their behavior, space, and time to optimize individual care for each child. Based on these observations and informal interviews, a list of caregiver strategies that are thought to be effective in increasing responsiveness in group childcare was developed (see Table 10.2). The same pilot caregivers participated in a focus group discussion with the Tuning In project staff to review and provide input for the revision of the Tuning In training manual. This resulted in changes to the training manual, including the addition of one within-team consultation session, in which caregivers working in the same room work together through a structured Tuning In activity, without the external consultant present. The purpose of the self-guided session is to increase collaboration and trust within the caregiving team and to reduce somewhat the reliance on the outside consultant.

A second revision suggested by the pilot study caregivers and adopted in the current version of Tuning In was to have each caregiver complete a temperament assessment for himself of herself, in addition to the assessments for two children. This process was included so that caregivers may compare their own temperamental characteristics with those of individual children in the classroom. It is expected that these assessments will lead to more discussion about how temperamental differences can make caring easier or more challenging, depending on the goodness of fit between child and caregiver. The third addition to the Tuning In manual was a problem-solving exercise designed to support caregivers' awareness of and application of sensitive caregiving strategies in group care.

The study is in the process of completing the clinical trial evaluation and beginning data analysis. Observed caregiver outcomes coded include sensitivity, intrusiveness, positive relationship, positive regard, negative regard, detachment, and cognitive stimulation. Staff education and experience are also assessed, as is staff personality (John & Srivastava, 1999), supportiveness of the workplace environment (Bloom, 1996), and the quality of relationships with parents (Elicker, Noppe, Noppe, & Fortner-Wood, 1997).

So far data have been collected for 37 professional infant-toddler caregivers (21 caregivers from the intervention group, 16 from the control group). Caregiver assignments were randomly stratified by center and type of program (university based, Early Head Start, or community childcare center). Participants range between 19 and 63 years of age, and all but one are females. Of 37 participants, most have high school education or higher, including 12 with bachelor's degrees and 2 with master's degrees. Thirteen participants have additional early childhood certificates or special training related to early care and education. Preliminary analysis of personality ratings shows that caregivers are typically high in conscientiousness and agreeableness, moderate in openness and extraversion, and low on neuroticism. When asked about the program's work environment, job satisfaction, and staff and parent relationships, participants typically reported they were moderately satisfied.

At the end of the four-week training sessions, the 21 caregivers in the intervention group completed an evaluation rating of their satisfaction with the Tuning In program. Satisfaction ratings were generally high, with means of 4 or higher (on a 5-point rating scale) on scales of finding the program useful, benefiting from the program, and understanding the concepts of sensitivity and responsiveness better at the end of the training. The most important challenges most caregivers mentioned in trying to be a more responsive caregiver were "too many children," "not enough time," "not knowing exactly what the child wants when the child can't communicate the need," and "knowing the best way to be effective in meeting the need."

When asked which Tuning In sessions and activities they found most useful, almost all of the caregivers indicated that watching the videotape clips helped them to "see their weaknesses, as well as strengths," "notice things ... missed before and learn how to correct them," "see from a different perspective," and also "see how children were responding." Among the new strategies and skills caregivers mentioned to have been acquired following the training were "being able to tune in to children's attempt at communication," "making sure to ... use eye contact and ... voice when fulfilling needs and wants of each child in the group care setting," "talking for the baby," and "try[ing] to think about the way a child's thinking before ... react[ing] to them. Go into a situation calm and ready to listen to each child."

The evaluation study also includes caregiver reports of individual child well-being (De Schipper, Van IJzendoorn, & Tavecchio, 2004) for two focal children in each childcare group of eight children. Preliminary analyses suggest that children's well-being as reported by caregivers increased over five weeks in general, but did not increase significantly more as a result of the Tuning In intervention.

Conclusions

Sensitive and responsive caregiving seems to be a key process variable in quality infant-toddler childcare that supports children's social-emotional development. Individualized care and sensitivity are thought to be critical, if a quality goal in childcare is for children to develop secure attachment relationships with their primary nonparental caregivers. In addition, positive interactions and sensitive care have been shown to be correlated with more mature concurrent functioning by children enrolled in childcare, and also to predict more advanced social-emotional and cognitive development in the years that follow. Therefore, a focused staff training intervention designed to increase sensitivity and responsiveness in caregivers may be an important tool for childcare program managers who wish to increase the process quality of childcare and support optimal social-emotional development in very young children. With further development, and depending on the outcomes of the formal evaluation currently under way, Tuning In may become a basic training program for beginning or more experienced caregivers in a variety of programs providing care and education for children in the first three years of life.

Acknowledgments

The authors acknowledge the contributions of many persons to the project, including all of the center directors, caregivers, and children, and Purdue University research assistants Olga Carbonell, Larissa Frias, Kyong-Ah Kwon, and Garene Kaloustian. The Tuning In project was supported by the Kinley Trust.

11

Extending the video-feedback intervention to sensitive discipline

The early prevention of antisocial behavior

Judi Mesman,[1] Mirjam N. Stolk,[1]
Jantien van Zeijl,[1] Lenneke R. A. Alink,[1]
Femmie Juffer,[1] Marian J. Bakermans-
Kranenburg,[1] Marinus H. van IJzendoorn,[1]
and Hans M. Koot[2]

[1]*Centre for Child and Family Studies,
Leiden University, the Netherlands*
[2]*Department of Developmental Psychology
and Developmental Psychopathology, Vrije
Universiteit Amsterdam, the Netherlands*

Antisocial behaviors such as aggression and delinquency have received considerable attention in the public debate about safety and crime prevention. These behaviors cause extensive damage to society, both material (e.g., vandalism, shoplifting) and personal (e.g., victims of violence). There is substantial evidence that early negative parent-child interaction patterns predict child externalizing problems (e.g., Belsky, Woodworth, & Crnic, 1996; Olson, Bates, Sandy, & Lanthier, 2000; Shaw, Owens, Giovannelli, & Winslow, 2001) and that early externalizing problems increase the risk for antisocial behavior in later childhood and adolescence (Campbell, 1995, 2002). Prevention efforts may therefore be most effective if they are targeted at parent-child interactions during early childhood. In this chapter, an intervention study is described that employs the Video-feedback Intervention to promote Positive Parenting (VIPP) method to enhance parental sensitivity and effective discipline, with the ultimate aims to decrease child externalizing problems and to prevent the development of later antisocial behavior. First, developmental issues regarding the prevalence and prediction of antisocial behavior are discussed. Second, different theoretical models with respect to the role of parenting in relation to child externalizing problems are presented. Finally, the overall design of the study is described as well as the global content of the program and the outcomes of the intervention.

The developmental significance of early externalizing problems

In the literature on developmental psychopathology, several different terms are used to describe essentially the same behavior pattern: *antisocial behavior, externalizing problems, behavior problems, conduct problems,* and *disruptive behavior problems.* The underlying construct refers to behaviors that are directed outward, go against social rules and expectations, and may be distressing or cause harm to other people. These include aggressive behaviors (e.g., hitting, biting, bullying), oppositional behaviors (e.g., disobedience, angry moods, defiance), delinquency (e.g., shoplifting, vandalism), and overactive behaviors (e.g., unable to sit still, trouble concentrating). The term *externalizing problems* seems to be most often used to describe these behaviors in young children, whereas *antisocial behavior* seems to be used mostly for older children, adolescents, and adults. In this paper, the same use of the terminology is adopted.

Externalizing behaviors are relatively common in early childhood and decline in frequency from the age of four or five years (Achenbach & Rescorla, 2000; Tremblay et al., 1999). Over half of 1½- to 3-year-olds show behaviors such as temper tantrums, disobedience, hitting, or angry moods (Achenbach & Rescorla, 2000; Koot & Verhulst, 1991). The high rate of externalizing behaviors in early childhood can be explained by the rapid developmental changes that occur during the first years of life. The child's increased mobility and growing need for autonomy, combined with increased parental limit setting, provide the ingredients for challenging and disruptive behaviors in toddlers and preschoolers (Campbell, 2002). Therefore, externalizing behaviors are quite common before the age of four years and can to a certain extent be regarded as age appropriate (Alink et al., 2006; Van Zeijl, Mesman, Stolk et al., 2006). This is not to say that externalizing *problems* are common as well. Based on criteria such as duration and severity, prevalence estimates of clinically significant externalizing problems in preschoolers range from 7% to 15% (Campbell, 1995, 2002).

Although externalizing behavior during the preschool years is relatively common, toddlers or preschoolers showing very high levels of these behaviors are at risk for antisocial problem behaviors in later childhood and adolescence (Campbell & Ewing, 1990; Lavigne et al., 1998; Mesman & Koot, 2001). In addition, it is mainly the early-onset group of children with externalizing problems that show the least favorable prognosis with respect to future antisocial outcomes (Moffitt, Caspi, Dickson, Silva, & Stanton, 1996). Therefore, externalizing problems in early childhood are of special interest to researchers and policy makers who are concerned with the early identification and prevention of antisocial behavior.

Parenting and the development of child externalizing problems

One of the most compelling issues regarding the early development of externalizing problems is the role of maladaptive parent-child interaction patterns. The relevance of investigating the association between parenting and child externalizing problems has been documented by many authors from a number of different theoretical viewpoints. In a comprehensive review by Shaw and Bell (1993), the different theories of parental contributors to antisocial behavior were examined with respect to their developmental and transactional properties. In other words, to what extent does a theory take into account the role of developmental processes and the role of reciprocal interactions between parents and children? These features are both crucial to prevention efforts, because they represent precisely those aspects of parent-child interactions that are most relevant to understanding the etiology of child problem behavior. Shaw and Bell (1993) concluded that two major theoretical frameworks of parent-child relationships include both developmental and transactional features: attachment theory and social learning theory. "They postulate reciprocal interactions of parent and child, and transformations in the form of normative changes in the child or changes in family processes" (Shaw & Bell, 1993, p. 493).

Attachment theory

Attachment theory was never just a theory of normal development, but also of psychopathology (Sroufe, Carlson, Levy, & Egeland, 1999). Indeed, Bowlby's ideas were inspired partly by his observations of early disruptions in mother-child relationships in a sample of young delinquents (Bowlby, 1944). In later years, several studies have shown that attachment insecurity and insensitive and unresponsive parenting in early childhood are related to behavior problems in children (e.g., Belsky et al., 1996; Greenberg, Speltz, DeKlyen, & Endriga, 1991; McCartney, Owen, Booth, Clarke-Stewart, & Vandell, 2004; Shaw et al., 2001).

Three models that include specific hypotheses about insecure attachment and associated parenting behaviors in relation to child problem behavior can be distinguished (Greenberg, 1999; Greenberg, Speltz, & DeKlyen, 1993; Van IJzendoorn, 1997). The first model under attachment theory is based on Bowlby's

(1973) original concept of the "internal working model" as a cognitive-affective schema of self and others that includes expectations regarding social interactions. Insensitive and unresponsive parenting may lead to the development of negative working models in children who as a result approach social situations with anger, mistrust, or anxiety (Main, 1995). This attributional bias in social interactions may result in externalizing problems such as oppositional behavior and reactive aggression (Greenberg, 1999).

The second model was formulated by Greenberg and colleagues and hypothesizes that externalizing behavior in young children is an attachment strategy aimed at regulating caregiver behavior when other strategies have proven ineffective (Greenberg & Speltz, 1988; Greenberg et al., 1993). A history of insensitive and unresponsive caregiving has led the child to adopt a strategy of highly negative behaviors, such as noncompliance and aggression, in an attempt to get attention from the parent or control the parent's behavior. This behavior may be effective in the short-term, but is likely to set the stage for the development of problematic family processes.

A third hypothesis regarding the process underlying the link between attachment and child problem behavior is based on the work of Richters and Waters (1991) and of Maccoby and Martin (1983). This hypothesis suggests that the child's readiness for socialization (i.e., willingness and motivation to comply with parent's rules and requests) is influenced by his or her early attachment experiences. A securely attached child who has experienced warm and contingent interactions with the caregiver is likely to be prosocially oriented and motivated to comply with that caregiver's requests. In contrast, an insecurely attached child with a history of experiencing unresponsive or hostile parenting is less likely to be motivated to behave desirably to parental rules or requests. In a related vein, it has been suggested that the association between early insecure attachment and the development of child externalizing problems is mediated by deficits in early moral development (Van IJzendoorn, 1997). Most externalizing behaviors are inherently antisocial (aggression, delinquency), suggesting a deficit in the early socialization process, specifically the process of moral development in terms of empathy and the internalization of norms. In their meta-analysis, Miller and Eisenberg (1988) found that empathic responding was negatively related to antisocial behavior. Moral development in its turn has been found to be influenced by the parent-child relationship. A number of studies have shown that insecure attachment and parental insensitivity are related to child noncompliance and lack of moral internalization (e.g., Kochanska, 1995; Van der Mark, Van IJzendoorn, & Bakermans-Kranenburg, 2002).

In addition to hypotheses about the processes linking insecure (versus secure) attachment to the development of problem behavior, several studies have shown that disorganized (versus organized) attachment is related to externalizing behavior outcomes in children (Van IJzendoorn, Schuengel, & Bakermans-Kranenburg, 1999). Disorganized attachment is thought to originate from frightening parenting behavior stemming from the parent's own traumatic personal experiences (Main & Hesse, 1990). In the Strange Situation Procedure (Ainsworth, Blehar, Waters, & Wall, 1978), disorganized attachment is characterized by the infant's lack of a coherent response to a stressful situation (Main & Solomon, 1990). Because the parent is both the source of comfort and the source of fear, the infant shows conflicting, incomplete, or apprehensive behaviors and does not show an organized behavioral strategy (Lyons-Ruth & Jacobvitz, 1999; Main & Solomon, 1990). It is as yet unclear whether the association between early disorganization and later externalizing problems is domain specific (Green & Goldwyn, 2002), or whether it reflects a general vulnerability to develop "odd, intrusive, controlling or incompetent social behaviors" (Lyons-Ruth & Jacobvitz, 1999, p. 539).

Coercion theory: A social learning perspective

Social learning theory was first put forward in the 1950s and 1960s as a framework to understand personality development (Bandura & Walters, 1963; Rotter, 1954). In this framework, reinforcement processes determine whether the occurrence of certain behaviors will increase or decrease in the future. In the following decades, the reinforcement principle was studied in relation to child aggression by several authors (e.g., Bandura, 1973; Lovaas, 1961; Rosekrans & Hartup, 1967), but it was especially the work of Patterson and his colleagues that clearly showed the importance of social learning principles in the development of child aggression by proposing the coercion theory (e.g., Patterson, 1971, 1976, 1982). Coercion theory hypothesizes that repeated experiences of microlevel coercive discipline interchanges between parent and child cumulate over time to establish a pattern of coercive family interaction that sets the stage for the development of antisocial behavior (Patterson, 1982).

The term *coercion* refers to the use of aversive or antisocial behaviors to exert short-term control over another person (Patterson, Reid, & Eddy, 2002). On a microsocial level, reinforcement processes determine the outcome of these interchanges and the likelihood that the behaviors are performed in the future. This can involve positive reinforcement when the coercive behavior is successful in obtaining a desired object, as well as negative reinforcement when the coercive behavior successfully removes an aversive stimulus (Snyder, 1995). Consider the following interaction sequence: A mother tells her child to clean up his toys (aversive stimulus); the child argues and whines (coercive behavior); the mother gets annoyed, scolds and yells, and repeats the demand (coercive discipline tactics);

the child argues even more, screams, and hits (coercive behavior); the mother gives in to avoid further negative behavior and withdraws the request (negative reinforcement of coercive behavior). This type of interaction is an example of what has been called the reinforcement trap. The parent gives in to the child to stop the negative behavior and this tactic has short-term success. However, in future interactions, the child is likely to repeat the coercive behavior (because it was successful before), and the mother is more likely to increase the severity of her coercive discipline tactics to obtain compliance. In this way, coercive dyadic interchanges escalate and are maintained by both partners. As Patterson (1976) put it, the child is both "victim and architect of a coercive system."

Several studies have shown that reinforcement processes in parental discipline predict aggressive, antisocial behaviors in children (Patterson, 1982; Snyder, Edwards, McGraw, Kilgore, & Holton, 1994; Snyder & Patterson, 1986) and that aggressive children tend to grow up in families where conflicts are frequent and family members are quick to initiate aggressive behavior and to respond in kind when others initiate such behaviors (Snyder & Stoolmiller, 2002). In addition to ineffective, coercive discipline strategies when the child is showing aversive behaviors, parents of aggressive children generally fail to provide positive reinforcement for prosocial and compliant behaviors (Patterson, 1976).

On a macrosocial level, coercion theory proposes that in the long run, the child's coercive behavior is likely to generalize to other social settings such as school, thus increasing the likelihood of peer rejection and academic failure (Patterson, Reid, & Dishion, 1992). In addition, these children are at increased risk for affiliation with deviant peers (Snyder, Horsch, & Childs, 1997), which may be a result not only of rejection by other peers, but also of reinforcement processes. Children with antisocial behavior problems may very well actively seek out people and situations likely to provide reinforcement for their aversive behaviors (Snyder, 1995). Finally, affiliation with deviant peers is a major risk for the escalation and maintenance of antisocial behavior (Snyder, 2002).

Implications for interventions

Although attachment theory and coercion theory originate from two separate research traditions, they actually have some important features in common. As several authors have noted, both theories emphasize the importance of contingent and nonaversive parent-child interactions (Patterson, 2002; Rothbaum & Weisz, 1994). For intervention efforts, attachment theory emphasizes parental insensitivity and unresponsiveness in daily parent-child interactions, whereas coercion theory provides coercive parental discipline tactics in conflict situations as target variables.

As noted by Shaw and Bell (1993), there is a gap between the developmental periods that attachment theory and coercion theory focus on. Whereas the former is mostly concerned with infancy and early childhood, the latter is generally applied to school-aged children and adolescents. However, despite the selective focus of previous studies in this area, the relevance of coercive and inconsistent discipline as posited by coercion theory need not be confined to older children. As soon as children's wishes and abilities start to conflict with the wishes of parents, the door is opened to coercive parent-child interactions. These can essentially take place from the time that infants are able to purposefully reach for objects that they are not allowed to touch, which is roughly during the second half of the first year. In other words, the parenting ingredients for the development of child externalizing problems are potentially fully present at the child's first birthday. Parenting interventions may therefore be most effective if targeted at parents of young children, when parental insensitivity and coercive discipline may set the stage for the development of externalizing problems.

Taking into account the theoretical and developmental issues discussed above, the intervention study presented in this chapter was inspired by both attachment theory and coercion theory. The SCRIPT study (Screening and Intervention of Problem behavior in Toddlerhood) was designed to test the effectiveness of an early childhood intervention program with a focus on both insensitive and coercive parenting behaviors in mothers of one- to three-year-old children. Because the toddler and early preschool years are characterized by rapid developmental changes, the study also examines potential differences between age groups with respect to the intervention process and its outcome. Finally, the study includes an accelerated longitudinal design that allows for growth curve analyses of the development of externalizing problems from age 12 to 60 months (Meredith & Tisak, 1990; Nesselroade & Baltes, 1979). For this chapter we focus on the effectiveness of the intervention. The research aims for the current study are:

1. To test the effectiveness of the intervention on parental sensitivity and discipline
2. To test whether the enhancement of parental sensitivity and discipline ability leads to a decrease in child externalizing problems
3. To investigate whether earlier preventive interventions are more effective than interventions at preschool age.

The SCRIPT study

Design

The SCRIPT project is a randomized experimental case-control intervention study with the goal to test the effectiveness of a video-based parenting intervention aimed at enhancing parental sensitivity and effective discipline strategies to reduce externalizing problems and increase empathic concern in one-, two-, and three-year-old children. To this end, the VIPP method was extended to address discipline strategies within the context of sensitivity enhancement. This adaptation of the VIPP method is named VIPP-SD (VIPP-Sensitive Discipline; see Chapter 2). The content of this intervention will be described later in this chapter.

General population screening

To obtain a sample of young children with behavior problems, a general population screening was conducted. The Child Behavior Checklist for children aged 1½ to 5 years (CBCL/1½–5; Achenbach & Rescorla, 2000) was used as a screening instrument. The Dutch translation of the preschool version has been found valid and reliable in a Dutch sample of two- to three-year-olds (Koot, Van den Oord, Verhulst, & Boomsma, 1997). Because there are no well-validated screening instruments for behavior problems in children younger than 18 months, and to achieve homogeneity of methods across ages, we decided to use the CBCL for all three age groups. Our results suggest that the CBCL can be successfully used to assess behavior problems in one-year-olds (Mesman et al., 2003; Van Zeijl, Mesman, Stolk et al., 2006).

For the screening phase, the addresses of 4,615 one- to three-year-old children were obtained from municipal registers from several cities and towns in the western region of the Netherlands. Specifically, children in the following age groups were selected: 10 to 12 months (1-year-olds), 22 to 26 months (2-year-olds), and 34 to 38 months (3-year-olds). Questionnaires measuring child and family characteristics (including the CBCL) were obtained from the primary caregivers of 2,409 children (response rate, 52.2%). The large majority of children were living with two parents, with the biological mother as the primary caregiver and a father figure (biological or stepfather) as the second caregiver. To ensure a homogenous sample, only children living in these families were eligible for the intervention study. This selection and the application of several other exclusion criteria (e.g., twins, serious medical condition in child or mother) resulted in the exclusion of 454 cases, leaving a target selection sample of 1,954 children. As expected, the mean scores on the CBCL Externalizing Problems scale for the three age groups were substantially higher for two- and three-year-old children than for the one-year-old infants. For each age group, children with scores above the 75th percentile on the CBCL syndrome Externalizing Problems (age 1, scores ≥ 13; age 2, ≥ 19; age 3, ≥ 20) were selected for the intervention study ($N = 438$). Parents of 246 children (56%) agreed to participate and were invited for a visit to the laboratory for the pretest. Nine families withdrew from the study after the pretest phase, resulting in a final sample of 237 children.

The intervention study

Three to four months after the screening phase, the selected mother-child dyads visited our laboratory for a two-hour session. Each session included different episodes designed to assess parental sensitivity and discipline strategies, child aggression, compliance, temperament, empathy, and attachment security. In addition, mothers completed the CBCL and a questionnaire about their own emotional problems. After the pretest session, participants were randomly assigned to either the intervention group or the control group. Families in the intervention group received four monthly home visits by a trained female home visitor followed by two booster sessions with two-month intervals (total duration, eight months). The content of the intervention program is described in the next section. The mothers in the control group were contacted by phone following the same time schedule as the home visits in the intervention group. During these telephone conversations, mothers were encouraged to talk about general topics regarding their child, such as eating, sleeping, and playing. Mothers in the control group received no advice or guidance. After the fourth session (intervention or control), both parents completed the CBCL.

One year after the pretest, mothers again visited the laboratory for the first posttest. The posttest included the same measures and procedures as the pretest laboratory session. In addition, saliva samples were obtained from mothers and children to assess cortisol levels as a measure of stress reactivity. Furthermore, mothers completed questionnaires regarding parenting attitudes, life events, and use of counseling services for parents. Mothers also completed an evaluation form asking their opinion about different aspects of the intervention (or control group) process. Finally, a second posttest was conducted one year after the first posttest, to test for potential long-term effects of the intervention. The procedures for the second posttest were identical to those of the first posttest.

The intervention study was primarily aimed at mother-child dyads. Fathers' involvement consisted of filling in questionnaires and participating in the two booster sessions of the intervention (see below). There were several reasons to focus primarily on mothers and to involve fathers only at a later stage in the intervention process. First, as mentioned above, in our screening sample mothers were almost always the primary caregivers (consistent with Dutch national trends; see Keuzenkamp, Hooghiemstra, Breedveld, & Merens, 2000), so we decided to focus on mothers for the intervention. Second, the presence of fathers during intervention sessions may make mothers feel less at ease, and therefore less open, and could also result in less attention for her specific needs (Bakermans-Kranenburg,

Van IJzendoorn, & Juffer, 2003). Third, in many cases it is very difficult to make appointments with fathers for home visits, because they almost always have full-time jobs outside the home. However, an advantage of involving fathers is that the intervention effects are more likely generalize to all parenting experiences of the child, instead of affecting just one parent. In addition, the two parents help and support each other in their efforts to implement new parenting skills (see Chapter 12). So to combine the best of both worlds, fathers were involved in the intervention, but only after mothers had had the opportunity to form a bond with the home visitor and feel at ease in the intervention process.

The sensitive discipline intervention (VIPP-SD)

The VIPP-SD intervention aims to enhance the mother's sensitivity and discipline strategies by increasing her (1) observation skills, (2) knowledge about parenting and the development of young children, and (3) empathy and understanding of her child. The ultimate goal is to decrease child behavior problems and increase empathy and compliance. The intervention program consists of three phases. In the first phase (sessions 1 and 2), the central goal is to get acquainted and to build a positive relationship with the mother. During these sessions, the emphasis is on the child's behavior, and positive parent-child interactions of the dyad involved are shown on videotape and reinforced (see Chapter 2). In the second phase (sessions 3 and 4), the home visitor actively works on improving negative maternal behavior by showing when and how positive parenting behaviors are successful, and discussing how these behaviors can be implemented in other situations. The third phase consists of two booster sessions (sessions 5 and 6) in which the topics of the first four sessions are covered again. Throughout the sessions, several elements are crucial to the intervention process, including creating a pleasant atmosphere, acknowledging the mother as the expert on her own child, focusing on positive mother-child interaction, and using the "speaking for the child" technique (see Chapter 2).

Each of first four sessions has its own theme with respect to sensitivity and discipline, and themes from past sessions are integrated into the following sessions. The specific themes and procedures of each session will be discussed in the next section. Because the general VIPP methods and the parental sensitivity intervention themes are already described in Chapter 2 and illustrated in a case study in Chapter 3, the focus is primarily on the parental discipline themes (the sensitive discipline component; see also Chapter 2). These themes are particularly aimed at providing alternatives for coercive discipline tactics during (potential) conflict situations.

Session 1

In the first session, distraction and inductive discipline are introduced as noncoercive responses to child difficult behavior or in potentially difficult situations. The video that is used for this session was taped during the pretest lab session and shows mother and child during a "do not" task that consists of the child not being allowed to touch attractive toys. After a few minutes (exact duration depends on the age of the child), the child is allowed to touch only the least attractive toy. After another short time interval, the mother and child are allowed to play with all the toys. Before showing the video, the home visitor explains that for young children active distraction is a way to help the child focus on something other than the forbidden action. After this explanation, the videotape of the "do not" task is viewed with the mother. The concept of inductive discipline is also introduced. Inductive discipline refers to techniques that emphasize the explanation of rules and the consequences of child behavior for others (Hoffman & Saltzstein, 1967). This form of discipline promotes child moral internalization, in contrast to discipline techniques that rely on power assertion and punishment (Hoffman, 1970). The home visitor explains the concept of induction to the mother. If the mother uses distraction or inductive discipline techniques in the videotaped "do not" task, these are pointed out and reinforced.

Session 2

A failure to provide positive reinforcement for prosocial and compliant behaviors is one of the parenting behaviors that Patterson (1982) describes as a risk factor for the development of child externalizing problems. Therefore, in the second session, positive reinforcement is the central theme. The video that is used for this session was taped during the first home visit (session 1) and shows the child playing alone, mother and child playing together, a cleanup task, and mother reading to the child. The home visitor encourages mothers to compliment their children when they are doing something right, instead of focusing only on bad behavior. Often, mothers ignore bad behavior, but fail to praise the child when he is being good. In addition, mothers often think that they compliment their child all the time, but when they start to make a conscious effort to do so more often, they notice that they really do not use positive reinforcement as frequently as they thought. Most mothers report almost immediate results when they have increased the number of compliments to their child. The home visitor's role is also to model this behavior, by praising the child when he or she is doing something right and by reinforcing the mother if she compliments the child. In this session, the home visitor also repeats the suggestions regarding the use of noncoercive discipline techniques such as induction and distraction as introduced in session 1. Using the videotaped cleanup task as an example, the technique of postponing is introduced. Instead of refusing and just saying no to a child's wish to play, mothers are encouraged to tell their children that they can play after they have cleaned up the toys.

Session 3

In the third session, the discipline theme is the sensitive time-out. The video that is used for this session was taped during the second home visit (session 2) and shows mother and child eating lunch or a snack. For many parents, this is a potentially challenging situation, because many young children do not eat as well as their parents would like. The home visitor explains that when a child throws a temper tantrum, a time-out may help the child to calm down. The mother can put the child in another (part of the) room, or the mother can choose to withdraw from the situation. The mother is advised to adapt the duration of the time-out on the child's age: one minute for a one-year-old child, two minutes for a two-year-old, and so forth. In addition, the home visitor suggests not to move the child out of sight (e.g., not close the door) to prevent the child from feeling abandoned or unsafe. The home visitor explains to the mother that for the time-out to work, it is important that she stays calm, that she explains that she will play with the child when he has calmed down, and that she ends the episode on a positive note, that is, appreciate that it was difficult for him and praise his efforts. Finally, it is important that both mother and child understand that the time-out is meant as a way of de-escalating the situation and normalizing interaction, not to punish the child. If the video shows the child having a temper tantrum during lunch, the home visitor can suggest the time-out as a way to calm the child. One mother applied this discipline tactic quite successfully by pushing the child's high chair away from the table when the child was being very difficult.

Session 4

The final discipline theme is empathy for the child. This theme is closely related to the concept of sensitivity, but is specifically aimed at enhancing the mother's understanding of the child's thoughts, feelings, and motives when the child is confronted with rules, do's, and don'ts. The video for this session shows mother and child playing together and building a tower together. The tower is somewhat difficult for young children, and they may get frustrated or upset when they do not manage to complete it. This frustration can easily lead to difficult behavior, which mothers often interpreted as naughty behavior ("he's just doing it to be annoying") because they were unaware of or insensitive to the child's frustration with the task. Mothers may then get angry and discipline the child, when empathy for the child's feelings would have been much more appropriate. The home visitor tells the mother that it is important to let the child know that she understands that these situations can be difficult for the child. The home visitor provides examples of phrases that the mother may use, such as "I understand that you do not like this" or "This is hard for you, isn't it?" The home visitor also explains that an important function of showing empathy for the child is that the child in turn learns to show empathy for others, which facilitates the development of prosocial behaviors.

Understanding the child and having empathy for the child should not be limited to feelings and behaviors. For successful discipline, understanding the child's cognitive limitations are just as important. Here two important parenting themes in Patterson's theory are elaborated: clear limit setting and consistent discipline. The home visitor explains that for young children it is very confusing if parents often change rules or are not consistent in maintaining these rules. The mother is advised to decide which rules are really important to her and to then make sure that she consistently reinforces these rules. Some discipline issues may be less important and should then not be presented as strict rules when in reality the parent is not motivated to reinforce them and as a result often gives in if the child challenges the rule.

Sessions 5 and 6

For the two booster sessions, fathers are also invited to be present and participate. The involvement of the father can strengthen the intervention effect and help mothers put their newly learned skills into practice (Bakermans-Kranenburg et al., 2003). In about half of the cases, fathers were present during the fifth or sixth session. The advice with respect to the themes of sessions 1 to 4 is repeated. In many cases, the fathers are enthusiastic about being able to participate in the session. They have often heard a lot about previous sessions from their wives and are eager to see "what it is like" and ask many questions. This gives the home visitor an opportunity to repeat all the themes from previous sessions for the father's benefit, without unintentionally implying that the mother had forgotten or not understood them the first time. Parents may also start to evaluate their respective behaviors and attitudes with respect to sensitivity and discipline practices. This can lead to interesting and helpful insights about each parent's role in relation to the child.

The home visitors' experiences confirm the expectation that the presence of fathers during intervention sessions can certainly be very supportive and helpful, but may in some cases be awkward or intrusive. In several cases the home visitors noticed that the mothers were more subdued and less outspoken when the fathers were present. The presence of the father can sometimes cause the mother to feel less confident and less inclined to be open about her parenting difficulties. In rare cases, the home visitor had to defend the mother, because the father was openly critical and unsupportive of her. It must be noted, however, that during the sessions only mothers' interactions with the children were filmed and discussed. Future studies may consider including the discussion of both mother-child and father-child interactions in the sessions to facilitate positive father involvement.

These booster sessions are very intensive for the home visitors because they try to work through as many themes from previous sessions as possible. The presence of the father often means many more questions to answer and investing in a positive relationship with a second person. In some ways, the booster sessions are easier because the bond with the mother has already been formed, and both home visitor and mother are now comfortable with each other. Often, mothers shared not only thoughts and insecurities about parenting issues with the home visitor, but also their experiences and feelings outside the parenting context. An important consequence of this intimacy is that the home visitor now has enough experience with the mother to offer advice specifically tailored to this mother's needs. This in turn will make it easier for the mother to receive and accept suggestions.

Age-specific challenges

The first five years of life are characterized by rapid developmental changes in physical, behavioral, social, and cognitive abilities, and the skills of, for example, a two-year-old are vastly more advanced than those of a one-year-old child. In addition, the family context may be subject to changes that are related to the age of the child. Because the SCRIPT study includes three age groups (one-, two-, and three-year-old children), the intervention process may be influenced by age-specific child and family characteristics. It is therefore important to be aware of age-specific issues that should be considered carefully during the intervention process.

One-year-old children

In the SCRIPT study, the one-year-old children are first seen at an average age of 16 months for the pretest lab session. The intervention sessions take place from age 18 to 26 months, and the posttest at age 28 months. Children generally have their second birthdays after the fourth or fifth intervention session.

One of the challenges of this age group is that the children are just starting to speak and are generally unable to express themselves clearly. Mothers of children in this age group often say that they find it very difficult to know what their child means by certain behaviors. This may lead to negative interpretations of behaviors that are really meant to get the parent's attention or to communicate frustration or unease. A related issue is that of age-appropriate expectations of children's abilities. Mothers sometimes tend to read too much hostile intent or too little need for closeness and proximity into their children's behaviors. It is important for the home visitor to make good use of the "speaking for the child" technique, which many mothers of very young children find very helpful.

Another challenge concerns the belief that it is unnecessary or premature to discipline one-year-old children. Many mothers feel that children this age do not understand discipline and that it is useless to try things like induction or postponement. During one home visit, a child had managed to get to one of the plants and happily started to grab hands full of earth. At this point, the mother told the home visitor that there was no point in intervening because the child would not understand, and that she would just clean up the mess later. In these situations the home visitor explained that even though the child may not always understand exactly what the mother says, it is helpful to get into the habit of explaining discipline situations early on. This way, both mother and child get used to communicating about challenging situations.

Two-year-old children

The two-year-old children in the SCRIPT study are first seen at an average age of 28 months for the pretest lab session. The intervention sessions take place from age 30 to 38 months, and the posttest at age 40 months.

In this age group, the birth of younger siblings is an important issue. In Dutch families, the time interval between the birth of two children is often two to three years. The arrival of a younger sibling may cause feelings of jealousy in the older child, which in turn may lead to negative and even aggressive behaviors toward the new child. In a study by Tremblay et al. (1999), physical aggression was more prevalent among preschoolers with siblings than preschoolers without siblings. Many parents in the intervention study mentioned that the child's behavior was particularly bad in relation to a younger brother or sister. Parents often find it difficult to divide their attention between the children, and one of the things that a home visitor may suggest is for the mother to try to spend some more one-on-one time with the older child. This will often have the effect of refueling children's ability to play by themselves without being jealous of or showing aggressive behaviors toward their sibling. In addition, the home visitor will point out that the discipline themes from session 1 (i.e., inductive discipline) and session 2 (i.e., positive reinforcement) are appropriate in these situations. The mother can explain to the child that aggressive behavior will hurt the child's brother or sister, and praise the child for instances when he or she is playing nicely with the younger sibling.

Three-year-old children

In the SCRIPT study, the three-year-old children are first seen at an average age of 40 months for the pretest lab session. The intervention sessions take place from age 42 to 50 months, and the posttest at age 52 months.

For parents of children in their fourth year of life, one of the biggest challenges regarding discipline is the fact that three-year-olds have mastered considerable verbal skills and are not afraid to use them in conflict situations. At this age, children talk back and challenge their parents' discipline attempts by using their own unshakeable logic. One mother's attempt to postpone buying her daughter an ice cream ("You can have an ice cream later") was immediately disqualified by her daughter who responded, "But I won't be hungry later!" For the home visitors, it is important to build mothers' confidence in their ability to cope with these situations and to provide alternatives for coercive interaction patterns.

Another challenge at this age is the upcoming transition to elementary school. Most children in the Netherlands go to elementary school at the age of four. In the SCRIPT study, the children in the oldest age group turn four toward the end of the intervention program. In the six months before that time, many mothers report that their children were especially difficult. Mothers feel that their children are getting too old for the childcare center or play group, while they are still too young for school, and that the children become bored easily, which leads to negative behavior. In addition to showing empathy for this predicament, the home visitor may suggest ways to engage the child in more challenging activities at home, for instance, by giving the child some "responsible tasks" in the household or by introducing more challenging games to play.

Effectiveness of the sensitive discipline intervention (VIPP-SD)
Effects on parenting and child behavior

Intervention effects were investigated on three levels: on the level of maternal attitudes toward sensitive parenting and discipline, on the level of actual parenting behavior, and on the level of the child's behavior (Van Zeijl, Mesman,

Van IJzendoorn et al., 2006). To assess intervention effects on maternal attitudes (measured at posttest only), a MANOVA was performed on attitudes toward sensitivity and sensitive discipline, with experimental condition as the between-subjects factor. The combined dependent variables were significantly affected by the intervention, $F (2, 234) = 11.00, p < .01$, partial $\eta^2 = .09$. Univariate tests revealed that mothers in the intervention group had more favorable attitudes toward sensitivity ($F [1, 235] = 18.88, p < .01$, partial $\eta^2 = .07$) and sensitive discipline ($F [1, 235] = 4.49, p < .05$, partial $\eta^2 = .02$) than control group mothers at the posttest.

A repeated-measures MANOVA with experimental condition as the between-subjects factor and time as the within-subjects factor was performed to assess intervention effects on observed parenting behavior: maternal sensitivity, positive discipline, and negative discipline. The interaction effect for experimental condition by time was significant, $F (3, 233) = 4.19, p < .01$, partial $\eta^2 = .05$. Univariate tests showed that intervention mothers showed an increase of positive discipline over time ($F [1, 235] = 8.33, p < .01$, partial $\eta^2 = .03$), whereas the control group mothers did not show such an increase (see Figure 11.1).

To test whether the intervention affected externalizing child behaviors (overactive, oppositional, and aggressive behaviors), a repeated-measures

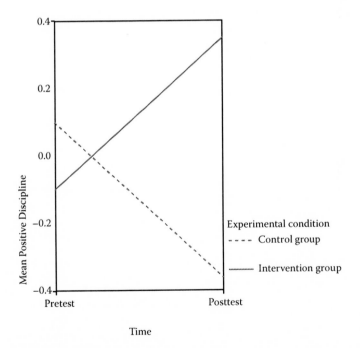

Figure 11.1   Regression lines for the interaction effect of time by experimental condition for maternal positive discipline.

MANCOVA was conducted, with experimental condition as the between-subjects factor and time as the within-subjects factor. Child temperament was entered as a covariate, because of the conceptual and statistical associations with externalizing behaviors. There was no interaction effect between experimental condition and time, F (3, 232) = 1.32, p = .27. However, the interaction of experimental condition by time by marital discord was significant, F (3, 227) = 3.02, p < .05, partial η^2 = .04. Univariate tests showed that the intervention was especially effective in decreasing overactive child behavior in families with more marital discord, F (1, 229) = 8.11, p < .01, partial η^2 = .03 (see Figure 11.2). Similarly, there was a significant interaction among experimental condition, time, and level of daily hassles, F (3, 227) = 2.77, p < .05, partial η^2 = .04. Particularly in families with more daily hassles, the intervention was effective in decreasing overactive child behavior, F (1, 229) = 6.79, p < .05, partial η^2 = .03 (see Figure 11.3). Treatment effectiveness was not different in the different age groups, and it was not related to child gender or temperament, maternal well-being, or professional training level of the intervener for any of the outcome variables.

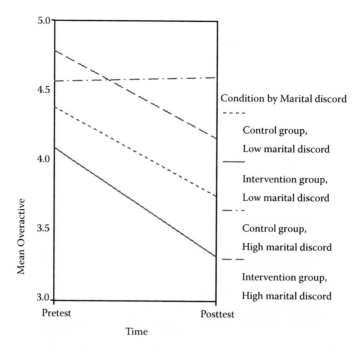

Figure 11.2   Regression lines for the interaction effect of time by experimental condition by marital discord for child overactive behavior.

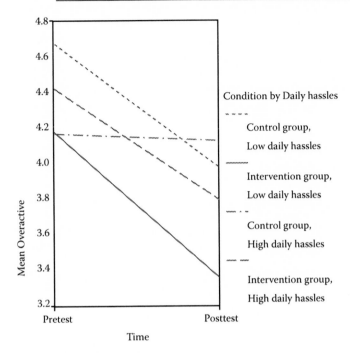

Figure 11.3   Regression lines for the interaction effect of time by experimental condition by daily hassles for child overactive behavior.

Process evaluation

Studies on (preventive) parenting interventions in early childhood mainly focus on program outcome, determining whether an intervention results in the desired effects. Equally relevant but underreported are the processes of these programs that may be crucial to their outcomes. Potentially important process elements of interventions include the relationship between mother and intervener (alliance), mothers' satisfaction with the program, maternal active implementation of skills (practicing or discussing the advice), father involvement, and program fidelity (for a description of process assessment see Stolk et al., in press).

Our results showed that the large majority of intervention participants found the video feedback informative (81%) and useful (76%). Further, 93% of the intervention mothers rated their relationship with the home visitor as (very) good. Almost half of the mothers in the intervention group (49%) reported having practiced the advice given during the sessions (reasonably) often or having read the booklet with advice after the intervention (47%). The large majority of mothers had discussed the advice with their partners (99%), with family members (83%), or with friends (75%). Fathers were invited to be present for the fifth and sixth intervention sessions (booster sessions). In 48% of the intervention sample, fathers did not make use of this invitation. Thirty-one percent of fathers were present in one intervention session, and 21% were present in both booster sessions. Finally, program fidelity was high: All participants received six home visits, each session was standardized in manuals, and intervener skills were extensively trained and supervised.

Results regarding the moderating role of process elements on intervention effectiveness showed that only mother-intervener alliance (as rated by the mother) was predictive of intervention outcome. Father involvement and maternal active implementation of skills were unrelated to the parenting outcomes of the intervention (for a full description of these results see Stolk et al., in press).

Discussion

VIPP-SD proved to be effective in enhancing maternal attitudes toward sensitivity and sensitive discipline, as well as increasing the use of positive discipline interactions in the intervention group compared to the control group (Van Zeijl, Mesman, Van IJzendoorn et al., 2006). However, the intervention program was not effective in decreasing negative discipline strategies such as physically interfering behavior, maybe because the intervention mainly reinforced positive interactions and effective parenting strategies. Observed sensitivity also remained unaffected. Thus, the VIPP-SD program proved to be effective in stimulating positive maternal attitudes toward sensitive child rearing and sensitive discipline, but observed behavioral changes were only noted for sensitive discipline, and not for sensitivity or negative discipline. It may be that because of the specific needs of our sample of children with high levels of externalizing problems, parents were more open to adapt their discipline strategies in conflict situations than to apply sensitive practices in other situations. Further, the intervention resulted in a decrease of overactive problem behaviors in children of families with high levels of marital discord or high levels of daily hassles (Van Zeijl, Mesman, Van IJzendoorn et al., 2006). The VIPP-SD program thus appeared to be most effective in families in greatest need of support. The intervention did not manage to decrease oppositional or aggressive problem behaviors. Overactive behaviors refer to the child's inclination for disruptive behavior, but to a less severe degree than oppositional or aggressive behaviors. The modest number of intervention sessions (four intervention sessions and two booster sessions) may have restricted its effectiveness to the less severe problem behaviors. Although there is some evidence that lower numbers of sessions may result in stronger intervention effects (Bakermans-Kranenburg et al., 2003), changes in children with high levels of quite severe problem behaviors may require a more intensive approach, and further investigations with varying numbers of intervention sessions are needed to test this hypothesis. Alternatively, the intervention effects on oppositional or aggressive behavior may become apparent or larger during the course of the child's later development (cf. Van Lier, Vuijk, & Crijnen, 2005). The effectiveness of the VIPP-SD intervention was not dependent on the specific age group (Van Zeijl, Mesman, Van IJzendoorn et al., 2006). Families with older children profited as much from the intervention as families with younger children. We may conclude that the home visitors adequately met the needs and challenges of families with children in the whole age range. Finally, program fidelity was high, and the large majority of participating mothers were positive about the intervention and the interveners.

Conclusions

The SCRIPT study in this chapter describes an intervention program aimed at enhancing parental sensitivity and effective discipline, reducing children's externalizing problems, and preventing future antisocial behavior. The intervention program is innovative in that it combines insights from two major theoretical frameworks with respect to the role of parent-child interactions in the development of child externalizing problems: attachment theory and coercion theory. The inclusion of three age groups allows for comparisons of effectiveness between ages, and potentially the identification of an optimal age for early interventions in this area. The experimental case-control design and the use of multiple methods (questionnaires and observations) and multiple informants (mothers, fathers, trained observers) ensure the scientific validity of this study. VIPP-SD proved to be effective in enhancing maternal attitudes toward positive parenting. Moreover, intervention mothers used more positive discipline interactions than control mothers, and the intervention resulted in a decrease of their children's overactive problem behavior. Finally, VIPP-SD was equally effective for all age groups from one to three years, and in some respects particularly effective for families with high stress levels.

Acknowledgments

This intervention study is part of the research project Screening and Intervention of Problem Behavior in Toddlerhood (SCRIPT). The authors thank all parents and children who participated in the study, as well as all students who assisted in various phases of the SCRIPT project. Judi Mesman is supported by the Netherlands Organization for Scientific Research (NWO VENI grant). The study is supported by grant 2200.0097 from Zorg Onderzoek Nederland (Netherlands Organization for Health Research and Development) to Marinus H. van IJzendoorn and Femmie Juffer.

12

Video-feedback intervention to promote positive parenting

Evidence-based intervention for enhancing sensitivity and security

Marinus H. van IJzendoorn,
Marian J. Bakermans-Kranenburg,
and Femmie Juffer

*Centre for Child and Family Studies,
Leiden University, the Netherlands*

This closing chapter briefly recapitulates the content and effectiveness of our approach of Video-feedback Intervention to promote Positive Parenting (VIPP). This preventive intervention program is an example of a focused and relatively brief intervention in the socioemotional domain that appears to be effective. The meta-analytic evidence for this type of intervention is summarized, including its potential to counteract the disorganizing influence of parents suffering from unresolved loss or other trauma. Then a profile of potentially effective interventions is provided. The role of fathers as intervention participants is discussed, and the issue of behavioral change versus representational continuity is addressed. We argue for a piecemeal approach to constructing effective interventions, starting with testing the effectiveness of small building blocks or intervention modules (less is more) that after successful evaluations might be combined into an even more effective overall broadband program for populations that are difficult to involve in intervention programs.

Video-feedback intervention to promote positive parenting

More than 20 years ago, a first attempt at enhancing parental sensitivity through an attachment-based videotaped model of sensitive parenting was implemented, but it proved to be ineffective (Lambermon & Van IJzendoorn, 1989). With videotaped model behavior parents remain focused on superficial appearances of the dyad involved. Parents need a mirror of their own daily interactions with their child to change their behavior. Based on attachment theory (Ainsworth, Blehar, Waters, & Wall, 1978; Bowlby, 1982), a preliminary version of the current video-feedback intervention program was developed in a study of families with adopted children (Juffer, 1993). This program was the first to use *in vivo* video feedback, and its effectiveness in the short- and long-term has been confirmed (see Chapter 9). After this successful probing, the current protocol of the VIPP approach was developed to break the intergenerational cycle of insecure attachment in a group of mothers who were at risk for developing an insecure attachment relationship with their child because of their own insecure mental representations of attachment (see Chapters 3 and 6).

To reach this goal, two types of interventions were developed and implemented — interventions directed at the behavioral level and interventions directed at the representational level — to pave the way for subsequent behavioral changes. The first program, Video-feedback Intervention to promote Positive Parenting (VIPP), aims at enhancing maternal sensitive behavior through providing personal video feedback, combined with brochures on sensitive responding in daily situations. The second intervention, VIPP-R (VIPP combined with representational methods), includes additional discussions about past and present attachment, aiming at affecting the mother's mental representation of attachment. Moreover, building a supporting relationship between the intervener and the mother was considered a crucial element of both types of intervention (Bowlby, 1988).

The two programs are short-term and home based. In both types of intervention there are specific themes for each session, and guidelines for each session are described in a detailed protocol (see Chapter 2; for a case study see Chapter 3). Both intervention modalities appeared to be effective in enhancing maternal sensitivity, in particular in families with highly reactive children (see Chapter 6). The study shows that some children may be more susceptible to the influence of parenting than other children, and that temperamental reactivity may be involved (Belsky, 1997, 2005). Furthermore, VIPP implemented in the baby's first year of life significantly protected children from developing clinical externalizing problem behaviors at preschool age (Klein Velderman et al., 2006b).

Multiple tests of VIPP

The VIPP programs have been used in several intervention studies on various samples in different countries. In Italy, they were implemented with two different clinical samples: preterm infants and infants affected by atopic dermatitis (see Chapter 7). In both groups the clinical characteristics of the child may hamper smooth and harmonious mother-infant interactions and increase the risk for the development of an insecure attachment relationship. In both clinical groups the children of insecure mothers appeared to profit most from the intervention enhancing attachment security, whereas children of secure mothers tended to become less secure. The brief attachment-based intervention was also effective in enhancing maternal sensitivity, again only in families with an insecure mother (see Chapter 7). In the United Kingdom, Woolley, Hertzmann, and Stein (see Chapter 8) used a VIPP-based intervention with video feedback to help mothers with postnatal eating disorders (of the bulimic type) with their infants during the first year of life. Mothers' extreme concerns about food, body shape, and weight have been found to interfere with their parenting, especially during mealtimes. In particular, they have difficulty noticing, interpreting, and sensitively responding to infant cues. Stein and colleagues (see Chapter 8) found promising outcomes for VIPP in this specific clinical sample.

Furthermore, Elicker, Georgescu, and Bartsch (see Chapter 10) translated VIPP into a program for professional childcare providers in the United States who work with children from birth to three years. The principles and methods of VIPP were adapted to create a four-week training program (called Tuning In) that is delivered to infant-toddler caregivers in childcare centers. The pilot study reported in Chapter 10 shows the feasibility of the VIPP approach in the context of group care. Whether the adapted program will be successful in enhancing the professional caregivers' sensitivity to the needs of the children in their care remains to be seen. Preliminary results of the large-scale randomized controlled trial are promising: Elicker and his colleagues report that the caregivers involved in this trial are enthusiastic about the potential of the adapted VIPP for training childcare providers in sensitivity in a group care setting.

Last, an intervention program was developed extending VIPP with components to enhance parental discipline strategies (promoting sensitive discipline; see Chapters 2 and 11). This VIPP-SD program is a synthesis of the Patterson and Bowlby approaches to parenting, and it showed to be especially effective in those families in which children are at risk for externalizing behavior problems and require structuring and limit setting in a warm, sensitive atmosphere. Whereas infants may only need sensitive parenting, toddlers in addition require careful structuring of their behavior, and they at times need strict but sensitive limit setting as well. The VIPP-SD program has been tested in the Netherlands in

a randomized case-control study aimed at reducing oppositional and externalizing problem behaviors in one-, two-, and three-year-olds (see Chapter 11). In
this large randomized controlled trial the effectiveness of VIPP-SD was demonstrated independent of children's age (van Zeijl, Mesman, Van IJzendoorn et al.,
2006; see Chapter 11).

Meta-analytic support for brief interventions with a behavioral focus

As presented in Chapters 4 and 5, a narrative review and a series of meta-analyses
on the effectiveness of interventions were conducted with reported results on
sensitivity and infant-parent attachment. The meta-analytic results showed that
randomized interventions that only focus on sensitive maternal behavior — like
our VIPP approach — are most effective in changing insensitive parenting as
well as infant attachment insecurity, although the size of the combined effects
remains in the small to modest range. Surprisingly, the most effective interventions not always use a large number of sessions with the families, and they do not
necessarily start early in life or even before birth. On the contrary, evidence was
found for fewer contacts (up to 16 sessions) being somewhat more effective, and
the same goes for interventions starting six months after birth or later. Effective
intervention modalities were effective regardless of the presence or absence of
multiple problems in the family (see Chapter 5).

What might explain the effectiveness of sensitivity-focused interventions such as
the VIPP? First, long-term and broadly focused support of multiproblem families
in coping with their daily hassles may be needed to enable them to subsequently
focus on sensitivity and representations. However, this broadband effort may
take too much time and energy away from a potentially effective, goal-directed
intervention approach. Second, sensitivity-focused interventions are characterized by well-defined and relatively modest aims. In broadband approaches
with multiple goals it may be more difficult to bring about a significant effect
on one of the many aspects that are included in the intervention. Third, the
average intervener may more easily understand and learn the protocol of sensitivity-focused interventions, and focused interventions thus may capitalize on
the intervener's expertise. Interventions with broader aims and methods need
intensively trained, highly qualified interveners (as, for example, in the Circle
of Security Project; Marvin, Cooper, Hoffman, & Powell, 2002), and they may
be rather scarce.

Fourth, treatment adherence or fidelity may diverge in the two types of interventions. Whereas it appears quite possible for interveners to stick to the protocol of a sensitivity-focused program, it may be much more difficult for them to

implement a long-term broadband intervention in a standard way. Last, interveners may easily become overburdened, and staff turnover may increase with the duration of the intervention (see Spieker, Nelson, DeKlyen, & Staerkel, 2005). Also, long-term interventions may create unfeasible obligations for the participating families, resulting in high attrition. The intervener's first impressions and satisfaction experienced during the first home visit were found to predict increases in maternal sensitivity in one of our studies (see Chapter 3), which also indicates the potentially deleterious effects of staff turnover and the need for continuity of interveners during the intervention process.

The most powerful aspect of sensitivity-focused interventions might be that the parent is taught to closely observe the child's signals and reactions. What we aim at with the video-feedback intervention of VIPP is enabling the parent to get the feedback from the child rather than from an intervener. When the parent begins to see the grateful smile of the child as a reaction to sensitive parenting (chain of sensitivity; see Chapter 2), the child takes the intervener's place. This mechanism of the children's reinforcement of their parents' successful interactive behaviors may partly explain the effects of relatively brief interventions, because the process of feedback is meant to continue after the intervener leaves the home. The parent is thus blessed with the most continuous intervener one can think of.

VIPP and disorganized attachment

Disorganized attachment arguably is the most insecure type of attachment, and it constitutes a risk factor for developing later psychopathology: Disorganized infants show signs of problematic regulation of negative emotions in stressful situations, they are more inclined to display externalizing behavior problems later in childhood, and they are at risk for a tendency to dissociate. Disorganized attachment has been defined as the (momentary) breakdown of the usual, organized (secure or insecure) attachment strategy (see Chapter 1). Although disorganized attachment should not be equated to reactive attachment disorder (Zeanah & Smyke, 2005), extreme indications of disorganization may be regarded as psychiatric attachment disturbance with more or less severe symptoms and consequences (Van IJzendoorn & Bakermans-Kranenburg, 2003). Disorganized attachment is suggested to be caused by frightening (or frightened) parental behavior (Main & Hesse, 1990) and by (shared or unique) environmental factors such as loss or trauma in the parents around the birth of their child (Main & Hesse, 1990; Schuengel, Bakermans-Kranenburg, & Van IJzendoorn, 1999). In a behavior genetic study some evidence was found for the predicted influence of unique environmental factors in determining disorganized attachments in twins (Bokhorst et al., 2003).

To explore the effectiveness of VIPP in reducing symptoms of disorganized attachments, the videotaped Strange Situations (Ainsworth et al., 1978) from the intervention study of adopted children were coded (see Chapter 9) with the system for disorganized attachment (Main & Solomon, 1990), and tested whether the brief behaviorally focused intervention also had managed to reduce attachment disorganization.The video-feedback intervention influenced attachment disorganization in a positive way, although the program was never intended to impact this type of attachment behavior (see Chapter 9). Because of the surprising nature of this outcome, we decided to conduct a meta-analysis on all intervention studies that reported on disorganization of attachment.

Ten studies were found with 15 preventive interventions that included disorganized attachment as an outcome measure (see Chapter 5). On the basis of contrast analyses we found that interventions may be most effective in decreasing disorganization in samples with high levels of disorganization, when they start after six months of infant's age, when it is the infant who is primarily at risk, and when a sensitivity-focused approach is used (Bakermans-Kranenburg, Van IJzendoorn, & Juffer, 2005). Two interventions with positive effects on disorganization had these four characteristics in common: The first study is on adopted children (see Chapter 9) and included a short-term attachment-based intervention with video feedback, and the second intervention is presented in Sajaniemi et al.'s (2001) study that explicitly aimed at enhancing the parents' ability to read the messages of their extremely low birth weight infants.

Effective sensitivity-focused interventions may have successfully affected parents' attention processes, directing and focusing the parents' attention to observations of their children in the here and now. Schuengel and his colleagues (1999) documented the protective role of mothers' secure mental representations of attachment in the development of infant disorganization. In the same vein, an infant may be a more salient focus of attention for sensitive mothers than for insensitive mothers. Close monitoring of infants leaves little room for signals and thoughts from other sources. Sensitive mothers may monitor their infants more closely and may thus experience fewer moments of absorption or intrusions of distracting thoughts. As suggested elsewhere (Bakermans-Kranenburg et al., 2005), interventions that teach parents to follow their children's lead or to observe their children by means of video-feedback focus parents' attention on the children's behavior, thereby diminishing dissociative processes in the presence of the children.

Fathers and siblings

Is it possible or desirable to involve fathers in attachment-based interventions? In our meta-analysis on attachment-based interventions (Bakermans-Kranenburg,

Van IJzendoorn, & Juffer, 2003), interventions involving fathers appeared to be significantly more effective than interventions focusing on mothers only. This outcome, however, is based on analyses with only three studies with fathers, comprising 81 participants. Several authors have argued that families should be considered a system (e.g., Cowan, 1997; Byng-Hall, 1999) and that interventions should use the system characteristics of the family to enhance the effectiveness of interventions. Egeland, Weinfeld, Bosquet, and Cheng (2000), for example, suggested that family interventions should involve mothers as well as fathers to strengthen mothers' influence and to stimulate family support for changes in maternal behavior.

Although the division of child-rearing tasks and roles is rather skewed even in modern families with two breadwinners (Van Dijk & Siegers, 1996), fathers do take part in rearing their children and may benefit from interventions as much as mothers do. Furthermore, fathers who are involved in preventive interventions may motivate their partners to continue participation and to practice new behaviors at home. In VIPP-SD we recommend including fathers in some of the later sessions, in which previously trained components of sensitivity are rehearsed with the mother (see Chapter 11). The presence of the father may enhance the effectiveness of the intervention as well as the permanence of the changes in maternal behavior.

It should be noted, however, that paternal involvement may be counterproductive as far as the mothers are concerned. In two of the three studies involving fathers, the effects on paternal sensitivity were large, but similar effects on maternal sensitivity were absent. In fact, in one study the mothers showed much less improvement in their sensitivity than the fathers (Scholz & Samuels, 1992), and in the other study the intervention effects were even negative for mothers (Dickie & Gerber, 1980). In the third study, separate effect sizes for mothers and fathers could not be computed (Metzl, 1980). Several explanations for these disappointing findings may be considered. First, if fathers are included in the intervention efforts, less attention might be paid to the mothers' needs and abilities. Second, when fathers are also involved in the intervention, mothers may underestimate the importance of their practicing new child-rearing insights and skills. Replications may shed light on the positive as well as the possible negative outcomes of interventions involving fathers and mothers.

Considering the family as a system also means that each of the siblings should be taken into account. In this respect, current intervention experiments may underestimate their influence because of the unstudied effects on other siblings in the family. It should be noted that our twin study on attachment and sensitivity found a rather impressive consistency of maternal sensitivity across the various children within the family (Fearon et al., 2000), confirming the consistency of maternal sensitivity found in an earlier study on siblings (Van IJzendoorn et al., 2000). In nontwin siblings, however, second-born children appeared to be treated on average substantially less sensitively than firstborn children (Van IJzendoorn et al., 2000). Therefore, interventions that succeed in enhancing maternal sensitivity to their firstborn infants may lead to enhanced shared sensitivity from which later-born children may profit as well.

Behavior and representation

Behaviorally focused interventions such as VIPP might create short-term changes in maternal behavior that are insufficiently ingrained in parents' attachment representations and parenting routines to affect the relationship with the infant. Interventions may create discrepancies between the representational and the behavioral level, that is, they may be effective in enhancing parental sensitivity without influencing parental representations (Van IJzendoorn, Juffer, & Duyvesteyn, 1995; see Figure 1.1 in Chapter 1). If parents only acquire new behavioral strategies to interact with their infant, they may not be able to cope with the attachment needs of the developing child. In that case, the generalizability of the intervention might be restricted. In the long run, the discrepancy between the representational level and the behavioral level may even be counterproductive, because the child may experience a discontinuity between the sensitive parent in the early years and the lack of parental sensitivity later on.

The parent's increased sensitivity may induce secure attachment behavior in the child and smooth infant-parent interactions, and these may, after some time, result in a favorable change at the level of the parent's representation (Fraiberg, Adelson, & Shapiro, 1975). Longitudinal follow-up studies are needed to test which of the two scenarios is more plausible. In the VIPP approach, the child may become the most important change agent as his or her behavior reinforces the efforts of parents to be more sensitive, and successfully synchronous interactions might lead to reshaping established working models of attachment relationships in the child as well as the adult. The differential effectiveness of VIPP and VIPP-R has not yet been established. It is not clear whether the representational component is needed at all to induce more permanent changes in sensitivity or attachment. Studies comparing the two approaches in different groups of parents and children should decide what works best for whom.

Reconciling focused and broadband interventions

In some groups VIPP might need to be embedded in a broader framework. For example, support of adolescent mothers in finding a job may be an essential ingredient of a behavioral intervention program, as it motivates the participants to keep participating in both the intervention and control groups. In line with the idea that treatments should be focused and well defined, the behavioral intervention is embedded in this contextual support, and the "hard core" of the intervention remains unique for the experimental group. In fact, we argue here for comparisons between two interventions, with one crucial intervention module added to one of these interventions. In these cases, broadband interventions may motivate participants to enter and stay in the intervention study, and at the same time they may deliver reliable and valid knowledge about the effectiveness of an important component of the intervention.

From a methodological perspective the focused approach should be preferred as well. Broadband interventions may be very effective on certain outcome measures, but it remains unclear exactly what ingredients are responsible for such effects. For example, the intervention project of Kagitcibasi (1996) proved to be rather effective, even after seven years, in terms of such pertinent outcome variables as school performance and school failure. However, the two-year-long intervention was a combination of center-based group parent training and home-based individual cognitive stimulation. For dissemination of the program and for enhancing its cost effectiveness, it is necessary to know whether the parent training or the cognitive stimulation was more effective, or whether the interaction between the two components was crucial to its success. A similar problem may arise with VIPP-based programs such as Tuning In (Chapter 10) if a large part of the program would involve supporting effective teamwork and better management of the childcare center.

Here we argue for a piecemeal approach to constructing effective interventions, starting with testing the effectiveness of small building blocks or intervention modules such as VIPP that, after successful evaluations, should be combined into an even more effective overall program. Such an approach may prevent foreclosure and political abuse of seemingly unsuccessful intervention packages (Spieker et al., 2005). Also, the modular approach may fit nicely into a stepwise upgrading of intervention intensity in real life, in which one might start with a single intervention module addressing the most common problems, and continue by adding more modules when the earlier intervention efforts appear to be insufficient.

Conclusions

VIPP is an intervention approach with a behavioral focus on parental sensitivity. The previous chapters showed how effective this approach is in various contexts and groups. VIPP is effective not only in nonclinical families, but also in families in which the parents or the children suffer from psychological or health problems. The VIPP protocol can easily be adapted to the specific needs and potentials of the (clinical) families or group care setting involved. We feel that the current evidence does not yet show the superiority of the intervention modality that is supplemented with representational discussions (VIPP-R): Purely behaviorally oriented interventions seem equally effective, and they are more cost effective.

Some parents and some children might be more susceptible to intervention efforts that change their behavior than other parents and children. This differential susceptibility may be linked to temperamental reactivity or perhaps to other constitutional factors of the children, or to insecure representations of childhood attachment experiences in the parents. Further research is needed into the crucial question of what works best for whom in what context. In general, however, the VIPP approach can be said to be successful, not only in enhancing sensitivity and security of attachment, but also in preventing externalizing problem behaviors.

The evidence base for VIPP is not restricted to the empirical studies reported in this book. Support for VIPP also resides in the findings of several meta-analyses documenting that behaviorally focused and rather brief interventions appear to be most effective (less is more) in enhancing maternal sensitivity as well as in promoting children's attachment security and preventing or reducing disorganized attachment. In the preparation of young parents for the difficult task of rearing children, VIPP may become an effective and indispensable tool to promote children's positive development and to prevent children's relational and behavioral problems.

Acknowledgments

This chapter is based on Van IJzendoorn, Bakermans-Kranenburg, and Juffer (2005).

References

References indicated with an asterisk refer to studies included in the narrative review (Chapter 4) and meta-analysis of attachment-based interventions (Chapter 5).

Abrams, K. Y. (2000). *Pathways to disorganization: A study concerning varying types of parental frightened and frightening behaviors as related to infant disorganized attachment.* Unpublished doctoral dissertation, University of California at Berkeley.

Abrams, K., Rifkin, A., & Hesse, E. (2006). Examining the role of parental frightened/ frightening subtypes in predicting disorganized attachment within a brief observation procedure. *Development and Psychopathology, 18,* 345–361.

Achenbach, T. M. (1991). *Manual for the Child Behavior Checklist/4-18 and 1991 profile.* Burlington: University of Vermont, Department of Psychiatry.

Achenbach, T. M., & Rescorla, L. A. (2000). *Manual for the ASEBA Preschool Forms and Profiles.* Burlington: University of Vermont, Research Center for Children, Youth and Families.

Ainsworth, M. D. S. (1967). *Infancy in Uganda: Infant care and the growth of love.* Oxford: Johns Hopkins Press.

Ainsworth, M. D. S. (1989). Attachment beyond infancy. *American Psychologist, 34,* 932–937.

Ainsworth, M. D. S., Bell, S. M., & Stayton, D. J. (1971). Individual differences in Strange Situation behavior of one-year-olds. In H. R. Schaffer (Ed.), *The origins of human relations* (pp. 17–56). London: Academic Press.

Ainsworth, M. D. S., Bell, S. M., & Stayton, D. J. (1974). Infant-mother attachment and social development: Socialization as a product of reciprocal responsiveness to signals. In M. P. M. Richards (Ed.), *The integration of a child into a social world* (pp. 99–135). London: Cambridge University Press.

Ainsworth, M. D. S., Blehar, M. C., Waters, E., & Wall, S. (1978). *Patterns of attachment. A psychological study of the Strange Situation.* Hillsdale, NJ: Lawrence Erlbaum.

Alink, L. R. A., Mesman, J., Van Zeijl, J., Stolk, M. N., Juffer, F., Koot, H. M., Bakermans-Kranenburg, M. J., & Van IJzendoorn, M. H. (2006). The early childhood aggression curve: Development of physical aggression in 10- to 50-month-old children. *Child Development, 77,* 954–966.

Anisfeld, A., Casper, V., Nozyce, M., & Cunningham, N. (1990). Does infant carrying promote attachment? An experimental study of the effects of increased physical contact on the development of attachment. *Child Development, 61,* 1617–1627.*

Armstrong, K. L., Fraser, J. A., Dadds, M. R., & Morris, J. (1999). A randomized, controlled trial of nurse home visiting to vulnerable families with newborns. *Journal of Paediatric Child Health, 35,* 237–244.*

Arnett, J. (1989). Caregivers in day-care centers: Does training matter? *Journal of Applied Developmental Psychology, 10,* 541–552.

Asch, S. E. (1946). Forming impressions of personality. *Journal of Abnormal and Social Psychology, 41,* 258–290.

Atkinson, L., Niccols, A., Paglia, A., Coolbear, J., Parker, K. C. H., Poulton, L., et al. (2000). A meta-analysis of time between maternal sensitivity and attachment assessments: Implications for internal working models in infancy/toddlerhood. *Journal of Social and Personal Relationships, 17,* 791–810.

Bakermans-Kranenburg, M. J., Juffer, F., & Van IJzendoorn, M. H. (1998). Intervention with video feedback and attachment discussions: Does type of maternal insecurity make a difference? *Infant Mental Health Journal, 19,* 202–219.*

Bakermans-Kranenburg, M. J., & Van IJzendoorn, M. H. (1993). A psychometric study of the Adult Attachment Interview: Reliability and discriminant validity. *Developmental Psychology, 29,* 870–879.

Bakermans-Kranenburg, M. J., Van IJzendoorn, M. H., & Juffer, F. (2003). Less is more: Meta-analyses of sensitivity and attachment interventions in early childhood. *Psychological Bulletin, 129,* 195–215.

Bakermans-Kranenburg, M. J., Van IJzendoorn, M. H., & Juffer, F. (2005). Disorganized infant attachment and preventive interventions: A review and meta-analysis. *Infant Mental Health Journal, 26,* 191–216.

Bandura, A. (1973). *Aggression. A social learning analysis.* Englewood Cliffs, NJ: Prentice-Hall.

Bandura, A., & Walters, R. H. (1963). *Social learning and personality development.* New York: Holt, Rinehart & Winston.

Barnard, K. E., Magyary, D., Summer, G., Booth, C. L., Mitchell, S. K., & Spieker, S. (1988). Prevention of parenting alterations for women with low social support. *Psychiatry, 51,* 248–253.*

Barnett, B., Blignault, I., Holmes, S., Payne, A., & Parker, G. (1987). Quality of attachment in a sample of 1-year-old Australian children. *Journal of the American Academy of Child and Adolescent Psychiatry, 26,* 303–307.*

Barrera, M. E., Rosenbaum, P. L., & Cunningham, C. E. (1986). Early home intervention with low-birth-weight infants and their parents. *Child Development, 57,* 20–33.*

Beckwith, L. (1988). Intervention with disadvantaged parents of sick preterm infants. *Psychiatry, 51,* 242–247.*

Beckwith, L. (2000). Prevention science and prevention programs. In Ch. H. Zeanah (Ed.), *Handbook of infant mental health* (2nd ed., pp. 439–456). New York: Guilford Press.

Belsky, J. (1997). Theory testing, effect-size evaluation, and differential susceptibility to rearing influences: The case of mothering and attachment. *Child Development, 68,* 598–600.

Belsky, J. (1999a). Modern evolutionary theory and patterns of attachment. In J. Cassidy & P. R. Shaver (Eds.), *Handbook of attachment: Theory, research, and clinical applications* (pp. 141–161). New York: Guilford Press.

Belsky, J. (1999b). Interactional and contextual determinants of attachment security. In J. Cassidy & P. R. Shaver (Eds.), *Handbook of attachment: Theory, research, and clinical applications* (pp. 249–264). New York: Guilford Press.

Belsky, J. (2005). The developmental and evolutionary psychology of intergenerational transmission of attachment. In C. S. Carter, L. Ahnert, K. E. Grossmann, S. B. Hrdy, M. E. Lamb, S. W. Porges, & N. Sacher (Eds.), *Attachment and bonding: A new synthesis* (pp. 169–178). Cambridge, MA: MIT Press.

Belsky, J., Woodworth, S., & Crnic, K. (1996). Trouble in the second year: Three questions about family interaction. *Child Development, 67,* 556–578.

Benasich, A. A., Brooks-Gunn, J., & Clewell, B. C. (1992). How do mothers benefit from early intervention programs? *Journal of Applied Developmental Psychology, 13,* 363–376.

Benoit, D., Madigan, S., Lecce, S., Shea, B., & Goldberg, S. (2001). Atypical maternal behavior toward feeding-disordered infants before and after intervention. *Infant Mental Health Journal, 22,* 611–626.*

Bimmel, N., Juffer, F., Van IJzendoorn, M. H., & Bakermans-Kranenburg, M. J. (2003). Problem behavior of internationally adopted adolescents: A review and meta-analysis. *Harvard Review of Psychiatry, 11,* 64–77.

Biringen, Z., Robinson, J., & Emde, R. N. (2000). The Emotional Availability Scales, 2nd edition. *Attachment and Human Development, 2,* 251–255.

Black, M. M., & Teti, L. O. (1997). Promoting mealtime communication between adolescent mothers and their infants through videotape. *Pediatrics, 99,* 432–437.*

Blair, C. (2002). Early intervention for low birth weight, preterm infants: The role of negative emotionality in the specification of effects. *Development and Psychopathology, 14,* 311–332.

Block, J. H., & Block, J. (1980). The role of ego-control and ego-resiliency in the organization of behavior. In W. A. Collins (Ed.), *Minnesota symposium on child psychology* (pp. 39–101). Hillsdale, NJ: Erlbaum.

Blok, H., Fukkink, R. G., Gebhardt, E. C., & Leseman, P. P. M. (2005). The relevance of delivery mode and other programme characteristics for the effectiveness of early childhood intervention. *International Journal of Behavioral Development, 29,* 35–47.

Bloom, P. J. (1996). The quality of work life in NAEYC accredited and non-accredited early childhood programs. *Early Education and Development, 7,* 301–317.

Bokhorst, C. L., Bakermans-Kranenburg, M. J., Fearon, P., Van IJzendoorn, M. H., Fonagy, P., & Schuengel, C. (2003). The importance of shared environment in mother-infant attachment security: A behavioral genetic study. *Child Development, 74,* 1769–1782.

Borenstein, M., Rothstein, D., & Cohen, J. (2000). *Comprehensive meta-analysis. A computer program for research synthesis.* Englewood, NJ: Biostat.

Bouchard, T. J., Jr., & Loehlin, J.C. (2001). Genes, evolution, and personality. *Behavior Genetics, 31,* 243–273.

Bowlby, J. (1944). Forty-four juvenile thieves: Their characteristics and home life. *International Journal of Psychoanalysis, 25,* 19–52.

Bowlby, J. (1969). *Attachment and loss* (Vol. 1). *Attachment.* New York: Penguin Books.

Bowlby, J. (1973). *Attachment and loss* (Vol. 2). *Separation: Anxiety and anger.* New York: Penguin Books.

Bowlby, J. (1980). *Attachment and loss* (Vol. 3). *Loss: Sadness and depression.* New York: Penguin Books.

Bowlby, J. (1982). *Attachment and loss* (Vol. 1). *Attachment* (2nd ed.). New York: Basic Books.

Bowlby, J. (1988). *A secure base: Clinical applications of attachment theory.* London: Routledge.

Bradley, R. H. (1993). Children's home environments, health, behavior, and intervention efforts: A review using the HOME inventory as a marker measure. *Genetic, Social, and General Psychology Monographs, 119,* 439–490.

Bradley, R. H. (2004, July 10–13). *Why some interventions work.* Paper presented at the biennial meeting of the ISSBD, Ghent, Belgium.

Bradley, R. H., Whiteside, L., Mundfrom, D. J., Casey, P. H., Caldwell, B. M., & Barrett, K. (1994). Inpact of the infant health and development program (IHDP) on the home environments of infants born prematurely and with low birthweight. *Journal of Educational Psychology, 86,* 531–541.

Brazelton, T. B. (1994). Touchpoints: Opportunities for preventing problems in the parent-child relationship. *Acta Paediatrica, 394,* 35–39.

Bretherton, I. (1991). The roots and growing points of attachment theory. In C. M. Parkes, J. Stevenson-Hinde, & P. Marris (Eds.), *Attachment across the life cycle* (pp. 9–32). London: Tavistock/Routledge.

Bridges, L. J., Palmer, S. A., Morales, M., Hurtado, M., & Tsai, D. (1992). Agreement between affectively based observational and parent-report measures of temperament at infant age 6 months. *Infant Behavior and Development, 16,* 501–506.

Brinker, R. P., Baxter, A., & Butler, L. S. (1994). An ordinal pattern analysis of four hypotheses describing the interactions between drug-addicted, chronically disadvantaged, and middle-class mother-infant dyads. *Child Development, 65,* 361–372.*

Bronfenbrenner, U. (1974). Is early intervention effective? *Teachers College Record, 76,* 279–303.

Brophy, H. E. (1997). Adolescent mothers and their infants: A home-based crisis prevention effort. *Dissertation Abstracts International, 58,* 3309.*

Brown, R. D. (1970). Experienced and inexperienced counselors' first impressions of clients and case outcomes: Are first impressions lasting? *Journal of Counseling Psychology, 17,* 550–558.

Bruch, H. (1973). *Eating disorders, obesity and anorexia nervosa and the person within.* New York: Basic Books.

Burchinal, M., Roberts, J., Nabors, L., & Bryant, D. (1996). Quality of center child care and infant cognitive and language development. *Child Development, 67,* 606–620.

Bustan, D., & Sagi, A. (1984). Effects of early hospital-based intervention on mothers and their preterm infants. *Journal of Applied Developmental Psychology, 5,* 305–317.*

Byng-Hall, J. (1999). Family and couple therapy: Toward greater security. In J. Cassidy & P. R. Shaver, *Handbook of attachment. Theory, research, and clinical applications* (pp. 625–648). New York: Guilford Press.

Caldwell, B. M., & Bradley, R. H. (1984). *Home observation for measurement of the environment.* Little Rock: University of Arkansas at Little Rock.

Campbell, S. B. (1995). Behavior problems in preschool children: A review of recent research. *Journal of Child Psychology and Psychiatry, 36*, 113–149.

Campbell, S. B. (2002). *Behavior problems in preschool children.* New York: Guilford Press.

Campbell, S. B., & Ewing, L. J. (1990). Follow-up of hard-to-manage preschoolers: Adjustment at age 9 and predictors of continuing symptoms. *Journal of Child Psychology and Psychiatry, 31*, 871–889.

Campos, J. J., Barrett, K., Lamb, M., Goldsmith, H., & Sternberg, C. (1983). Socioemotional development. In P. H. Mussen (Eds.), *Infancy and developmental psychology* (pp. 783–915). New York: Wiley.

Capps, L., Sigman, M., & Mundy, P. (1994). Attachment security in children with autism. *Development and Psychopathology, 6*, 249–261.

Capurso, M. (2001). *Gioco e studio in ospedale [Play and study at hospital].* Trento, Italy: Erikson.

Carter, J. C., & Fairburn, C. G. (1995). Treating binge eating problems in primary care. *Addictive Behaviors, 20*, 765–772.

Carter, S. L., Osofsky, J. D., & Hann, D. M. (1991). Speaking for the baby: A therapeutic intervention with adolescent mothers and their infants. *Infant Mental Health Journal, 12*, 291–301.

Cassibba, R., Van IJzendoorn, M. H., Bruno, S., & Coppola, G. (2004). Attachment of mothers and children with recurrent asthmatic bronchitis. *Journal of Asthma, 41*, 419–431.

Cassibba, R., Van IJzendoorn, M. H., Coppola, G., Bruno, S., Costantini, A., Gatto, S., et al. (In preparation). *Enhancing maternal sensitivity and infant attachment security in families with dermatitis and premature children: A short-term intervention study with video-feedback.*

Cassidy, J. (1999). The nature of the child's ties. In J. Cassidy & P. R. Shaver (Eds.), *Handbook of attachment: Theory, research, and clinical applications* (pp. 3–20). New York: Guilford Press.

Chaffin, M., Hanson, R., Saunders, B. E., Nichols, T., Barnett, D., Zeanah, C., et al. (2006). Report of the APSAC Task Force on attachment therapy, reactive attachment disorder, and attachment problems. *Child Maltreatment, 11*, 76–89.

Cicchetti, D., Toth, S. L., & Rogosch, F. A. (1999). The efficacy of toddler-parent psychotherapy to increase attachment security in offspring of depressed mothers. *Attachment and Human Development, 1*, 34–66.*

Cohen, J. (1988). *Statistical power analysis for the behavioral sciences* (rev. ed.). New York: Academic Press.

Cohen, N. J., Muir, E., Parker, C. J., Brown, M., Lojkasek, M., Muir, R., et al. (1999). Watch, wait, and wonder: Testing the effectiveness of a new approach to mother-infant psychotherapy. *Infant Mental Health Journal, 20*, 429–451.*

Constantino, J. N., Hashemi, N., Solis, E., Alon, T., Haley, S., McClure, S., et al. (2001). Supplementation of urban home visitation with a series of group meetings for parents and infants: Results of a "real-world" randomized, controlled trial. *Child Abuse and Neglect, 25*, 1571–1581.*

Cooper, H. (1998). *Synthesizing research.* Thousand Oaks, CA: Sage.

Cooper, P., Coker, S., & Fleming, C. (1994). Self-help for bulimia nervosa: A preliminary report. *International Journal of Eating Disorders, 16*, 401–404.

Cooper, P. J., & Murray, L. (1997). The impact of psychological treatments of postpartum depression on maternal mood and infant development. In L. Murray & P. J. Cooper (Eds.), *Postpartum depression and child development* (pp. 201–261). New York: Guilford.*

Cost, Quality & Child Outcomes Study Team. (1995). *Cost, quality, and child outcomes in child care centers: Executive summary* (2nd ed.) Denver: Economics Department, University of Colorado.

Cowan, P. A. (1997). Beyond meta-analysis: A plea for a family systems view of attachment. *Child Development, 68,* 601–603.

Cox, J. L., Holden, J. M., & Sagovsky, R. (1987). Detection of postnatal depression: Development of the 10-item Edinburgh Postnatal Depression Scale. *British Journal of Psychiatry, 150,* 782–786.

Cox, M. S., Hopkins, J., & Hans, S. (2000). Attachment in preterm infants and their mother: neonatal risk status and maternal representations. *Infant Mental Health Journal, 21,* 464–480.

Crittenden, P. M. (1992). Quality of attachment in preschool years. *Development and Psychopathology, 4,* 209–241.

Crnic, K. A., Ragozin, A. S., Greenberg, M. T., Robinson, N. M., & Basham, R. B. (1983). Social interaction and developmental competence of preterm and full-term infants during the first year of life. *Child Development, 54,* 1199–1210.

Crockenberg, S. B. (1981). Infant irritability, mother responsiveness, and social support influences on the security of infant-mother attachment. *Child Development, 52,* 857–865.

Crowell, J. A., Waters, E., Treboux, D., O'Connor, E., Colondowns, C., Feider, O., et al. (1996). Discriminant validity of the Adult Attachment Interview. *Child Development, 67,* 2584–2599.

Das Eiden, R., & Reifman, A. (1996). Effects of Brazelton demonstrations on later parenting: A meta-analysis. *Journal of Pediatric Psychology, 21,* 857–868.

DeGarmo, D. S., Patterson, G. R., & Forgatch, M. S. (2004). How do outcomes in a specified parent training intervention maintain or wane over time? *Prevention Science, 5,* 73–89.

De Schipper, J. C., van IJzendoorn, M. H., & Tavecchio, L. W. C. (2004). Stability in center day care: Relations with children's well-being and problem behavior in day care. *Social Development, 13, 531–550.*

De Wolff, M., & Van IJzendoorn, M. H. (1997). Sensitivity and attachment: A meta-analysis on parental antecedents of infant attachment. *Child Development, 68,* 571–591.

Dickie, J. R., & Gerber, S. C. (1980). Training in social competence: The effect on mothers, fathers, and infants. *Child Development, 51,* 1248–1251.*

Dozier, M., Lindhiem, O., & Ackerman, J. P. (2005). Attachment and biobehavioral catch-up. An intervention targeting empirically identified needs of foster infants. In L. J. Berlin, Y. Ziv, L. Amaya-Jackson, & M. T. Greenberg, *Enhancing early attachments. Theory, research, intervention, and policy* (pp. 178–194). New York: Guilford Press.

Dozier, M., Stovall, K. C., Albus, K. E., & Bates, B. (2001). Attachment for infants in foster care: The role of caregiver state of mind. *Child Development, 72,* 1467–1477.

Duinkerken, A., & Geerts, H. (2000). Awareness required: The information and preparation course on intercountry adoption in the Netherlands. In P. Selman (Ed.), *Intercountry adoption: Developments, trends and perspectives* (pp. 368–388). London: British Agencies for Adoption and Fostering (BAAF).

Easterbrooks, M. A. (1989). Quality of attachment to mother and to father: Effects of perinatal risk status. *Child Development, 60,* 825–830.

Egeland, B., Adam, E., Ogawa, J., & Korfmacher, J. (1995, April). *Adult attachment: Implications for the therapeutic process in a home visitation intervention.* Paper presented at the Biennial Meeting of the Society for Research in Child Development, Indianapolis.

Egeland, B., & Erickson, M. F. (1993). Attachment theory and findings: Implications for prevention and intervention. In S. Kramer & H. Parens (Eds.), *Prevention in mental health: Now, tomorrow, ever?* (pp. 21–50). Northvale, NJ: Jason Aronson.*

Egeland, B., & Erickson, M. F. (2004). Lessons from STEEP: Linking theory, research, and practice for the well-being of infants and parents. In A. J. Sameroff, S. C. McDonough, & K. L. Rosenblum (Eds.), *Treating parent-infant relationship problems. Strategies for intervention* (pp. 213–242). New York: Guilford Press.

Egeland, B., Erickson, M. F., Clemenhagen-Moon, J., Hiester, M. K., & Korfmacher, J. (1990). *24 months tools coding manual: Project STEEP revised 1990 from mother-child project scales* (manuscript). Minneapolis: University of Minnesota.

Egeland, B., Weinfield, N. S., Bosquet, M., & Cheng, V. K. (2000). Remembering, repeating, and working through: Lessons from attachment-based interventions. In J. D. Osofsky & H. E. Fitzgerald (Eds.), *Handbook of infant mental health* (Vol. 4). *Infant mental health in groups at high risk* (pp. 35–89). New York: John Wiley.*

Eisenberg, A. R. (1992). Conflicts between mothers and their young children. *Merrill-Palmer Quarterly, 38,* 21–43.

Elicker, J., Fortner-Wood, C., & Noppe, I. C. (1999). The context of infant attachment in family child care. *Journal of Applied Developmental Psychology, 20,* 319–336.

Elicker, J., Noppe, I. C., Noppe, L. D., & Fortner-Wood, C. (1997). The Parent-Caregiver Relationship Scale: Rounding out the relationship system in infant child care. *Early Education and Development, 8,* 83–100.

Elicker, J., Ruprecht, K., & Wittenborn, A. (2004, June). *Staff and parent conceptions of relationships in Early Head Start.* Poster presentation at the annual National Head Start Research Conference, Washington, DC.

Erickson, M. F., Korfmacher, J., & Egeland, B. R. (1992). Attachments past and present: Implications for therapeutic intervention with mother-infant dyads. Special issue: Developmental approaches to prevention and intervention. *Development and Psychopathology, 64,* 22–31.

Erickson, M. F., & Kurz-Riemer, K. (1999). *Infants, toddlers, and families. A framework for support and intervention.* New York: Guilford Press.

Erickson, M. F., Sroufe, L. A., & Egeland, B. (1985). The relationship between quality of attachment and behavior problems in preschool in a high-risk sample. *Monographs of the Society for Research in Child Development, 50,* 147–166.

Fagot, B. I. (1997). Attachment, parenting, and peer interactions of toddler children. *Developmental Psychology, 33,* 489–499.

Fairburn, C. G. (2002). Cognitive-behavioral therapy for bulimia nervosa. In C. G. Fairburn & K. D. Brownell (Eds.), *Eating disorders and obesity: A comprehensive handbook* (2nd ed.). New York: Guilford Press.

Fairburn, C. G., & Beglin, S. J. (1994). Assessment of eating disorders: Interview or self-report questionnaire? *International Journal of Eating Disorders, 16,* 363–370.

Fairburn, C. G., & Cooper, Z. (1993). The Eating Disorder Examination, 12th edition. In C. G. Fairburn & G. T. Wilson (Eds.), *Binge eating: Nature, assessment, and treatment* (pp. 317–360). New York: Guilford Press.

Farran, D. C. (1990). Effects of intervention with disadvantaged and disabled children: A decade review. In J. P. Shonkoff & S. J. Meisels (Eds.), *Handbook of early childhood intervention* (pp. 501–539). Cambridge: Cambridge University Press.

Farran, D. C. (2000). Another decade of intervention for children who are low income or disabled: What do we know now? In J. P. Shonkoff & S. J. Meisels (Eds.), *Handbook of early childhood intervention* (2nd ed., pp. 510–548). Cambridge: Cambridge University Press.

Fava Vizziello, G. (2003). *Psicopatologia dello sviluppo* [Developmental psychopathology]. Bologna, Italy: Il Mulino.

Fearon, R. M. P., Van IJzendoorn, M. H., Fonagy, P., Bakermans-Kranenburg, M. J., Schuengel, C., & Bokhorst, C. L. (2006). In search of shared and non-shared environmental factors in security of attachment: A behavior-genetic study of the association between sensitivity and attachment security. *Developmental Psychology, 42,* 1026–1040.

Field, T. (2002). Infants' need for touch. *Human Development, 45,* 100–103.

Field, T. M., Scafidi, F., Pickens, J., Prodromidis, M., Pelaez-Nogueras, M., Torquati, J., et al. (1998). Polydrug-using adolescent mothers and their infants receiving early intervention. *Adolescence, 33,* 117–143.*

Field, T. M., Widmayer, M., Stringer, S., & Ignatoff, E. (1980). Teenage, lower-class, black mothers and their preterm infants: An intervention and developmental follow-up. *Child Development, 51,* 426–436.*

Fisher-Fay, A., Goldberg, S., Simmons, R., & Levison, R. (1988). Chronic illness and infant-mother attachment: cystic fibrosis. *Developmental and Behavioral Pediatrics, 9,* 266–270.

Fleming, A. S., Klein, E., & Corter, C. (1992). The effects of a social support group on depression, maternal attitudes and behavior in new mothers. *Journal of Child Psychology and Psychiatry, 33,* 685–698.*

Fox, N. A., Leavitt, L. A., & Warhol, J. G. (1999). *The role of early experience in infant development.* USA: Johnson & Johnson Pediatric Institute.

Fraiberg, S., Adelson, E., & Shapiro, V. (1975). Ghosts in the nursery: A psychoanalytic approach to the problems of impaired infant-mother relationships. *Journal of the American Academy of Child Psychiatry, 14,* 387–422.

Fraley, R. C. (2002). Attachment stability from infancy to adulthood: Meta-analysis and dynamic modeling of developmental mechanisms. *Personality and Social Psychology Review, 6,* 123–151.

Frodi, A., & Thompson, R. (1985). Infants' affective responses in the Strange Situation: Effects of prematurity and of quality of attachment. *Child Development, 56,* 1280–1290.

Gelfland, D. M., Teti, D. M., Seiner, S. A., & Jameson, P. B. (1996). Helping mothers fight depression: Evaluation of a home-based intervention program for depressed mothers and their infants. *Journal of Clinical Child Psychology, 25*, 406–422.*

George, C., Kaplan, N., & Main, M. (1985). *Adult Attachment Interview* (unpublished manuscript).

Goldberg, S., & Di Vitto, B. (1995). Parenting children born preterm. In M. H. Bornstein (Ed.), *Handbook of parenting* (pp. 329–354). Hillsdale, NJ: Lawrence Erlbaum.

Goldberg, S., Gotowiec, A., & Simmons, R. J. (1995). Infant-mother attachment and behavior problems in healthy and chronically ill preschoolers. *Development and Psychopathology, 7*, 267–282.

Goldberg, S., Morris, P., Simmons, R. J., Fowler, R. S., & Levinson, H. (1990a). Chronic illness in infancy and parenting stress: A comparison of three groups of parents. *Journal of Pediatric Psychology, 15*, 347–358.

Goldberg, S., Perrotta, M., Minde, K., & Corter, C. (1986). Maternal behavior and attachment in low-birth-weight twins and singletons. *Child Development, 57*, 34–46.

Goldberg, S., Simmons, R. J., Newman, J., Campbell, K., & Fowler, R. S. (1991). Congenital heart disease, parental stress, and infant-mother relationships. *Journal of Pediatrics, 119*, 661–666.

Goldberg, S., Washington, J., Morris, P., Fisher-Fay, A., & Simmons, R. J. (1990b). Early diagnosed chronic illness and mother-child relationships in the first two years. *Canadian Journal of Psychiatry, 35*, 726–733.

Goldsmith, H. H., & Alansky, J. A. (1987). Maternal and infant predictors of attachment: A meta-analytic review. *Journal of Consulting and Clinical Psychology, 55*, 805–816.

Goldsmith, H. H., Lemery, K. S., Buss, K. A., & Campos, J. J. (1999). Genetic analyses of focal aspects of infant temperament. *Developmental Psychology, 35*, 972–985.

Goldsmith, H. H., & Rothbart, M. K. (1996). *Laboratory Temperament Assessment Battery (LAB-TAB): Prelocomotor and locomotor versions.* Madison, WI: University of Wisconsin.

Goossens, F. A., & Van IJzendoorn, M. H. (1990). Quality of infants attachments to professional caregivers. Relation to infant-parent attachment and day-care characteristics. *Child Development, 61*, 832–837.

Gowen, J. W., & Nebrig, J. B. (1997). Infant-mother attachment at risk: How early intervention can help. *Infants and Young Children, 9*, 62–78.*

Green, J., & Goldwyn, R. (2002). Annotation: Attachment disorganisation and psychopathology: new findings in attachment research and their potential implications for developmental psychopathology in childhood. *Journal of Child Psychology and Psychiatry, 43*, 835–846.

Greenberg, M. T. (1999). Attachment and psychopathology in childhood. In J. Cassidy & P. R. Shaver (Eds.), *Handbook of attachment. Theory, research, and clinical applications* (pp. 469–496). New York: Guilford Press.

Greenberg, M. T., & Speltz, M. L. (1988). Contributions of attachment theory to the understanding of conduct problems during the preschool years. In J. Belsky & T. Nezworski (Eds.), *Clinical implications of attachment* (pp. 177–218). Hillsdale, NJ: Erlbaum.

Greenberg, M. T., Speltz, M. L., & DeKlyen, M. (1993). The role of attachment in the early development of disruptive behavior problems. Development and Psychopathology, 5, 191–213.

Greenberg, M. T., Speltz, M. L., DeKlyen, M., & Endriga, M. C. (1991). Attachment security in preschoolers with and without externalizing behavior problems: A replication. Development and Psychopathology, 3, 413–430.

Haft, W. L., & Slade, A. (1989). Affect attunement and maternal attachment: A pilot study. Infant Mental Health Journal, 10, 157–172.

Hamill, P. V. V., Drizd, T. A., Johnson, C. L., Reed, R. B., & Roche, A. F. (1977). NCHS growth curves for children birth–18 years (Series 11, No. 165, DHEW Publication [PHS] 78-1650). Hyattsville, MD: National Center for Health Statistics, Vital and Health Statistics.

Hamilton, C. E. (2000). Continuity and discontinuity of attachment from infancy through adolescence. Child Development, 71, 690–694.

Hamilton, M. L. (1972). Evaluation of a parent and child center program. Child Welfare, 51, 248–258.*

Hansburg, H. G. (1980). Adolescent separation anxiety: A method for the study of adolescent separation problems. New York: Krieger.

Harris, J. R. (1998). The nurture assumption. London: Bloomsbury.

Harlow, H. F. (1958). The nature of love. American Pychologist, 13, 673–685.

Hausfather, A., Toharia, A., LaRoche A., & Engelsmann, F. (1997). Effects of age entry, day-care quality, and family characteristics on preschool behavior. Journal of Child Psychology and Psychiatry, 38, 441–448.

Havermans, A., & Verheule, C. (2001). Evaluatie preventie-project Video Interactie Begeleiding bij interlandelijke adoptie [Evaluation preventive project Video Interaction Guidance in families with internationally adopted children]. Utrecht, the Netherlands: Stichting Adoptie Voorzieningen.

Hedges, L. V., & Olkin, I. (1985). Statistical methods for meta-analysis. London: Academic Press.

Heinicke, C. M., Beckwith, L., & Thompson, A. (1988). Early intervention in the family system: A framework and review. Infant Mental Health Journal, 9, 111–141.

Heinicke, C. M., Fineman, N. R., Ruth, G., Recchia, S. L., Guthrie, D., & Rodning, C. (1999). Relationship-based intervention with at-risk mothers: Outcome in the first year of life. Infant Mental Health Journal, 20, 349–374.*

Hesse, E. (1999). The Adult Attachment Interview: Historical and current perspectives. In J. Cassidy & P. R. Shaver (Eds.), Handbook of attachment: Theory, research, and clinical applications (pp. 395–433). New York: Guilford Press.

Hesse, E., & Main, M. (2006). Frightened, threatening, and dissociative (FR) parental behavior as related to infant D attachment in low-risk samples: Description, discussion, and interpretations. Development and Psychopathology, 18, 309–343.

Hobfoll, S. E., & Lerman, M. (1988). Personal relationships, personal attributes, and stress resistance: Mothers' reactions to their child's illness. American Journal of Community Psychology, 16, 565–589.

Hoffman, M. L. (1970). Moral development. In P. H. Mussen (Ed.), Carmichael's handbook of child development (Vol. 2). New York: Wiley.

Hoffman, M. L. (1984). Empathy, its limitations, and its role in a comprehensive moral theory. In J. L. Gewirtz & W. Kurtines (Eds.), *Morality, moral development, and moral behavior* (pp. 283–302). New York: Wiley.

Hoffman, M. L. (2000). *Empathy and moral development. Implications for caring and justice*. Cambridge: Cambridge University Press.

Hoffman, M. L., & Saltzstein, H. D. (1967). Parent discipline and the child's moral development. *Journal of Personality and Social Psychology, 5*, 45–57.

Howes, C. (1997). Children's experiences in center-based child care as a function of teacher background and adult-child ratio. *Merrill-Palmer Quarterly, 43*, 404–425.

Howes, C. (1999). Attachment relationships in the context of multiple caregivers. In J. Cassidy & P. R. Shaver (Eds.), *Handbook of attachment. Theory, research, and clinical applications* (pp. 671–687). New York: Guilford.

Howes, C., & Ritchie, S. (2002). *A matter of trust: Connecting teachers and learners in the early childhood classroom*. New York: Teachers College Press.

Howes, C., & Smith, E. (1995). Relations among child care quality, teacher behavior, teacher's play activities, emotional security and cognitive activity in child care. *Early Childhood Research Quarterly, 10*, 381–404.

Hunter, J. E., & Schmidt, F. L. (1996). Cumulative research knowledge and social policy formation: The critical role of meta-analysis. *Psychology, Public Policy, and Law, 2*, 324–347.

Huxley, P., & Warner, R. (1993). Primary prevention of parenting dysfunction in high-risk cases. *American Journal of Orthopsychiatry, 63*, 582–588.*

Ievers, C.E., Drotar, D., Dahms, W.T., Doershuk, C.F., & Stern, R.C. (1994). Maternal child-rearing behavior in three groups: cystic fibrosis, insulin-dependent diabetes mellitus, and healthy children. *Journal of Pediatric Psychology, 19*, 681–687.

Jacobsen, T., & Hofmann, V. (1997). Children's attachment representations: Longitudinal relations to school behavior and academic competency in middle childhood and adolescence. *Developmental Psychology, 33*, 703–710.

Jacobson, S. W., & Frye, K. F. (1991). Effect of maternal social support on attachment: Experimental evidence. *Child Development, 62*, 572–582.*

Jaffari-Bimmel, N., Juffer, F., Van IJzendoorn, M. H., Bakermans-Kranenburg, M. J., & Mooijaart, A. (2006). Social development from infancy to adolescence: Longitudinal and concurrent factors in an adoption sample. *Developmental Psychology, 42*, 1143–1153.

John, O. P., & Srivastava, S. (1999). The Big Five taxonomy: History, measurement, and theoretical perspectives. In L. E. Pervin & O. P. John (Eds.), *Handbook of personality: Theory and research* (2nd ed., pp. 102–138). New York: Guilford Press.

Johnson, D. (2000). Medical and developmental sequelae of early childhood institutionalization in Eastern European adoptees. In C. A. Nelson (Ed.), *The effects of early adversity on neurobehavioral development. The Minnesota symposia on child psychology* (Vol. 31, pp. 113–162). Mahwah, NJ: Lawrence Erlbaum.

Juffer, F. (1993). *Verbonden door adoptie. Een experimenteel onderzoek naar hechting en competentie in gezinnen met een adoptiebaby* [Attached through adoption. An experimental study of attachment and competence in families with adopted babies]. Amersfoort, the Netherlands: Academische Uitgeverij.

Juffer, F. (2006). Children's awareness of adoption and their problem behavior in families with 7-year-old internationally adopted children. *Adoption Quarterly*, 9, 1–22.

Juffer, F., Bakermans-Kranenburg, M. J., & Van IJzendoorn, M. H. (2005a). Enhancing children's socioemotional development: A review of intervention studies. In D. M. Teti (Ed.), *Handbook of research methods in developmental science* (pp. 213–232). Oxford: Blackwell.

Juffer, F., Bakermans-Kranenburg, M. J., & Van IJzendoorn, M. H. (2005b). The importance of parenting in the development of disorganized attachment: Evidence from a preventive intervention study in adoptive families. *Journal of Child Psychology and Psychiatry*, 46, 263–274.*

Juffer, F., Hoksbergen, R. A. C., Riksen-Walraven, J. M. A., & Kohnstamm, G. A. (1997). Early intervention in adoptive families: Supporting maternal sensitive responsiveness, infant-mother attachment, and infant competence. *Journal of Child Psychology and Psychiatry*, 38, 1039–1050.*

Juffer, F., Metman, A. H., & Andoetoe, I. (1986). *Het eerste levensjaar* [*The first year of life*]. Utrecht, the Netherlands: Utrecht University.

Juffer, F., & Rosenboom, L. G. (1997). Infant-mother attachment of internationally adopted children in the Netherlands. *International Journal of Behavioral Development*, 20, 93–107.

Juffer, F., Stams, G. J. J. M., & Van IJzendoorn, M. H. (2004). Adopted children's problem behavior is significantly related to their ego resiliency, ego control, and sociometric status. *Journal of Child Psychology and Psychiatry*, 45, 697–706.

Juffer, F., & Van IJzendoorn, M. H. (2005). Behavior problems and mental health referrals of international adoptees: A meta-analysis. *JAMA*, 293, 2501–2515.

Juffer, F., & Van IJzendoorn, M. H. (2007). A longitudinal study of Korean adoptees in the Netherlands: Infancy to middle childhood. In K. J. S. Bergquist, M. E. Vonk, D. S. Kim, & M. D. Feit (Eds.), *International Korean adoption: A fifty-year history of policy and practice*. (pp. 263–276). Binghamton, NY: The Haworth Press.

Juffer, F., Van IJzendoorn, M. H., & Bakermans-Kranenburg, M. J. (1997). Intervention in transmission of insecure attachment: A case-study. *Psychological Reports*, 80, 531–543.

Kagitcibasi, C. (1996). *Family and human development across cultures: A view from the other side*. Hillsdale, NJ: Lawrence Erlbaum.

Kang, R., Barnard, K., Hammond, M., Oshio, S., Spencer, C., Thibodeaux, B., et al. (1995). Preterm infant follow-up project: A multi-site field experiment of hospital and home intervention programs for mothers and preterm infants. *Public Health Nursing*, 12, 171–180.*

Katz, L. G. (2000, April). *Parenting and teaching in perspective* (ERIC Document Reproduction Service ED439835). Paper presented at the Parent-Child 2000 Conference, London.

Kerns, K. A. (1994). A developmental model of the relations between mother-child attachment and friendship. In R. Erber & R. Gilmour (Eds.), *Theoretical frameworks for personal relationships* (pp. 129–156). New York: Lawrence Erlbaum.

Keuzenkamp, S., Hooghiemstra, E., Breedveld, K., & Merens, A. (2000). *De kunst van het combineren. Taakverdeling onder partners* [*The art of combining. The division of roles between partners*]. The Hague, the Netherlands: Sociaal Cultureel Planbureau.

Kitzman, H., Olds, D. L., Henderson, C. R., Hanks, C., Cole, R., Tatelbaum, R., et al. (1997). Effects of prenatal and infancy home visitation by nurses on pregnancy outcomes, childhood injuries, and repeated childbearing: A randomized trial. *JAMA, 278,* 644–652.*

Klein Velderman, M., Bakermans-Kranenburg, M. J., Juffer, F., & Van IJzendoorn, M. H. (2006a). Effects of attachment-based interventions on maternal sensitivity and infant attachment: Differential susceptibility of highly reactive infants. *Journal of Family Psychology, 20,* 266–274.

Klein Velderman, M., Bakermans-Kranenburg, M. J., Juffer, F., Van IJzendoorn, M. H., Mangelsdorf, S. C., & Zevalking, J. (2006b). Preventing preschool behavior problems through video-feedback intervention in infancy. *Infant Mental Health Journal, 27,* 466–493.

Kochanska, G. (1995). Children's temperament, mothers' discipline, and security of attachment: Multiple pathways to emerging internalization. *Child Development, 61,* 597–615.

Koniak-Griffin, D., Ludington-Hoe, S., & Verzemnieks, I. (1995). Longitudinal effects of unimodal and multimodal stimulation on development and interaction of healthy infants. *Research in Nursing and Health, 18,* 27–38.*

Koot, H. M., Van den Oord, E. J. C. G., Verhulst, F. C., & Boomsma, D. I. (1997). Behavioral and emotional problems in young preschoolers: Cross-cultural testing of the validity of the Child Behavior Checklist/2-3. *Journal of Abnormal Child Psychology, 25,* 183–196.

Koot, H. M., & Verhulst, F. C. (1991). Prevalence of problem behavior in Dutch children aged 2–3. *Acta Psychiatrica Scandinavica, 83* (Suppl. 367), 1–37.

Krupka, A. (1995). *The quality of mother-infant interactions in families at risk for maladaptive parenting.* Dissertation, University of Western Ontario, Ontario.*

Lafreniere, P. J., & Capuano, F. (1997). Preventive intervention as means of clarifying direction of effects in socialization: Anxious-withdrawn preschoolers case. *Development and Psychopathology, 9,* 551–564.*

Lagerberg, D. (2000). Secondary prevention in child health: Effects of psychological intervention, particularly home visitation, on children's development and other outcome variables. *Acta Paediatric Supplements, 434,* 43–52.

Lambermon, M. W. E. (1991). *Video of folder? Korte- en lange-termijn-effecten van voorlichting over vroegkinderlijke opvoeding* [Video or booklet? Short-term and long-term effects of information about early childhood education]. Unpublished doctoral dissertation, Leiden University, Leiden, the Netherlands.

Lambermon, M. W. E., & Van IJzendoorn, M. H. (1989). Influencing mother-infant interaction through videotaped or written instruction: Evaluation of a parent education program. *Early Childhood Research Quarterly, 4,* 449–458.*

Larson, C. P. (1980). Efficacy of prenatal and postpartum home visits in child health and development. *Pediatrics, 66,* 191–197.*

Lavigne, J. V., Arend, R., Rosenbaum, D., Binns, H. J., Kaufer-Cristoffel, K., & Gibbons, R. D. (1998). Psychiatric disorders with onset in the preschool years. I. Stability of diagnoses. *Journal of the American Academy of Child and Adolescent Psychiatry, 37,* 1246–1254.

Leifer, M., Wax, L. C., Leventhal-Belfer, L., Fouchia, A., & Morrison, M. (1989). The use of multitreatment modalities in early intervention: A quantitative case study. *Infant Mental Health Journal, 10,* 100–116.

Leitch, D. B. (1999). Mother-infant interaction: Achieving synchrony. *Nursing Research, 48,* 55–58.

Lester, B. M., & Zeskind, P. S. (1979), The organization and assessment of crying in the infant at risk. In T. M. Field, A. M. Sostek, S. Goldberg, & H. H. Shuman (Eds.), *Infants born at risk* (pp. 121–144). New York: Spectrum.

Letourneau, N. (2000). Promoting optimal parent-infant interactions with keys to caregiving. *NCAST National News, 16,* 1–6.*

Lieberman, A. F. (1992). Infant-parent psychotherapy with toddlers. *Development and Psychopathology, 4,* 559–574.

Lieberman, A. F. (2004). Child-parent psychotherapy: A relationship-based approach to the treatment of mental health disorders in infancy and early childhood. In Sameroff, A. J., McDonough, S. C., & Rosenblum, K. L., (Eds.), *Treating parent-infant relationship problems* (pp. 97–122). New York: Guilford Press.

Lieberman, A. F., & Pawl, J. H. (1993). Infant-parent psychotherapy. In C. H. Zeanah (Ed.), *Handbook of infant mental health* (pp. 427–442). New York: Guilford Press.

Lieberman, A. F., Weston, D. R., & Pawl, J. H. (1991). Preventive intervention and outcome with anxiously attached dyads. *Child Development, 62,* 199–209.*

Lieberman, A. F., & Zeanah, C. H. (1999). Contributions of attachment theory to infant-parent psychotherapy and other interventions with infants and young children. In J. Cassidy & P.R. Shaver (Eds.), *Handbook of attachment: Theory, research, and clinical applications* (pp. 555–574). New York: Guilford Press.

Lojkasek, M., Cohen, N., & Muir, E. (1994). Where is the infant in infant intervention? A review of the literature on changing troubled mother-infant relationships. *Psychotherapy, 31,* 208–220.

Lovaas, O. I. (1961). Effect of exposure to symbolic aggression on aggressive behavior. *Child Development, 32,* 37–44.

Love, J. M., Kisker, E. E., Ross, C. M., Shochet, P. Z., Brooks-Gunn, J., Paulsell, D., et al. (2002). *Making a difference in the lives of infants and toddlers and their families: The impacts of Early Head Start* (Vol. I, final technical report). Princeton, NJ: Mathematica Policy Research.

Luster, T., Perlstadt, H., McKinney, M., Sims, K., & Juang, L. (1996). The effects of a family support program and other factors on the home environment provided by adolescent mothers. *Family Relations, 45,* 255–264.*

Lyons-Ruth, K., Bronfman, E., & Parsons, E. (1999). Maternal disrupted affective communication, maternal frightened or frightening behavior, and infant disorganized attachment strategies. *Monographs of the Society for Research in Child Development, 64,* 172–192.

Lyons-Ruth, K., Connell, D. B., & Grunebaum, H. U. (1990). Infants at social risk: Maternal depression and family support services as mediators of infant development and security of attachment. *Child Development, 61,* 85–98.*

Lyons-Ruth, K., & Jacobvitz, D. (1999). Attachment disorganization: Unresolved loss, relational violence, and lapses in behavioral and attentional strategies. In J. Cassidy & P.R. Shaver (Eds.), *Handbook of attachment. Theory, research, and clinical applications* (pp. 520–554). New York: Guilford.

Maccoby, E. E., & Martin, J. A. (1983). Socialization in the context of the family: Parent-child interaction. In E. M. Hetherington (Ed.), *Socialization, personality, and social development* (Vol. 4, pp. 1–101). New York: Wiley.

Macey, T. J., Harmon, R. J., & Easterbrooks, M. A. (1987). Impact of premature birth on the development of the infant in the family. *Journal of Consulting and Clinical Psychology, 55*, 846–852.

MacLeod, J., & Nelson, G. (2000). Programs for the promotion of family wellness and the prevention of child maltreatment: A meta-analytic review. *Child Abuse and Neglect, 24*, 1127–1149.

Madden, J., O'Hara, J., & Levenstein, P. (1984). Home again: Effects of the mother-child home program on mother and child. *Child Development, 55*, 636–647.*

Madrid, A., & Schwartz, M. (1991). Maternal-infant bonding and pediatric asthma: An initial investigation. *Pre- and Peri-Natal Psychology, 5*, 347–358.

Mahoney, G., & Powell, A. (1988). Modifying parent-child interaction: Enhancing the development of handicapped children. *Journal of Special Education, 22*, 82–96.*

Main, M. (1995). Recent studies in attachment: Overview, with selected implications for clinical work. In S. Goldberg, R. Muir, & J. Kerr (Eds.), *Attachment theory: Social, developmental, and clinical perspectives* (pp. 407–474). New York: Analytic Press.

Main, M. (1999). Epiloque. Attachment theory: Eighteen points with suggestions for future studies. In J. Cassidy & P. R. Shaver (Eds.), *Handbook of attachment. Theory, research, and clinical applications* (pp. 845–887). New York: Guilford.

Main, M., & Goldwyn, R. (1994). *Adult attachment rating and classification system* (unpublished manuscript). Berkeley: University of California.

Main, M., & Hesse, E. (1990). Parents' unresolved traumatic experiences are related to infant disorganized attachment status: Is frightened and/or frightening parental behavior the linking mechanism? In M. T. Greenberg, D. Cichetti, & E. Cummings (Eds.), *Attachment in the preschool years: Theory, research, and intervention* (pp. 161–182). Chicago: University of Chicago Press.

Main, M., Kaplan, N., & Cassidy, J. (1985). Security in infancy, childhood and adulthood: A move to the level of representation. *Monographs of the Society for Research in Child Development, 50*, 66–104.

Main, M., & Solomon, J. (1990). Procedures for identifying infants as disorganized/disoriented during the Ainsworth Strange Situation. In M. T. Greenberg, D. Cicchetti, & E. M. Cummings (Eds.), *Attachment in the preschool years. Theory, research, and intervention* (pp. 121–182). Chicago: University of Chicago Press.

Marcovitch, S., Goldberg, S., Gold, A., Washington, J., Wasson, C., Krekewich, K., et al. (1997). Determinants of behavioral problems in Romanian children adopted in Ontario. *International Journal of Behavioral Development, 20*, 17–32.

Marvin, R., Cooper, G., Hoffman, K., & Powell, B. (2002). The circle of security project: Attachment-based intervention with caregiver-preschool child dyads. *Attachment and Human Development, 4*, 107–124.

Marvin, R. S., & Pianta, R. C. (1996). Mothers' reactions to their child's diagnosis: Relations with security of attachment. *Journal of Clinical Child Psychology, 25,* 436–445.

McCallum, M. S., & McKim, M. K. (1999). Recurrent otitis media and attachment security: A path model. *Early Education and Development, 10,* 517–533.

McCartney, K. (1984). Effects of the quality of the day-care environment on children's language development. *Developmental Psychology, 20,* 244–260.

McCartney, K., Owen, M. T., Booth, C. L., Clarke-Stewart, A., & Vandell, D. L. (2004). Testing a maternal attachment model of behavior problems in early childhood. *Journal of Child Psychology and Psychiatry, 45,* 765–778.

McDonough, S. (2004). Interaction guidance: Promoting and nurturing the caregiving relationship. In A. J. Sameroff, S. C. McDonough, & K. L. Rosenblum (Eds.), *Treating parent-infant relationship problems. Strategies for intervention* (pp. 79–96). New York: Guilford Press.

Meij, J. Th. (1992). *Sociale ondersteuning, gehechtheidskwaliteit en vroegkinderlijke competentie-ontwikkeling [Social support, attachment, and early competence].* Dissertation, Catholic University, Nijmegen, the Netherlands.*

Meredith, W., & Tisak, J. (1990). Latent curve analysis. *Psychometrika, 55,* 107–122.

Mesman, J., & Koot, H. M. (2001). Early preschool predictors of preadolescent internalizing and externalizing DSM-IV diagnoses. *Journal of the American Academy of Child and Adolescent Psychiatry, 40,* 1029–1036.

Mesman, J., Koot, H. M., Stolk, M., Van Zeijl, J., Bakermans-Kranenburg, M. J., Juffer, F., et al. (2003, April). *Externalizing problems at age 1 year compared to ages 2–3 years: Prevalence and correlates.* Paper presented at the biennial conference of the Society for Research of Child Development, Tampa, FL.

Metzl, M. N. (1980). Teaching parents a strategy for enhancing infant development. *Child Development, 51,* 583–586.*

Meyer, E. C., Coll, C. T. G., Lester, B. M., Boukydis, C. F. Z., McDonough, S. M., & Oh, W. (1994). Family-based intervention improves maternal psychological well-being and feeding interaction of preterm infants. *Pediatrics, 93,* 241–246.*

Miller, P. A., & Eisenberg, N. (1988). The relation of empathy to aggressive and externalizing/antisocial behavior. *Psychological Bulletin, 103,* 324–344.

Minde, K. (1999). Mediating attachment patterns during a serious medical illness. *Infant Mental Health Journal, 20,* 105–122.

Minde, K. (2000). Prematurity and serious medical conditions in infancy: Implications for development, behaviour and intervention. In C. H. Zeanah (Ed.), *Handbook of infant mental health* (pp. 176–194). New York: Guilford Press.

Minde, K., Goldberg, S., Perrotta, M., Washington, J., Lojkasek, M., Corter, C., et al. (1989). Continuities and discontinuities in the development of 64 very small premature infants to 4 years of age. *Journal of Child Psychology and Psychiatry, 30,* 391–404.

Moffitt, T. E., Caspi, A., Dickson, N., Silva, P., & Stanton, W. (1996). Childhood-onset versus adolescent-onset antisocial conduct problems in males: Natural history from ages 3 to 18 years. *Development and Psychopathology, 8,* 399–424.

Mrazek, D. A., Casey, B., & Anderson, I. (1987). Insecure attachment in severely asth-matic preschool children: Is it a risk factor? *Journal of the American Academy of Child and Adolescent Psychiatry, 26,* 516–520.

Muir, E. (1992). Watching, waiting, and wondering: Applying psychoanalytic principles to mother-infant intervention. *Infant Mental Health Journal, 13,* 319–328.

Mullen, B. (1989). *Advanced basic meta-analysis.* Hillsdale, NJ: Erlbaum.

Murray, L., & Carothers, A. D. (1990). The validation of the Edinburgh Postna-tal Depression Scale on a community sample. *British Journal of Psychiatry, 157,* 288–290

Nesselroade, J. R., & Baltes, P. B. (Eds.). (1979). *Longitudinal research in the study of behavior and development.* New York: Academic Press.

NICHD Early Child Care Research Network. (1996). Characteristics of infant child care: Factors contributing to positive caregiving. *Early Childhood Research Quar-terly, 11,* 269–306.

NICHD Early Child Care Research Network. (2000). Characteristics and quality of child care for toddlers and preschoolers. *Applied Developmental Science, 4,* 116–135.

Nickman, S. L., Rosenfeld, A. A., Fine, P., Macintyre, J. C., Pilowsky, D. J., Howe, R. A., et al. (2005). Children in adoptive families: Overview and update. *Journal of the American Academy of Child and Adolescent Psychiatry, 44,* 987–995.

Noppe, I. C., Elicker, J., Fortner-Wood, C., Shin, J. Y., & Zhang, Y. (2001, April). *Infants' attachment security with parents and child care providers: Toddlers' social and cognitive outcomes.* Poster presented at the Biennial Meeting of the Society for Research in Child Development, Minneapolis.

O'Connor, Th. G., & Nilsen, W. J. (2005). Models versus metaphors in translating attachment theory to the clinic and community. In L. J. Berlin, Y. Ziv, L. Amaya-Jackson, & M. T. Greenberg (Eds.), *Enhancing early attachments. Theory, research, intervention, and policy* (pp. 313–326). New York: Guilford Press.

O'Connor, Th. G., & Zeanah, C. H. (2003). Attachment disorders: Assessment strate-gies and treatment approaches. *Attachment and Human Development, 5,* 223–244.

Olds, D. L., Henderson, C. R., Chamberlin, R., & Tatelbaum, R. (1986). Preventing child abuse and neglect: A randomized trial of nurse home visitation. *Pediatrics, 78,* 65–77.*

Olson, S. L., Bates, J. E., Sandy, J. M., & Lanthier, R. (2000). Early developmental pre-cursors of externalizing behavior in middle childhood and adolescence. *Journal of Abnormal Child Psychology, 28,* 119–133.

Onozawa, K., Glover, V., Adams, D., Modi, N., & Kumar, R. C. (2001). Infant massage improves mother-infant interaction for mothers with postnatal depression. *Journal of Affective Disorders, 63,* 201–207.*

Oser, C., & Cohen, J. (2003). *America's babies: The ZERO TO THREE Policy Center data book.* Washington, DC: Zero to Three.

Palti, H., Otrakul, A., Belmaker, E., Tamir, D., & Tepper, D. (1984). Children's home environments: Comparison of a group exposed to a stimulation intervention pro-gram with controls. *Early Child Development and Care, 13,* 193–212.*

Parks, M. L. (1983/1984). Maternal sensitivity to infant cues: Impact of group interven-tion for adolescent mothers (doctoral dissertation, University of Michigan). *Dis-sertation Abstracts International, 44,* DA8402353.*

Patterson, G. R. (1971). *Families: Applications of social learning to family life*. Champaign: Research Press Company.

Patterson, G. R. (1976). The aggressive child: Victim and architect of a coercive system. In E. J. Mash, L. A. Hamerlynch, & L. C. Hardy (Eds.), *Behavior modification and families* (pp. 267–316). New York: Brunner/Mazel.

Patterson, G. R. (1982). *Coercive family process*. Eugene, OR: Castilia.

Patterson, G. R. (2002). The early development of coercive family process. In J. B. Reid, G. R. Patterson, & J. Snyder (Eds.), *Antisocial behavior in children and adolescents* (pp. 25–44). Washington, DC: American Psychological Association.

Patterson, G. R., Reid, J. B., & Dishion, T. J. (1992). *A social interactional approach* (Vol. 4). *Antisocial boys*. Eugene, OR: Castalia.

Patterson, G. R., Reid, J. B., & Eddy, J. M. (2002). A brief history of the Oregon model. In J. B. Reid, G. R. Patterson, & J. Snyder (Eds.), *Antisocial behavior in children and adolescents. A developmental analysis and model for intervention* (pp. 3–21). Washington, DC: American Psychological Association.

Pearson, J. L., Cohn, D. A., Cowan, P. A., & Cowan, C. P. (1994). Earned- and continuous-security in adult attachment: Relation to depressive symptomatology and parenting style. *Development and Psychopathology, 6*, 359–373.

Pederson, D. R., & Moran, G. (1996). Expression of the attachment relationship outside the Strange Situation. *Child Development, 67*, 915–927.

Pederson, D. R., Moran, G., Sitko, C., Campbell, K., Ghesquire, K., & Acton, H. (1990). Maternal sensitivity and the security of infant-mother attachment: A Q-sort study. *Child Development, 61*, 1974–1983.

Peisner-Feinberg, E. S., & Burchinal, M. R. (1997). Relations between preschool children's child care experiences and concurrent development: The Cost, Quality, and Outcomes Study. *Merril Palmer Quarterly, 43*, 451–467.

Pless, I. B., & Pinkerton, P. (1975). *Chronic childhood disorder: Promoting patterns of adjustment*. Chicago: Yearbook Medical.

Plunkett, J. W., Klein, T., & Meisels, S. J. (1988). The relationship of preterm infant-mother attachment to stranger sociability at 3 years. *Infant Behavior and Development, 11*, 83–96.

Plunkett, J. W., Meisels, S. J., Stiefel, G. S., Pasick, P. L., & Roloff, D. W. (1986). Patterns of attachment among preterm infants of varying biological risk. *Journal of the American Academy of Child Psychiatry, 25*, 794–800.

Poehlmann, J., & Fiese, B. H. (2001). The interaction of maternal and infant vulnerabilities on developing attachment relationships. *Development and Psychopathology, 13*, 1–11.

Raudenbush, S. W. (1984). Magnitude of teacher expectancy effects of pupil IQ as a function of the credibility of expectancy induction: A synthesis of findings from 18 experiments. *Journal of Educational Psychology, 76*, 85–97.

Richters, J. E., & Waters, E. (1991). Attachment and socialization: The positive side of social influence. In M. Lewis & S. Feinman (Eds.), *Social influences and socialization from infancy* (pp. 185–213). New York: Plenum Press.

Richters, J. E., Waters, E., & Vaughn, B. E. (1988). Empirical classification of infant-mother relationships from interactive behavior and crying during reunion. *Child Development, 59*, 512–522.

Riksen-Walraven, J. M. A. (1978). Effects of caregiver behavior on habituation rate and self-efficacy in infants. *International Journal of Behavioral Development, 1,* 105–130.*

Riksen-Walraven, J. M. A., Meij, J. Th., Hubbard, F. O., & Zevalkink, J. (1996). Intervention in lower-class Surinam-Dutch families: Effects on mothers and infants. *International Journal of Behavioral Development, 19,* 739–756.*

Riksen-Walraven, J. M. A., & Van Aken, M. A. G. (1997). Effects of two mother-infant intervention programs upon children's development at 7, 10, and 12 years. In W. Koops, J. B. Hoeksma, & D. C. van den Boom (Eds.), *Development of interaction and attachment: traditional and non-traditional approaches* (pp. 79–92). Amsterdam: North Holland.

Robertson, J., & Robertson, J. (1989). *Separation and the very young.* London: Free Association Books.

Robert-Tissot, C., Cramer, B., Stern, D. N., Serpa, S. R., Bachmann, J. P., Palacio-Espasa, F., et al. (1996). Outcome evaluation in brief mother-infant psychotherapies: Report on 75 cases. *Infant Mental Health Journal, 17,* 97–114.*

Rode, S., Chang, P., Fisch, R., & Sroufe, L. (1981). Attachment patterns of infants separated at birth. *Developmental Psychology, 17,* 188–191.

Rodning, C., Beckwith, L., & Howard, J. (1990). Characteristics of attachment organization and play organization in prenatally drug-exposed toddlers. *Development and Psychopathology, 1,* 277–289.

Rogers, S., Ozonoff, S., & Maslin-Cole, C. (1991). A comparative study of attachment behavior in young children with autism or other psychiatric disorders. *Journal of American Academy of Child and Adolescent Psychiatry, 30,* 483–488.

Rosekrans, M. A., & Hartup, W. W. (1967). Imitative influences of consistent and inconsistent response consequences to a model on aggressive behavior in children. *Journal of Personality and Social Psychology, 7,* 429–434.

Rosenboom, L. G. (1994). *Gemengde gezinnen, gemengde gevoelens? Hechting en competentie van adoptiebaby's in gezinnen met biologisch eigen kinderen* [Mixed families, mixed feelings? Attachment and competence of adopted infants in families with biological children]. Dissertation, Utrecht University, Utrecht, the Netherlands.*

Rosenthal, R. (1963). On the social psychology of the psychological experiment: The experimenter's hypothesis as unintended determinant of experimental results. *American Scientist, 51,* 268–283.

Rosenthal, R. (1991). *Meta-analytic procedures for social research.* Beverly Hills, CA: Sage Publications.

Rosenthal, R. (1995). Writing meta-analytic reviews. *Psychological Bulletin, 118,* 183–192.

Rosenthal, R. (2002). The Pygmalion effect and its mediating mechanisms. In J. Aronson (Ed.), *Improving academic achievement: Impact of psychological factors on education* (pp. 25–36). San Diego: Academic Press.

Rosenthal, R., & Jacobson, L. (1966). Teachers' expectancies: Determinants of pupils' IQ gains. *Psychological Reports, 19,* 115–118.

Rosnow, R. L., & Rosenthal, R. (1989). Statistical procedures and the justification of knowledge in psychological science. *American Psychologist, 44,* 1276–1284.

Ross, G. S. (1984). Home intervention for premature infants of low-income families. *American Journal of Orthopsychiatry, 54,* 263–270.*

Rothbart, M. K. (1981). Measurement of temperament in infancy. *Child Development, 52,* 569–578.

Rothbart, M. K. (1986). Longitudinal observation of infant temperament. *Developmental Psychology, 22,* 356–365.

Rothbaum, F., & Weisz, J. R. (1994). Parental caregiving and child externalizing behavior in nonclinical samples: A meta-analysis. *Psychological Bulletin, 116,* 55–74.

Rotter, J. B. (1954). *Social learning and clinical psychology.* Englewood Cliffs, NJ: Prentice-Hall.

Rowe, D. C. (1994). *The limits of family influence.* New York: Guilford.

Rutgers, A. H., Bakermans-Kranenburg, M. J., Van IJzendoorn, M. H., & Van Berckelaer-Onnes, I. A. (2004). Autism and attachment: A meta-analytic review. *Journal of Child Psychology and Psychiatry, 45,* 1123–1134.

Rutter, M., Andersen-Wood, L., Becket, C., Bredenkamp, D., Castle, J., Dunn, J., et al. (1998). Developmental catch-up, and deficit, following adoption after severe global early privation. *Journal of Child Psychology and Psychiatry, 39,* 465–476.

Sagi, A., Van IJzendoorn, M. H., Scharf, M., & Koren-Karie, N. (1994). Stability and discriminant validity of the Adult Attachment Interview: A psychometric study in young Israeli adults. *Developmental Psychology, 30,* 771–777.

Sajaniemi, N., Mäkelä, J., Salokorpi, T., von Wendt, L., Hämäläinen, T., & Hakamies-Blomqvist, L. (2001). Cognitive performance and attachment patterns at four years of age in extremely low birth weight infants after early intervention. *European Child & Adolescent Psychiatry, 10,* 122–129.*

Schneider, B. H., Atkinson, L., & Tardif, C. (2001). Child-parent attachment and children's peer relations: A quantitative review. *Developmental Psychology, 37,* 86–100.

Scholz, K., & Samuels, C. A. (1992). Neonatal bathing and massage intervention with fathers, behavioral effects 12 weeks after birth of the first baby: The Sunraysia Australia intervention project. *International Journal of Behavioral Development, 15,* 67–81.*

Schuengel, C., Bakermans-Kranenburg, M. J., & Van IJzendoorn, M. H. (1999). Frightening maternal behavior linking unresolved loss and disorganized infant attachment. *Journal of Consulting and Clinical Psychology, 67,* 54–63.

Schuler, M. E., Nair, P., Black, M. M., & Kettinger, L. (2000). Mother-infant interaction: Effects of a home intervention and ongoing maternal drug use. *Journal of Clinical Child Psychology, 29,* 424–431.*

Seifer, R., Clark, G. N., & Sameroff, A. J. (1991). Positive effects of interaction coaching on infants with developmental disabilities and their mothers. *American Journal on Mental Retardation, 96,* 1–11.*

Shapiro, T., Sherman, M., Calamari, G., & Koch, D. (1986). Attachment in autism and other developmental disorders. *Journal of American Academy of Child and Adolescent Psychiatry, 26,* 480–484.

Shaw, D. S., & Bell, R. Q. (1993). Developmental theories of parental contributors to antisocial behavior. *Journal of Abnormal Child Psychology, 21,* 493–518.

Shaw, D. S., Owens, E. B., Giovannelli, J., & Winslow, E. B. (2001). Infant and toddler pathways leading to early externalizing disorders. *Journal of the American Academy of Child and Adolescent Psychiatry, 40,* 36–43.

Sheeran, T., Marvin, R. S., & Pianta, R. C. (1997). Mothers' resolution of their child's diagnosis and self-reported measures of parenting stress, marital relations, and social support. *Journal of Pediatric Psychology, 22,* 197–212.

Shonkoff, J. P., & Phillips, D. A. (Eds.). (2001). *From neurons to neighborhoods. The science of early childhood development.* Washington, DC: National Academy Press.

Singer, L. T., Fulton, S., Davillier, M., Koshy, D., Salvator, A., & Baley, J. E. (2003). Effects on infant risk status and maternal psychological distress on maternal-infant interactions during the first year of life. *Journal of Developmental and Behavioral Pediatrics, 24,* 233–241.

Snyder, J. (1995). Coercion: A two-level theory of antisocial behavior. In W. O'Donohue & L. Krasner (Eds.), *Theories of behavior therapy. Exploring behavior change* (pp. 313–348). Washington, DC: American Psychological Association.

Snyder, J. (2002). Reinforcement and coercion mechanisms in the development of antisocial behavior: Peer relationships. In J. B. Reid, G. R. Patterson, & J. Snyder (Eds.), *Antisocial behavior in children and adolescents. A developmental analysis and model for intervention* (pp. 123–146). Washington, DC: American Psychological Association.

Snyder, J., Edwards, P., McGraw, K., Kilgore, K., & Holton, A. (1994). Escalation and reinforcement in mother-child conflict: Social processes associated with the development of physical aggression. *Development and Psychopathology, 6,* 305–321.

Snyder, J., Horsch, E., & Childs, J. (1997). Peer relationships of young children: Affiliative choices and the shaping of agressive behavior. *Journal of Clinical Child Psychology, 26,* 145–156.

Snyder, J., & Patterson, G. R. (1986). The effects of consequences of patterns of social interaction: A quasi-experimental approach to reinforcement in natural interaction. *Child Development, 57,* 1257–1268.

Snyder, J., & Stoolmiller, M. (2002). Reinforcement and coercion mechanisms in the development of antisocial behavior: The family. In J. B. Reid, G. R. Patterson, & J. Snyder (Eds.), *Antisocial behavior in children and adolescents. A developmental analysis and model for intervention* (pp. 101–122). Washington, DC: American Psychological Association.

Spangler, G., & Grossmann, K. E. (1993). Biobehavioral organization in securely and insecurely attached infants. *Child Development, 64,* 1439–1450.

Spieker, S., Nelson, D., DeKlyen, M., & Staerkel, F. (2005). Enhancing early attachments in the context of Early Head Start: Can programs emphasizing family support improve rates of secure infant-mother attachments in low-income families? In L. J. Berlin, Y. Ziv, L. Amaya-Jackson, & M. T. Greenberg (Eds.), *Enhancing early attachments. Theory, research, intervention, and policy (pp.* 250–275). New York: Guilford Press.

Spiker, D., Ferguson, J., & Brooks-Gunn, J. (1993). Enhancing maternal interactive behavior and child social competence in low birth weight, premature children. *Child Development, 64,* 754–768.*

Sroufe, L. A. (1988). *Child development: Its nature and course.* New York: McGraw-Hill.

Sroufe, L. A., Carlson, E. A., Levy, A. K., & Egeland, B. (1999). Implications of attachment theory for developmental psychopathology. *Development and Psychopathology, 11*, 1–13.

Sroufe, L. A., Carlson, E., & Shulman, S. (1993). Individuals in relationships: Development from infancy through adolescence. In D. C. Funder, R. D. Parke, C. Tomlinson-Keasey, & K. Widaman (Eds.), *Studying lives through time: Personality and development* (pp. 315–342). Washington, DC: American Psychological Association.

Sroufe, L. A., Egeland, B., Carlson, E. A., & Collins, W. A. (2005). *The development of the person. The Minnesota study of risk and adaptation from birth to adulthood.* New York: Guilford Press.

Sroufe, L. A., Egeland, B., & Kreutzer, T. (1990). The fate of early experience following developmental change: longitudinal approaches to individual adaptation in childhood. *Child Development, 61*, 1363–1373.

Stams, G. J. J. M., Juffer, F., Rispens, J., & Hoksbergen, R. A. C. (2000). The development and adjustment of 7-year-old children adopted in infancy. *Journal of Child Psychology and Psychiatry, 41*, 1025–1037.

Stams, G. J. J. M., Juffer, F., & Van IJzendoorn, M. H. (2002). Maternal sensitivity, infant attachment, and temperament in early childhood predict adjustment in middle childhood: The case of adopted children and their biologically unrelated parents. *Developmental Psychology, 38*, 806–821.

Stams, G. J. J. M., Juffer, F., Van IJzendoorn, M. H., & Hoksbergen, R.A.C. (2001). Attachment-based intervention in adoptive families in infancy and children's development at age seven: two follow-up studies. *British Journal of Developmental Psychology, 19*, 159–180.

Steele, H. (2003). Holding therapy is not attachment therapy: Editor's introduction to this invited special issue. *Attachment and Human Development, 5*, 219–220.

Stein, A., Lee, J., Woolley, H., Wheatcroft, R., Cooper, P., & Murray, L. (In preparation). *The peer interaction of children of mothers with eating disorders: a follow-up study.*

Stein, A., Murray, L., Cooper, P. J., & Fairburn, C. G. (1996). Infant growth in the context of maternal eating disorders and maternal depression: A comparative study. *Psychological Medicine, 26*, 569–574.

Stein, A., Woolley, H., Cooper, S. D., & Fairburn, C. G. (1994). An observational study of mothers with eating disorders and their infants. *Journal of Child Psychology and Psychiatry, 35*, 733–748.

Stein, A., Woolley, H., & McPherson, K. (1999). The evolution of conflict between mothers with eating disorders and their infants during mealtimes. *British Journal of Psychiatry, 175*, 455–461.

Stein, A., Woolley, H., Murray, L., Cooper, P., Cooper, S., Noble, F., et al. (2001). Influence of psychiatric disorder on the controlling behavior of mothers with 1-year-old infants: A study of women with maternal eating disorder, postnatal depression and a healthy comparison group. *British Journal of Psychiatry, 179*, 157–162.

Stein, A., Woolley, H., Senior, R., Hertzmann, L., Lovel, M., Lee, J., et al. (2006). Treating disturbances in the relationship between mothers with bulimic eating disorders and their infants: A randomized, controlled trial of video feedback. *American Journal of Psychiatry, 163*, 899–906.

Stevenson-Hinde, J. (2005). The interplay between attachment, temperament, and maternal style: A Madingley perspective. In K. E. Grossmann, K. Grossmann, & E. Waters (Eds.), *Attachment from infancy to adulthood: The major longitudinal studies* (pp. 198–222). New York: Guilford Press.

Stolk, M. N., Mesman, J., Van Zeijl, J., Alink, L. R. A., Bakermans-Kranenburg, M. J., Van IJzendoorn, M. H., Juffer, F., & Koot, H. M. (In press). Early parenting intervention aimed at maternal sensitivity and discipline: A process evaluation. *Journal of Community Psychology.*

St. Pierre, R. G., & Layzer, J. I. (1999). Using home visits for multiple purposes: The comprehensive child development program. *The Future of Children, 9,* 134–151.*

Suomi, S. J. (1999). Attachment in rhesus monkeys. In J. Cassidy & P. R. Shaver (Eds.), *Handbook of attachment: Theory, research, and clinical applications* (pp. 181–197). New York: Guilford Press.

Tabachnick, B. G., & Fidell, L. S. (2001). *Using multivariate statistics.* New York: Harper & Row.

Tessier, R., Cristo, M., Velez, S., Giron, M., Figueroa de Calume, Z., Ruiz-Paláez, J. G., et al. (1998). Kangaroo mother care and the bonding hypothesis. *Pediatrics, 102,* e17.*

Thompson, R. A. (1999). Early attachment and later development. In J. Cassidy & P. R. Shaver (Eds.), *Handbook of attachment. Theory, research, and clinical applications* (pp. 265–286). New York: Guilford Press.

Tieman, W., Van der Ende, J., & Verhulst, F. C. (2005). Psychiatric disorders in young adult intercountry adoptees: An epidemiological study. *American Journal of Psychiatry, 162,* 592–598.

Tremblay, R. E., Japel, C., Perusse, D., Boivin, M., Zoccolillo, M., Montplaisir, J., et al. (1999). The search for the age of "onset" of physical aggression: Rousseau and Bandura revisited. *Criminal Behavior and Mental Health, 9,* 8–23.

True, M. M., Pisani, L., & Oumar, F. (2001). Infant-mother attachment among the Dogon of Mali. *Child Development, 72,* 1451–1466.

Van Aken, M. A., & Riksen-Walraven, J. M. A. (1992). Parental support and the development of competence in children. *International Journal of Behavioral Development, 15,* 101–123.

Van den Boom, D. C. (1988). *Neonatal irritability and the development of attachment: Observation and intervention.* Leiden, the Netherlands: Leiden University.

Van den Boom, D. C. (1994). The influence of temperament and mothering on attachment and exploration: An experimental manipulation of sensitive responsiveness among lower-class mothers with irritable infants. *Child Development, 65,* 1457–1477.*

Van der Mark, I. L., Van IJzendoorn, M. H., & Bakermans-Kranenburg, M. J. (2002). Development of empathy in girls during the second year of life: Associations with parenting, attachment, and temperament. *Social Development, 11,* 451–468.

Van Dijk, L., & Siegers, J. J. (1996). The division of childcare among mothers, fathers, and nonparental careproviders in Dutch two-parent families. *Journal of Marriage and the Family, 58,* 1018–1028.

Van IJzendoorn, M. H. (1995). Adult attachment representations, parental responsiveness, and infant attachment: A meta-analysis on the predictive validity of the Adult Attachment Interview. *Psychological Bulletin, 117,* 387–403.

Van IJzendoorn, M. H. (1997). Attachment, emergent morality, and aggression: Toward a developmental socioemotional model of antisocial behavior. *International Journal of Behavioral Development, 21,* 703–727.

Van IJzendoorn, M. H., & Bakermans-Kranenburg, M. J. (2003). Attachment disorders and disorganized attachment: Similar and different. *Attachment and Human Development, 5,* 313–320.

Van IJzendoorn, M. H., Bakermans-Kranenburg, M. J., & Juffer, F. (2005). Why less is more: From the Dodo bird verdict to evidence-based interventions on sensitivity and early attachments. In L. J. Berlin, Y. Ziv, L. Amaya-Jackson, & M. T. Greenberg, *Enhancing early attachments. Theory, research, intervention, and policy* (pp. 297–312). New York: Guilford Press.

Van IJzendoorn, M. H., Bakermans-Kranenburg, M. J., & Juffer, F. (In press). Plasticity of growth in height, weight and head circumference: Meta-analytic evidence for massive catch-up of children's physical growth after international adoption. *Journal of Developmental and Behavioral Pediatrics.*

Van IJzendoorn, M. H., Goldberg, S., Kroonenberg, P. M., & Frenkel, O. J. (1992). The relative effects of maternal and child problems on the quality of attachment: A meta-analysis on the quality of attachment in clinical samples. *Child Development, 63,* 840–858.

Van IJzendoorn, M. H., & Juffer, F. (2005). Adoption is a successful natural intervention enhancing adopted children's IQ and school performance. *Current Directions in Psychological Science, 14,* 326–330.

Van IJzendoorn, M. H., & Juffer, F. (2006). The Emanuel Miller Memorial Lecture 2006: Adoption as intervention. Meta-analytic evidence for massive catch-up and plasticity in physical, socio-emotional, and cognitive development. *Journal of Child Psychology and Psychiatry, 47,* 1228–1245.

Van IJzendoorn, M. H., Juffer, F., & Duyvesteyn, M. G. C. (1995). Breaking the intergenerational cycle of insecure attachment: A review of the effects of attachment-based interventions on maternal sensitivity and infant security. *Journal of Child Psychology and Psychiatry, 36,* 225–248.

Van IJzendoorn, M. H., Juffer, F., & Klein Poelhuis, C. W. (2005). Adoption and cognitive development: A meta-analytic comparison of adopted and non-adopted children's IQ and school performance. *Psychological Bulletin, 131,* 301–316.

Van IJzendoorn, M. H., & Kroonenberg, P. M. (1988). Cross-cultural patterns of attachment: A meta-analysis of the Strange Situation. *Child Development, 59,* 147–156.

Van IJzendoorn, M. H., & Kroonenberg, P. M. (1990). Cross-cultural consistency of coding the Strange Situation. *Infant Behavior and Development, 13,* 469–485.

Van IJzendoorn, M. H., Moran, G., Belsky, J., Pederson, D., Bakermans-Kranenburg, M. J., & Kneppers, K. (2000). The similarity of siblings' attachments to their mother. *Child Development, 71,* 1084–1096.

Van IJzendoorn, M. H., & Sagi, A. (1999). Cross-cultural patterns of attachment: Universal and contextual dimensions. In J. Cassidy & P. R. Shaver (Eds.), *Handbook of attachment. Theory, research, and clinical applications* (pp. 713–734). New York: Guilford.

Van IJzendoorn, M. H., Sagi, A., & Lambermon, M. (1992). The multiple caregiver paradox: Data from Holland and Israel. In R. C. Pianta (Ed.)., *Beyond the parent: The role of other adults in children's lives. New Directions for Child Development, 57,* 5–27.

Van IJzendoorn, M. H., Schuengel, C., & Bakermans-Kranenburg, M. J. (1999). Disorganized attachment in early childhood: Meta-analysis of precursors, concomitants, and sequelae. *Development and Psychopathology, 11,* 225–249.

Van Lier, P. A., Vuijk, P., & Crijnen, A. A. (2005). Understanding mechanisms of change in the development of antisocial behavior: The impact of a universal intervention. *Journal of Abnormal Child Psychology, 33,* 521–535.

Van Londen, W. M., Juffer, F., & Van IJzendoorn, M. H. (2001, April). *Intergenerational transmission of attachment in adoptive families.* Poster presented at the Biennial Meeting of the Society for Research in Child Development, Minneapolis.

Van Zeijl, J., Mesman, J., Stolk, M. N., Alink, L. R. A., Van IJzendoorn, M. H., Bakermans-Kranenburg, M. J., Juffer, F., & Koot, H. M. (2006). Terrible ones? Assessment of externalizing behaviors in infancy with the Child Behavior Checklist. *Journal of Child Psychology and Psychiatry, 47,* 801–810.

Van Zeijl, J., Mesman, J., Van IJzendoorn, M. H., Bakermans-Kranenburg, M. J., Juffer, F., Stolk, M. N., Koot, H. M., & Alink, L. R. A. (2006). Attachment-based intervention for enhancing sensitive discipline in mothers of one- to three-year-old children at risk for externalizing behavior problems: A randomized controlled trial. *Journal of Consulting and Clinical Psychology, 74,* 99–1005.

Vaughn, B., Goldberg, S., Atkinson, L., Marcovitch, S., MacGregor, D., & Seifer, R. (1994). Quality of toddler-mother attachment in children with Down syndrome: Limits to interpretation of Strange Situation behavior. *Child Development, 65,* 95–108.

Vaughn, B. E., & Waters, E. (1990). Attachment behavior at home and in the laboratory: Q-sort observations and Strange Situation classifications of one-year-olds. *Child Development, 61,* 1965–1973.

Verhulst, F. C., Althaus, M., & Versluis-den Bieman, H. J. (1990). Problem behavior in international adoptees. I. An epidemiological study. *Journal of the American Academy of Child and Adolescent Psychiatry, 29,* 94–103.

Verschueren, K., & Marcoen, A. (1999). Representation of self and socioemotional competence in kindergartners: Differential and combined effects of attachment to mother and father. *Child Development, 70,* 183–201.

Viswanath, K., Kahn, E., Finnegan, J. R., Jr., Hertog, J., & Potter, J. D. (1993). Motivation and the "knowledge gap": Effects of a campaign to reduce diet-related cancer risk. *Communication Research, 20,* 546–563.

Vonk, R. (1998). *De eerste indruk: Bekijken en bekeken worden [The first impression: Watching and being watched].* Amsterdam: Boom.

Vorria, P., Papaligoura, Z., Dunn, J., Van IJzendoorn, M. H., Steele, H., Kontopoulou, A., et al. (2003). Early experiences and attachment relationships of Greek infants raised in residential group care. *Journal of Child Psychology and Psychiatry, 44,* 1208–1220.

Wagner, M. M., & Clayton, S. L. (1999). The parents as teachers program: Results from two demonstrations. *The Future of Children, 9,* 91–115.*

Wasik, B. H., Ramey, C. T., Bryant, D. M., & Sparling, J. J. (1990). A longitudinal study of two early intervention strategies: Project CARE. *Child Development, 61,* 1682–1696.*

Wasserman, G. A., Lennon, M. C., Allen, R., & Shilansky, M. (1987). Contributors to attachment in normal and physically handicapped infants. *Journal of the American Academy of Child and Adolescent Psychiatry, 26,* 9–15.

Waters, E., & Deane, K. (1985). Defining and assessing individual differences in attachment relationships: Q-methodology and the organization of behavior in infancy and early childhood. *Monographs of the Society for Research in Child Development, 50,* 41–65.

Waters, E., Hamilton, C. E., & Weinfield, N. S. (2000). The stability of attachment security from infancy to adulthood and early adulthood: General introduction. *Child Development, 71,* 678–683.

Waters, E., Merrick, S., Treboux, D., Crowell, J., & Albersheim, L. (2000). Attachment security in infancy and early adulthood: A twenty-year longitudinal study. *Child Development, 71,* 684–689.

Waters, E., Treboux, D., & Crowell, C. F. J. (In press). *Scoring Secure Base instrument.* Stony Brook: State University of New York, Department of Psychology.

Waters, E., Vaughn, B. E., Posada, G., & Kondo-Ikemura, K. (1995). Caregiving, cultural, and cognitive perspectives on secure-base behavior and working models: New growing points of attachment theory and research. *Monographs of the Society for Research in Child Development, 60* (2–3, Serial No. 244).

Waters, E., Weinfield, N. S., & Hamilton, C. E. (2000). The stability of attachment security from infancy to adolescence and early adulthood: General discussion. *Child Development, 71,* 703–706.

Webster-Stratton, C., Reid, M. J., & Hammond, M. (2004). Treating children with early-onset conduct problems: Intervention outcomes for parent, child, and teacher training. *Journal of Clinical Child and Adolescent Psychology, 33,* 105–124.

Weiner, A., Kuppermintz, H., & Guttmann, D. (1994). Video home training (the Orion project): A short-term preventive and treatment intervention for families with young children. *Family Process, 33,* 441–453.*

Weinfield, N. S., Sroufe, L. A., Egeland, B., & Carlson, E. A. (1999). The nature of individual differences in infant-caregiver attachment. In J. Cassidy & P. R. Shaver (Eds.), *Handbook of attachment: Theory, research, and clinical applications* (pp. 68–88). New York: Guilford Press.

Weinfield, N. S., Whaley, G. J. L., & Egeland, B. (2004). Continuity, discontinuity, and coherence in attachment from infancy to late adolescence: Sequelae of organization and disorganization. *Attachment and Human Development, 6,* 73–97.

West, M., Livesley, W. J., Reiffer, L., & Sheldon, A. (1986). The place of attachment in the life events model of stress and illness. *Canadian Journal of Psychiatry, 31,* 202–207.

Whitebook, M., Howes, C., & Phillips, D. (1989). *Who cares? Child care teachers and the quality of care in America* (final report). Oakland, CA: Child Care Employee Project.

Whitt, J. K., & Casey, P. H. (1982). The mother-infant relationship and infant development: The effect of pediatric intervention. *Child Development, 53,* 948–956.*

Wijnroks, L. (1994). *Dimensions of mother-infant interaction and the development of social and cognitive competence in preterm infants.* Dissertation, University of Groningen, Groningen, the Netherlands.*

Wille, E. (1991). Relation of preterm birth with quality of infant-mother attachment at one year. *Infant Behavior and Development, 14,* 227–240.

Willemsen-Swinkels, S. H. N., Bakermans-Kranenburg, M. J., Buitelaar, J. K., Van IJzendoorn, M. H., & Van Engeland, H. (2000). Insecure and disorganised attachment in children with a pervasive developmental disorder: Relationship with social interaction and heart rate. *Journal of Child Psychology and Psychiatry, 41*, 759–767.

Williams, H. C., Burney, P. G. J., & Hay, R. J. (1994). The UK working party's diagnostic criteria for atopic dermatitis. Derivation of a minimum set of discriminators for atopic dermatitis. *British Journal of Dermatology, 131*, 834–839.

Williamson, G. M., Walters, A. S., & Shaffer, D. R. (2002). Caregiver models of self and others, coping, and depression: predictors of depression in children with chronic pain. *Health Psychology, 21*, 405–410.

Wolke, D. (1993). The treatment of problem crying behaviour. In I. St. James-Roberts, G. Harris, & D. Messer (Eds.), *Infant crying, feeding and sleeping: Development, problems and treatments* (pp. 44–79). New York: Harvester Wheatsheaf.

Zahn-Waxler, C., Iannotti, R. J., Cummings, E. M., & Denham, S. (1990). Antecedents of problem behaviors in children of depressed mothers. *Development and Psychopathology, 2*, 271–291.

Zahr, L. K. (2000). Home-based intervention after discharge for Latino families of low-birth-weight infants. *Infant Mental Health Journal, 21*, 448–463.*

Zangheri, F., Cassibba, R., Ferriani, E., & Fabrici, C. (2002). L'attaccamento madre-bambino in soggetti affetti da dermatite atopica [Mother-child attachment in children affected by atopic dermatitis]. *Età Evolutiva, 71*, 43–51.

Zaslow, M. J., & Eldred, C. A. (Eds.). (1998). *Parenting behavior in a sample of young mothers in poverty: Results of the New Chance observational study.* New York: Manpower Demonstration Research Corporation.*

Zawadski, B., Strelau, J., Oniszcenko, W., Riemann, R., & Angleitner, A. (2001). Genetic and environmental influences on temperament. *European Psychologist, 6*, 272–286.

Zeanah, C. H., & Smyke, A. T. (2005). Building attachment relationships following maltreatment and severe deprivation. In L. J. Berlin, Y. Ziv, L. Amaya-Jackson, & M. T. Greenberg (Eds.), *Enhancing early attachments. Theory, research, intervention, and policy* (pp. 195–216). New York: Guilford Press.

Zeanah, C. H., Smyke, A. T., Koga, S. F., & Carlson, E. (2005). Attachment in institutionalized and community children in Romania. *Child Development, 76*, 1015–1028.

Ziegenhain, U., Wijnroks, L., Derksen, B., & Dreisörner, R. (1999). Entwicklungspsychologische Beratung bei jugendlichen Müttern und ihren Säuglingen: Chancen früher Förderung der Resilienz [Psychological counseling for adolescent mothers and their infants: Chances for early promotion of resilience]. In G. Opp & A. Freytag (Eds.), *Von den Stärken der Kinder: Erziehung zwischen Risiko und Resilienz [Competent children: Child-rearing between risk and resilience]*. München: Reinhardt.*

Zigler, E. F., & Hall, N. W. (2000). *Child development and social policy: Theory and applications.* Boston: McGraw-Hill.

Index

Heart disease, 91–92
Het eerste levensjaar (The First Year of Life), 130, 143
Home Observation for Measurement of the Environment (HOME), 63
Home-visiting family support services, 55–56
Hospitalization, of child, 93

I

Illness
    distribution of attachment patterns, 96–98
    impact on infant-parent attachment, 91
    psychiatric, 115
    as risk factor for attachment, 94
Inductive discipline, 181, 182
Infant. See also Preterm infant
    child development album, 130
    classification of attachment behavior, 82
    effect of bulimic mother on feeding, 115
    enhancing and manipulating parental sensitivity, 72
    intervention addressing mealtime conflict, 119
    mental health problems in, 54
    mother's concern for manner of eating, 132
    mothers with postnatal eating disorder, 112–113
    negative association of feeding, 113–114
    prevention deviant developmental pathways, 59
    self-feeding, 113, 114, 115–116, 119–120, 134, 135
    significance of signals, 131
    techniques to explore perspective of, 121–123
    weight of, 112–113
Infant attachment security
    associating with positive outcomes, 37

    association of parental sensitivity with, 62
    classification of, 82
    efficacy of intervention on, 102
    meta-analysis enhancing, 73
Infant Behavior Questionnaire (IBQ)
    assessment of temperament, 83
    for Leiden VIPP and VIPP-R study, 79
    for VIPP program, 24–25
Infant-mother attachment, 82
Infant-parent attachment
    illness as risk factor for development of, 91–92
    intervention to enhance adoptive families, 139
Insecure-ambivalent children, 3, 4
Insecure attachment. See Attachment security
Insecure-avoidant children, 2–3
Insecure-dismissing parents, 4
Insecure-disorganized children, 3
Insecure-preoccupied parents, 4
Insecure-unresolved parents, 4
Interaction guidance method, 11
Internal working model, 174
Intervention. See also Leiden study; SCRIPT study; VIPP program
    addressing mealtime conflict, 116–117
    association of focus and number of sessions, 67, 69
    in attachment, 5
    attachment-based, 1
    characteristics of, 67
    child-parent psychotherapy as, 54–55
    coding of studies, 64–65, 68
    combined effect size of, 66, 67
    design affects outcome, 66
    directing at behavioral and representational level, 4
    effectiveness of, 60, 70, 73, 83–86
    effect on disorganized attachment, 70, 71
    effect size of, 65
    effect size on attachment, 72

Printed in the United Kingdom
by Lightning Source UK Ltd.
128798UK00001BA/2/A